COLLECTOR'S
VALUE GUIDE™

Department 56®
Villages

The Heritage Village Collection®
The Original Snow Village®

Collector Handbook and
Secondary Market Price Guide

FIFTH EDITION

Department 56® Villages

This publication is *not* affiliated with Department 56®, Inc. or any of its affiliates, subsidiaries, distributors or representatives. Any opinions expressed are solely those of the authors, and do not necessarily reflect those of Department 56®, Inc. The Heritage Village Collection®, The Original Snow Village®, Dickens' Village®, New England Village®, Christmas in the City® and Storybook Village® are registered trademarks of Department 56®, Inc. Alpine Village Series™, North Pole Series™, Disney Parks Village™, Little Town of Bethlehem™ and Historical Landmark Series™ are trademarks of Department 56®. Charles Dickens' Signature Series© and the American Architecture Series© are copyrights of Department 56. Product names and product designs are the property of Department 56®, Inc., Eden Prairie, MN. Photographs by CheckerBee, Inc.

Managing Editor:	Jeff Mahony	Creative Director:	Joe T. Nguyen
Associate Editors:	Melissa A. Bennett	Production Supervisor:	Scott Sierakowski
	Jan Cronan	Senior Graphic Designers:	Lance Doyle
	Gia C. Manalio		Susannah C. Judd
	Paula Stuckart		David S. Maloney
Contributing Editor:	Mike Micciulla		Carole Mattia-Slater
Editorial Assistants:	Jennifer Filipek	Graphic Designers:	Jennifer J. Bennett
	Nicole LeGard Lenderking		Sean-Ryan Dudley
	Joan C. Wheal		Kimberly Eastman
Research Assistants:	Timothy R. Affleck		Jason C. Jasch
	Priscilla Berthiaume		Angi Shearstone
	Heather N. Carreiro		David Ten Eyck
	Beth Hackett	Web Graphic Designer:	Ryan Falis
	Victoria Puorro		
	Steven Shinkaruk		
Web Reporters:	Samantha Bouffard		
	Ren Messina		

ISBN 1-888-914-79-3

CheckerBee PUBLISHING

306 Industrial Park Road • Middletown, CT 06457
www.CollectorBee.com

Table Of Contents

5   Introducing The Collector's Value Guide™

6   Department 56® Overview

9   The Heritage Village Collection® Overview

13   What's New For The Heritage Village Collection®

20   Recent Retirements

22   The Heritage Village Collection® Top Ten

24   How To Use Your Collector's Value Guide™

25   Value Guide – Department 56® Villages

       25 Dickens' Village – Buildings

       49 New England Village – Buildings

       60 Alpine Village – Buildings

       64 Christmas in the City – Buildings

       73 North Pole – Buildings

       81 Disney Parks Village – Buildings

       83 Little Town of Bethlehem – Buildings

       84 Heritage Village – Accessories

       90 Dickens' Village – Accessories

      101 New England Village – Accessories

      107 Alpine Village – Accessories

      109 Christmas in the City – Accessories

      114 North Pole – Accessories

      119 Disney Parks Village – Accessories

      120 Little Town of Bethlehem – Accessories

      121 Heritage Village – Hinged Boxes

      122 Heritage Village – Ornaments

126 Future Releases

127 Total Value Of My Collection

129 The Original Snow Village® Overview

131 What's New For The Original Snow Village®

135 Recent Retirements

136 The Original Snow Village® Top Ten

138 How To Use Your Collector's Value Guide™

139 Value Guide – Department 56® Villages

      139 Snow Village – Buildings

      175 Snow Village – Accessories

      197 Snow Village – Ornaments

199	Future Releases
200	Total Value Of My Collection
201	Other Department 56® Collectibles Overview
203	What's New For Other Department 56® Collectibles
206	How To Use Your Collector's Value Guide™
207	Value Guide – Department 56® Villages
	207 Bachman's Hometown Series – Buildings
	207 Meadowland – Buildings
	207 Miscellaneous – Buildings
	209 Monopoly – Buildings
	211 Seasons Bay – Buildings
	213 Storybook Village – Buildings
	216 Meadowland – Accessories
	216 Miscellaneous – Accessories
	217 Seasons Bay – Accessories
	217 General
	217 Spring
	218 Summer
	219 Fall
	219 Winter
	220 Storybook Village – Accessories
	220 Storybook Teapots
222	Future Releases
223	Total Value Of My Collection
224	Secondary Market Overview
228	Insuring Your Collection
229	Caring For Your Collection
230	Variations
233	Production, Packaging and Pricing
234	Department 56® Product Spotlight
236	On The Road With Department 56®
237	Display Ideas
241	Display Success With "Dr. S"
245	Current Display Pieces
249	Glossary
251	Numerical Index
259	Alphabetical Index

Introducing The Collector's Value Guide™

Welcome to the fifth edition of the Collector's Value Guide™ for Department 56® Villages. Inside you will find detailed information about the wonderful world of The Heritage Village Collection®, The Original Snow Village® and other Department 56 collectibles. With this reference guide, you'll learn how this popular collectible has grown from a holiday tradition to became a year-round home decorating phenomenon.

This guide is filled with color photographs of Department 56 buildings and accessories, along with essential information about each piece including stock numbers, issue and retirement dates, secondary market values and original prices. Our Collector's Value Guide™ is designed to help you keep track of your collection, keep up with the secondary market and gain insight into the different aspects of collecting Department 56 Villages.

Look Inside To Find:

- 🎄 The Most Recent Introductions And Retirements

- 🎄 The Ten Most Valuable *Heritage Village* Pieces

- 🎄 The Ten Most Valuable *Snow Village* Pieces

- 🎄 How To Shop The Secondary Market

- 🎄 Exciting New Display Ideas

- 🎄 More Display Shortcuts from "Dr. S"

- 🎄 A Look At Other Department 56 Products & More!

Department 56® Overview

*F*or almost 25 years, Department 56 has provided collectors with images of quaint towns, historic villages and urban streets through their expanding collection of lighted buildings and accessories. While the original buildings were designed for winter and holiday displays, more recent releases have captured the beauty and charm of houses throughout the year.

Identified in 1976 as "Department 56," the company was originally part of a retail store named Bachman's. A leading designer, importer and distributor of giftware, Bachman's began as a family-owned farm in the late 1800s and expanded into a floral business early in the 20th century. As the company grew, the number of departments increased, which created the need for a numbering system to identify specific areas of the company. Department 56 was the name assigned to Bachman's division of Wholesale Gift Imports.

In The Beginning

The man in charge of this new department, Ed Bazinet, created a line of six miniature lighted buildings that resembled a quaint snow-covered village. Response was immediate and positive – the buildings were so much in demand that, within three years, there were 31 buildings, 10 of which were retired. These "Snow Village" pieces were a such hit that they were being imitated by other companies, which caused the name of the Department 56 line to be changed to "The Original Snow Village®."

In 1984, Department 56 was incorporated and became separate from Bachman's. That same year, *The Dickens' Village Series®*, the first of several lines in what would become The Heritage Village Collection®, was introduced. Depicting Charles Dickens' Victorian-era England, its success spurred the release of two more lines in 1986, *The New England Village®* series and *The Alpine Village Series®*. The very next year, *Christmas in the City®* and *Little Town of Bethlehem™* were released. In

1988, the first *Dickens' Village* retirements were announced and two years later the *North Pole Series*™ was introduced.

As the popularity of village collecting grew, Department 56 continued down the road of expansion. The *Disney Parks Village*™ series was released in 1994, marking the first time a licensed village entered the collection; while a year later, the "Homes for the Holidays" program introduced new collectors to the villages. The event was a success and continues today as "Discover Department 56," offering special gift sets to launch collections. In 1996, the addition of *Storybook Village*® brought to life the stories we heard as children. And when the *Seasons Bay*™ series debuted in 1998, collectors were instantly charmed by the early 20th-century vacation resort by the bay. *Elf Land*™ was also introduced that year as an extension of the *North Pole* village.

The current Department 56 village collection can be viewed in its entirety at the company's new retail store in Minnesota. Located in the massive Mall of America in Bloomington, the store gives collectors an up-close view to every village and product currently available, not to mention some great display ideas! Collectors can also go straight to the source to get a look at their favorite pieces at the showroom in Department 56's headquarters in Eden Prairie, Minnesota. Visitors are welcome to browse the showroom each Friday afternoon during the summer months.

Business Is Booming

So how did Department 56 get to Eden Prairie? In 1991, the company relocated to its current headquarters in response to the tremendous growth the company was experiencing. One year later, another big change came when the company was purchased by Forstmann Little Co. and its stock was made public. Collectors now had the opportunity to invest directly in the company. The initial offering was completed in 1993 and the stock was listed on the New York Stock Exchange under the ticker symbol "DFS." More changes came in 1997, as founder Ed Bazinet stepped down and Susan Engel, President and CEO, took his place.

Collector Devotion

The Department 56 villages have a widespread following and many collectors have expressed their devotion by forming fan clubs. In order to unify and organize these clubs in both the United States and Canada, the National Council of "56" Clubs was founded in 1992. Although these clubs are not sponsored by Department 56, the company both acknowledges and supports them. As a token of appreciation to collectors' loyalty to the line, the company released the "Collectors' Club House," (set/2) available exclusively for members in 1998.

"Little Things Mean A Lot"

In recent years, Department 56 has introduced many exciting innovations to enhance its villages. This includes "Brite Lites," neon-like signs which cast a glow throughout the villages, a village snow machine that creates realistic snow storms and acrylic icicles that hang from the buildings. Life-like motion has also been added through several animated pieces like "The Carnival Carousel" and accessories like the "Village Animated Skating Pond" or the "Village Animated Ski Mountain." A few buildings even come with smoking chimneys! And to add more excitement to the villages, several buildings with detailed, three-dimensional interiors were released for the first time at the end of 1999.

As the production process has been refined through the years, the pieces have become smaller and more detailed. Buildings are being made with attachments and different materials like metal, acrylic and sisal are being incorporated into both buildings and accessories. Other pieces gaining in popularity, brick roads, grassy ground cover or blue sky backdrops, are "extras" that are quite essential for any display.

Something For Everyone

Department 56 isn't just about villages. The company specializes in many other collectibles including *Snowbabies*™, *Snowbunnies*®, *Silhouette Treasures*™ Collection and *Candle Crown*™ Collections.

The Heritage Village Collection® Overview

*I*n 1984, Department 56 introduced a set of buildings called "The Original Shops Of Dickens' Village" (set/7), marking the first pieces from the *Dickens' Village Series* and the first releases separate from The Original Snow Village collection. As the years progressed, Department 56 continued to break new ground by releasing several additional, stand-alone villages. Soon, these village pieces were categorized into one large grouping, titled Heritage Village. Today, seven villages comprise Heritage Village, all of which are connected through their matte exterior finish.

Dickens' Village Series®

From the original shops released in 1984, *Dickens' Village* has grown to include the types of structures that you would expect to find in Charles Dickens' Victorian England, including cozy cottages, welcoming inns, friendly taverns, bustling outdoor markets and an ever expanding variety of shops. In addition to the buildings, a line of complementary accessories have been released which are sure to enhance any *Dickens' Village* display.

With a subset of *Dickens' Village*, the *Historical Landmark Series*™, collectors can add a touch of realism to their village by displaying mini-replicas of famous landmarks. The series began in 1997 and has included such famous attractions as "Big Ben" (set/2), the "Tower of London" (set/5) and for 2000, the new "The Old Royal Observatory" (set/2).

Along with the *Historical Landmark Series*, several other pieces have been released into *Dickens' Village* in other series as well, including themed releases both for buildings and accessories. In fact, there are even some series which have been discontinued from the line, such as the *Charles Dickens' Signature Series*. Another series, *The 12*

Days Of Dickens' Village, reaches completion this year with the release of "The 12 Days Of Dickens' Village Sign."

New England Village®

As with *Dickens' Village*, *New England Village* also began as a set. Issued in 1986, it included four shops, a church, a town hall and a schoolhouse. This was only the beginning of a rapidly growing village which displays the rustic charm of the holiday season in New England. These quaint pieces bring us back to a simpler time when people lived and worked in small, tight-knit communities – seafaring communities which thrived along the coastline, while industrial and farm communities provided wares and produce inland.

New England Village pieces are easy to identify by their dark colors and simple architecture. A line of accompanying accessories are available that perfectly complement the simple New England structures, bringing life to the small town.

Alpine Village Series®

The snowy climate of the Alps makes *Alpine Village* perfect for holiday displays. This traditional European village, full of shops and charming chalets, was introduced in 1986 as a set of five buildings. Currently, with just over 20 buildings, this is one of the smaller villages, although it continues to grow at a steady pace. This year, two additional buildings have been introduced to the line, one of which is the "Glockenspiel," which towers over the community with its ornate time-keeping mechanism and adds sound to the quiet mountain town as it plays the tune "Emperor Waltz."

As in years past, 2000 also showcases scenes from the perennial holiday classic, *The Sound Of Music®*. While not an official series, fans of the movie can relish adding a new piece to their collection with "*The Sound Of Music®* Wedding Church." Other pieces from the village which have harkened back to cinematic features include several based around childhood favorite, *Heidi*.

Christmas in the City®

With its tall, narrow, brick buildings and the hustle and bustle of holiday shoppers, there's no doubt it's *Christmas in the City*. This nostalgic look at life in an American metropolis offers plenty of shopping, entertainment and eateries. First introduced in 1987 with only six buildings, *Christmas in the City* has grown rapidly to include almost 60 buildings. This year, the five new introductions are a bakery, a beauty salon, a laundromat with an eatery attached, a pub and the residence of the foreign consul.

Similar to most big cities, every building in *Christmas in the City* is a least two-stories tall and is fashioned out of brick and concrete. Most come adorned with holiday decorations and all are similar in look and feel, though each has its own unique personality, perfectly displayed in its tall windows, wrought iron gates and signage. Accessories available include shoppers, cars and carriages, all united by themes of glamour and glitz reminiscent of a bygone era.

North Pole Series™

The *North Pole Series* is truly a winter wonderland! These brightly-colored buildings bring warmth and cheer to the snowy North Pole landscape. This village began in 1990 with only three buildings – two of which ("Elf Bunkhouse" and "Reindeer Barn") where from the set, "North Pole" (set/2). Though the village started out rather small, it has now grown to include more than 40 different buildings and just as many accessories, several of which are multiple-piece sets. Here's your chance to see Santa, Mrs. Claus and all of the elves hard at work, and at play! There are a lot of gifts to be made each year before Christmas and Santa and his elves need more than just "Santa's Workshop" to get the job done. *Elf Land*, is a subseries the *North Pole Series*, which consists of smaller buildings made specially for the elves, so Santa's helpers can now kick back and relax in style.

Disney Parks Village™

The *Disney Parks Village* series was released in 1994 with four buildings and only two more where released the following year.  These pieces were first made available at Disney World in Florida, as well as Disneyland in California. These replicas of actual buildings were intended to capture the magic of the Disney theme parks and to serve as special momentos. After only two years of production, the entire collection, including the four accessories released, retired in 1996.

Little Town of Bethlehem™

Little Town of Bethlehem was introduced in 1987 as a complete set of 12 pieces, made up of three buildings and nine accessories. The set was retired in 1999, but this year, three new buildings were introduced under the name, *Little Town of Bethlehem*, along with five accessory sets. "The Innkeeper's Caravansary" provides a stopping place for weary travelers, "Gatekeeper's Dwelling" depicts a rustic home, while "Nativity" (set/2) is a set of two pieces illustrating the scene in the stable following the birth of Jesus. The accessory pieces help to complete the scene at this *Little Town of Bethlehem.*

What's New For The Heritage Village Collection®

*O*n December 10, 1999, Department 56 announced the following new *Heritage Village* releases.

DICKENS' VILLAGE BUILDINGS

ALDEBURGH MUSIC BOX SHOP ... With snow on the roof and a wreath above the door, this store invites shoppers to come inside. ("Aldeburgh Music Box Shop" will also be available in a limited edition gift set.)

THE CHINA TRADER ... The bright reds, blues and yellows of "The China Trader" building invite the passersby to enter and swap fine English china.

LEED'S OYSTER HOUSE ... For a night of fine dining, residents of *Dickens' Village* would be wise to choose a delectable seafood entree at "Leed's Oyster House."

MARGROVE ORANGERY ... This glass-roofed structure is a precursor to the greenhouse which was used to maintain orange trees during long winter months.

McSHANE COTTAGE (SET/2) ... This cozy cottage invites neighbors in from the snow, as geese wander around looking for a way into the matching henhouse.

OLD QUEENSBRIDGE STATION (SET/2) ... How do the people in the community travel in and out of *Dickens' Village*? "Old Queensbridge Station" (set/2) provides the answer.

THE OLD ROYAL OBSERVATORY (SET/2) ... Why not learn more about the stars at "The Old Royal Observatory" (set/2), a tall, three-story brick structure from the *Historic Landmark Series*.

The Spider Box Locks . . . An open treasure box entices shoppers as they walk near "The Spider Box Locks" which is festively decorated for the Christmas season.

Staghorn Lodge . . . Guests staying in this hunter's lodge are sure to relish quiet nights by the fire.

Wingham Lane Parrot Seller . . . *Dickens' Village* residents yearning for a unique companion will find exotic birds for sale at this Wingham Lane shop.

Dickens' Village Accessories

The queen in "The Queen's Parliamentary Coach" catches a glimpse of the "Members of Parliament" (set/2) as she passes the "King's Road Market Cross." She notices someone "Meeting Family At The Railroad Station" (set/4) and, a bit farther down the road, a fruit tree being transported by "Master Gardeners" (set/2), as well as a couple "Under The Bumbershoot." *Dickens' Village* is full of wonderful trinkets from "A Treasure From The Sea" (set/2) to "Fine Asian Antiques" (set/2) which explains why there is such a "Busy Railway Station" (set/3). As the queen exits town, she passes "The Locomotive Shed & Water Tower" and "The 12 Days of Dickens' Village Sign." The *Dickens' Village* ornament released this year from the *Classic Ornament Series* is "Victoria Station."

New England Village Buildings

Hale & Hardy House . . . Every light in the "Hale & Hardy House" is burning bright, welcoming the villagers in from the cold.

Harper's Farmhouse . . . Tuckered out after a day full of chores, the Harper family relaxes in front of the fireplace in their charming farmhouse.

TRINITY LEDGE ... Patriotic pride is evident with the red and white lighthouse of as it stands tall next to a cozy yellow home.

PLATT'S CANDLES & WAX ... "Platt's Candles & Wax" offers villagers a wide selection of holiday candles in this cozy shop.

 P.L. WHEELER'S BICYCLE SHOP ... It's easy to get around *New England Village* with a bike rented from "P.L. Wheeler's Bicycle Shop."

NEW ENGLAND VILLAGE ACCESSORIES

Today is a remarkably busy day in *New England Village*. Let's follow the boy in "Pennyfarthing Pedaling" as he travels across town. First, he passes a "Doctor's House Call" (set/2) where the doctor has just arrived and two seamen can be seen tying "The Sailors' Knot." The sailors are close friends with "The Woodworker" who is carving in his red barn. Another villager and her daughter are busy "Making The Christmas Candles" (set/3). The sounds of children shouting "Let's Go One More Time" (set/3) can be heard as they slide down the snow covered hills. And just before the journey ends, we have to wait for the "Dairy Delivery Sleigh" to cross the bright red "Mill Creek Crossing."

ALPINE VILLAGE BUILDINGS

GLOCKENSPIEL . . . Inspired by the German musical instrument, "Glockenspiel" is a tower with a built-in clock. The large window just under the roof reveals the excitement inside.

 The Sound Of Music® WEDDING CHURCH ... Paying tribute to the all-time movie classic, *The Sound of Music®*, this ornate church features two delightful bell towers.

ALPINE VILLAGE ACCESSORIES

One of the "Alpine Villagers" plays the accordion for the teenage lovers dancing in "The Sound of Music® Gazebo," while "Sisters Of The Abbey" are watching a man "Leading The Bavarian Cow."

CHRISTMAS IN THE CITY BUILDINGS

5TH AVENUE SALON . . . All of the sophistication 5th Avenue is famous for can be seen here in this elegant salon. The blue trim complements the large window panes and yellow exterior of the building.

CLARK STREET AUTOMAT . . . Villagers can satisfy their appetite while they wait for their clothes to dry at the "Clark Street Automat."

THE CONSULATE (SET/2, LE-2000) . . . The American flag flies high in front of this beautiful brick structure.

LAFAYETTE'S BAKERY . . . It is difficult to ignore the mouth-watering pastries displayed in the windows of "Lafayette's Bakery" or resist turning in as you smell their delicious aroma.

MOLLY O'BRIEN'S IRISH PUB . . . Step right in to "Molly O'Brien's Irish Pub" where the residents of the city happily eat and drink away their troubles. The two-story brick building features a shamrock on the front door.

Christmas in the City Accessories

Let's go see what's happening on the "Busy City Sidewalks" (set/4). One family celebrates the holiday by "Visiting The Nativity" (set/3), while another is "Picking Out The Christmas Tree" (set/3). Others are buying some "Fresh Flowers For Sale" (set/2). A small boy notices the "Excellent Taste" (set/2) in choice of pastry at the local bakery. Blending in with the sounds of the city, someone cheers, "All In Together Girls" at three children jumping rope. The *Christmas in the City* ornament released this year from the *Classic Ornament Series* is "Hollydale's Department Store."

North Pole Buildings

COLD CARE CLINIC...The most universal illness at the North Pole is the common cold. A red flag with a white cross tops the "Cold Care Clinic," a member of the *Elf Land* series.

ELF MOUNTAIN SKI RESORT ... Ever wonder what elves do on their days off? The "Elf Mountain Ski Resort" gives Santa's helpers the option of a full day of skiing followed by a relaxing evening by the fireplace.

JACK IN THE BOX PLANT NO. 2 (LE-2000) ... The pastel colors of this North Pole building are as perfect as the toys that are created inside. With a train coming through the roof and other toys scattered about, the excitement from inside the factory can not be contained.

MINI-DONUT SHOP ... The large, glazed donut that hangs in the center of this *Elf Land* building brings attention to the three-story "Mini-Donut Shop."

NORTHERN LIGHTS TINSEL MILL . . . The wide, red blades of the "Northern Lights Tinsel Mill" are easily spotted over the snowy hills.

THE PEANUT BRITTLE FACTORY . . . Candy is an essential part of the holidays and what could be more fitting to satisfy that sweet tooth than some tasty peanut brittle.

NORTH POLE ACCESSORIES

Santa enjoys having "A Happy Harley Day" and when the elves aren't "Tangled In Tinsel," they play in the snow like "Downhill Daredevils" (set/2). You can see the "Elves On Track" (set/3) or watch Santa in his "Canine Courier." Elves can also be found in chairs with their feet up like "Ski Bums" and with Santa roasting "Marshmallows Around The Campfire" (set/3). While children wait patiently for a "Photo With Santa," Mrs. Claus gives him a dose of medicine and shouts, "Open Wide!" "Check This Out" – the elves spend the day playing games!

The *North Pole* ornament released this year for the *Classic Ornament Series* is "Real Plastic Snow Factory."

LITTLE TOWN OF BETHLEHEM BUILDINGS

INNKEEPER'S CARAVANSARY . . . Lights coming from the second floor of this oddly shaped building provide a sense of belonging for those looking for a place to stay.

NATIVITY (SET/2) ... The "Nativity" (set/2) is a familiar scene with Mary and Joseph leaning over the baby Jesus in his crib.

GATEKEEPER'S DWELLING ... Sleeping peacefully in his cozy two-story home, the gatekeeper has left his lights on to welcome weary travelers.

LITTLE TOWN OF BETHLEHEM ACCESSORIES

The *Little Town of Bethlehem* would not be complete without "The Good Shepherd & His Animals" (set/6) watching over the town. "Heralding Angels" (set/3) spread heavenly sounds just outside the "Town Gate" (set/2), while "Wise Men From The East" (set/2) stop to take a rest near the "Town Well & Palm Trees" (set/3).

GENERAL HERITAGE VILLAGE ACCESSORIES

"Dorothy's Skate Rental" is a new addition to the Heritage Village accessories as well as the joker in "Hear Ye, Hear Ye." The "Family Winter Outing" (set/3) taking place "Through The Woods" (set/4) fits perfectly into the winter collections. "Village Monuments" (set/3) wraps up the new Heritage Village accessories.

Recent Retirements

*D*epartment 56 announced that the following Heritage Village pieces retired on November 5, 1999. Each year the retirements are made public in *USA Today*, as well as on the web site (*www.department56.com*). Collectors can also receive word by pre-registering to receive an e-mail directly from the company on the morning of retirements. Each piece is listed below with issue year in parenthesis.

DICKENS' VILLAGE

❑ Butter Tub Barn (1996)
❑ Butter Tub Farmhouse (1996)
❑ Chancery Corner (1999, set/8)
❑ Dursley Manor (1995)
❑ East Indies Trading Co. (1997)
❑ Heathmoor Castle (LE-1999)
❑ J. Lytes Coal Merchant (1997)
❑ Leacock Poulterer (1997)
❑ The Melancholy Tavern (1996)
❑ Mulberrie Court Brownstones (1996)
❑ North Eastern Sea Fisheries Ltd. (1998)
❑ The Old Curiosity Shop (1987)
❑ The Olde Camden Town Church (1996)
❑ Quilly's Antiques (1996)
❑ Tattyeave Knoll (1998)

NEW ENGLAND VILLAGE

❑ East Willet Pottery (1997)
❑ Navigational Charts & Maps (1996)
❑ Semple's Smokehouse (1997)
❑ Van Guilder's Ornamental Ironworks (1997)

ALPINE VILLAGE

❑ Kamm Haus (1995)
❑ St. Nikolaus Kirche (1991)

CHRISTMAS IN THE CITY

❑ Grand Central Railway Station (1996)
❑ The Grand Movie Theater (1998)
❑ Hi-De-Ho Nightclub (1997)
❑ Riverside Row Shops (1997)
❑ Wintergarten Café (1999)

LITTLE TOWN OF BETHLEHEM

❑ Little Town Of Bethlehem (1987, set/12)

NORTH POLE

❑ The Glacier Gazette (1997)
❑ Hall Of Records (1996)
❑ Marie's Doll Museum (1999)
❑ Post Office (1992)
❑ Santa's Rooming House (1995)
❑ Santa's Visiting Center (1999, set/6)
❑ Weather & Time Observatory (1995)

GENERAL HERITAGE VILLAGE ACCESSORIES

❑ Poinsettia Delivery Truck (1997)
❑ Stars And Stripes Forever (1998)
❑ Victoria Station Train Platform (1990)

DICKENS' VILLAGE ACCESSORIES

- ❏ Ashley Pond Skating Party (1997, set/6)
- ❏ Brixton Road Watchman (1995, set/2)
- ❏ Chelsea Lane Shoppers (1993, set/4)
- ❏ Delivering Coal For The Hearth (1997, set/2)
- ❏ Five Golden Rings (1995, set/2, *V, The 12 Days Of Dickens' Village*)
- ❏ Four Calling Birds (1995, set/2, *IV, The 12 Days Of Dickens' Village*)
- ❏ Holiday Travelers (1990, set/3)
- ❏ A Partridge In A Pear Tree (1995, set/4, *I, The 12 Days Of Dickens' Village*)
- ❏ Six Geese A-Laying (1995, set/2, *VI, The 12 Days Of Dickens' Village*)
- ❏ Tending The Cold Frame (1998, set/3)
- ❏ Tending The New Calves (1996, set/3)
- ❏ Three French Hens (1995, set/3, *III, The 12 Days Of Dickens' Village*)

NEW ENGLAND VILLAGE ACCESSORIES

- ❏ Christmas Bazaar . . . Flapjacks & Hot Cider (1997, set/2)
- ❏ Christmas Bazaar . . . Handmade Quilts (1996, set/2)
- ❏ Christmas Bazaar . . . Sign (1997, set/2)
- ❏ Christmas Bazaar . . . Toy Vendor & Cart (1997, set/2)
- ❏ Christmas Bazaar . . . Woolens & Preserves (1996, set/2)
- ❏ Harvest Pumpkin Wagon (1995)

ALPINE VILLAGE ACCESSORIES

- ❏ Polka Fest (1994, set/3)
- ❏ Silent Night (1995, music box)

CHRISTMAS IN THE CITY ACCESSORIES

- ❏ Big Smile For The Camera (1997, set/2)
- ❏ Going Home For The Holidays (1996, set/3)
- ❏ Let's Go Shopping In The City (1997, set/3)
- ❏ Spirit Of The Season (1997)
- ❏ Steppin' Out On The Town (1997, set/5)

NORTH POLE ACCESSORIES

- ❏ A Busy Elf (1995)
- ❏ Early Rising Elves (1996, set/5)
- ❏ End Of The Line (1996, set/2)
- ❏ North Pole Express (1996, set/3)
- ❏ Testing The Toys (1992, set/2)

CHRISTMAS IN THE CITY ORNAMENTS

- ❏ Dorothy's Dress Shop (1998)

The Heritage Village Collection® Top Ten

*T*his section lists the ten most valuable Heritage Village pieces as established by their value on the secondary market. Our market meter shows the percentage increase of each piece's value over the issue price.

Dickens' Village Mill (LE-2,500)
Dickens' Village • #6519-6
Issued: 1985 • Retired: 1986
Issue Price: $35 • Value: $5,000
Market Meter: +14,186%

Norman Church (LE-3,500)
Dickens' Village • #6502-1
Issued: 1986 • Retired: 1987
Issue Price: $40 • Value: $3,340
Market Meter: +8,250%

Cathedral Church Of St. Mark (LE-3,024)
Christmas in the City • #5549-2
Issued: 1991 • Retired: 1993
Issue Price: $120 • Value: $2,100
Market Meter: +1,650%

Chesterton Manor House (LE-7,500)
Dickens' Village • #6568-4
Issued: 1987 • Retired: 1988
Issue Price: $45 • Value: $1,475
Market Meter: +3,178%

The Original Shops Of Dickens' Village (set/7)
Dickens' Village • #6515-3
Issued: 1984 • Retired: 1988
Issue Price: $175 • Value: $1,300
Market Meter: +643%

New England Village (set/7)
New England Village ✦ #6530-7
Issued: 1986 ✦ Retired: 1989
Issue Price: $170 ✦ Value: $1,175
Market Meter: +591%

Smythe Woolen Mill (LE-7,500)
New England Village ✦ #6543-9
Issued: 1987 ✦ Retired: 1988
Issue Price: $42 ✦ Value: $1,100
Market Meter: +2,519%

Josef Engel Farmhouse
Alpine Village ✦ #5952-8
Issued: 1987 ✦ Retired: 1989
Issue Price: $33 ✦ Value: $980
Market Meter: +2,870%

Dickens' Cottages (set/3)
Dickens' Village ✦ #6518-8
Issued: 1985 ✦ Retired: 1988
Issue Price: $75 ✦ Value: $950
Market Meter: +1,167%

Palace Theatre
Christmas in the City ✦ #5963-3
Issued: 1987 ✦ Retired: 1989
Issue Price: $45 ✦ Value: $920
Market Meter: +1,944%

How To Use Your Collector's Value Guide™

1. Locate your piece in the Value Guide. The Heritage Village Collection is listed in the following order: *Dickens' Village, New England Village, Alpine Village, Christmas in the City, North Pole, Disney Parks Village Series* and *Little Town of Bethlehem*. In the section following the villages, each village's accessories are listed. Pieces are listed

Ashbury Inn
Issued: 1991 • Retired: 1995
#5555-7 • Original Price: $55
Market Value: $74

alphabetically within each section; however, buildings that are part of a set are shown individually after the set. To help you locate your pieces we have provided numerical and alphabetical indexes in the back of the book (beginning on page 251).

2. Find the market value of your piece. If there is a variation with secondary market value, you will also find that value noted (store exclusives are also listed in the same manner). If no market value has been established for a piece, it is listed as "N/E" (not established). Pieces currently available at stores reflect the retail price.

Dickens' Village Buildings		
Date Purchased	Price Paid	Value
1. 5/21/92	55.00	74.00
2.		
3.		
4.		
5.		
Totals	55.00	74.00

3. Record the year purchased, retail price you paid and the secondary market value in the corresponding boxes at the bottom of the page.

4. Calculate the value for the page by adding all of the boxes in each column. Be sure to use a pencil so you can change the totals as your collection grows.

5. Transfer the totals from each page to the "Total Value of My Collection" worksheets for Heritage Village, beginning on page 127.

6. Add the totals together to determine the overall value of your collection.

DICKENS' VILLAGE – BUILDINGS

In 1999, 15 *Dickens' Village* buildings were retired, while 12 new buildings were introduced to the collection. There are currently 25 *Dickens' Village* buildings that are available to collectors through retail outlets. The most valuable piece on the secondary market is the "Dickens' Village Mill," which was limited to 2,500 pieces.

1

New!

Aldeburgh Music Box Shop
Issued: 1999 • Current
#58441 • Original Price: $60
Market Value: $60

2

New!

**Aldeburgh Music Box Shop
(set/3, LE-35,000)**
Issued: 1999 • Current
#58442 • Original Price: $85
Market Value: $85

3

Ashbury Inn
Issued: 1991 • Retired: 1995
#5555-7 • Original Price: $55
Market Value: $74

4

Ashwick Lane Hose & Ladder
Issued: 1997 • Current
#58305 • Original Price: $54
Market Value: $54

5

a   *b*

Barley Bree (set/2)
Issued: 1987 • Retired: 1989
#5900-5 • Original Price: $60
Market Value: $365

**Dickens' Village
Buildings**

	Date Purchased	Price Paid	Value
1.			
2.			
3.			
4.			
5.			
Totals			

25

Dickens' Village — Buildings

5a

Barn
Issued: 1987 • Retired: 1989
#5900-5 • Original Price: $30
Market Value: N/E

5b

Farmhouse
Issued: 1987 • Retired: 1989
#5900-5 • Original Price: $30
Market Value: N/E

6

Barmby Moor Cottage
Issued: 1997 • Current
#58324 • Original Price: $48
Market Value: $48

7

Big Ben (set/2)
The Historical Landmark Series
Issued: 1998 • Current
#58341 • Original Price: $95
Market Value: $95

8

Bishops Oast House
Issued: 1990 • Retired: 1992
#5567-0 • Original Price: $45
Market Value: $82

9

Blenham Street Bank
Issued: 1995 • Retired: 1998
#58330 • Original Price: $60
Market Value: $74

Dickens' Village Buildings

	Date Purchased	Price Paid	Value
5a.			
5b.			
6.			
7.			
8.			
9.			
Totals			

10

Version 2

Version 1

Blythe Pond Mill House
Issued: 1986 • Retired: 1990
#6508-0 • Original Price: $37
Market Value:
1 – $270 *("Blythe Pond")*
2 – $125 *("By The Pond")*

11

Boarding & Lodging School ("18", LE-1993)
Charles Dickens' Signature Series
Issued: 1993 • Retired: 1993
#5809-2 • Original Price: $48
Market Value: $152

12

Boarding & Lodging School ("43")
Issued: 1994 • Retired: 1998
#5810-6 • Original Price: $48
Market Value: $60

13

Brick Abbey
Issued: 1987 • Retired: 1989
#6549-8 • Original Price: $33
Market Value: $360

14

Butter Tub Barn
Issued: 1996 • Retired: 1999
#58338 • Original Price: $48
Market Value: $50

15

Butter Tub Farmhouse
Issued: 1996 • Retired: 1999
#58337 • Original Price: $40
Market Value: $44

Dickens' Village Buildings

	Date Purchased	Price Paid	Value
10.			
11.			
12.			
13.			
14.			
15.			
Totals			

Dickens' Village – Buildings

16

C. Fletcher Public House (LE-12,500)
Issued: 1988 • Retired: 1989
#5904-8 • Original Price: $35
Market Value: $525

17

Chadbury Station And Train
Issued: 1986 • Retired: 1989
#6528-5 • Original Price: $65
Market Value: $395

18

Chancery Corner
(set/8, Event Piece)
Issued: 1999 • Retired: 1999
#58352 • Original Price: $65
Market Value: N/E

19

Chesterton Manor House (LE-7,500)
Issued: 1987 • Retired: 1988
#6568-4 • Original Price: $45
Market Value: $1,475

20

New!

The China Trader
Issued: 1999 • Current
#58447 • Original Price: $72
Market Value: $72

21

Christmas Carol Cottage
(with magic smoking element)
The Christmas Carol Revisited
Issued: 1996 • Current
#58339 • Original Price: $60
Market Value: $60

Dickens' Village Buildings

	Date Purchased	Price Paid	Value
16.			
17.			
18.			
19.			
20.			
21.			
22.			
Totals			

22

a   b   c

Christmas Carol Cottages (set/3)
Issued: 1986 • Retired: 1995
#6500-5 • Original Price: $75
Market Value: $135

22a

The Cottage Of Bob Cratchit & Tiny Tim
Issued: 1986 • Retired: 1995
#6500-5 • Original Price: $25
Market Value: $65

22b

Fezziwig's Warehouse
Issued: 1986 • Retired: 1995
#6500-5 • Original Price: $25
Market Value: $45

22c

Scrooge & Marley Counting House
Issued: 1986 • Retired: 1995
#6500-5 • Original Price: $25
Market Value: $54

23

Cobblestone Shops (set/3)
Issued: 1988 • Retired: 1990
#5924-2 • Original Price: $95
Market Value: $355

23a

Booter And Cobbler
Issued: 1988 • Retired: 1990
#5924-2 • Original Price: $32
Market Value: $120

23b

T. Wells Fruit & Spice Shop
Issued: 1988 • Retired: 1990
#5924-2 • Original Price: $32
Market Value: $100

23c

The Wool Shop
Issued: 1988 • Retired: 1990
#5924-2 • Original Price: $32
Market Value: $175

Dickens' Village – Buildings

Dickens' Village Buildings

	Date Purchased	Price Paid	Value
22a.			
22b.			
22c.			
23.			
23a.			
23b.			
23c.			
Totals			

24

Cobles Police Station
Issued: 1989 • Retired: 1991
#5583-2 • Original Price: $37.50
Market Value: $150

25

Counting House & Silas Thimbleton Barrister
Issued: 1988 • Retired: 1990
#5902-1 • Original Price: $32
Market Value: $92

26

Version 2

Version 1

Crooked Fence Cottage
Issued: 1997 • Current
#58304 • Original Price: $60
Market Value:
1 – *N/E ("Se̱ires" on bottomstamp)*
2 – *$60 ("Se̱ries" on bottomstamp)*

27

Crown & Cricket Inn (LE-1992)
Charles Dickens' Signature Series
Issued: 1992 • Retired: 1992
#5750-9 • Original Price: $100
Market Value: $165

28

a *b* *c*

David Copperfield (set/3)
Issued: 1989 • Retired: 1992
#5550-6 • Original Price: $125
Market Value:
1 – *$247 (with Peggotty's version 1)*
2 – *$187 (with Peggotty's version 2)*

28a

Betsy Trotwood's Cottage
Issued: 1989 • Retired: 1992
#5550-6 • Original Price: $42.50
Market Value: $68

28b

Mr. Wickfield Solicitor
Issued: 1989 • Retired: 1992
#5550-6 • Original Price: $42.50
Market Value: $100

Dickens' Village Buildings

	Date Purchased	Price Paid	Value
24.			
25.			
26.			
27.			
28.			
28a.			
28b.			
Totals			

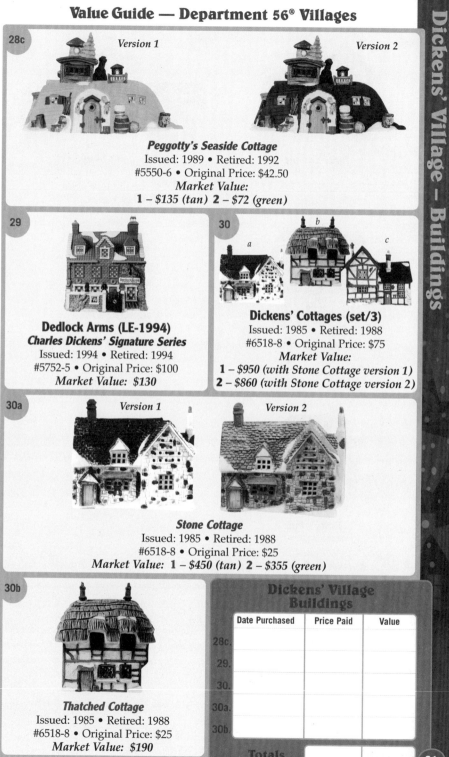

28c

Version 1   Version 2

Peggotty's Seaside Cottage
Issued: 1989 • Retired: 1992
#5550-6 • Original Price: $42.50
Market Value:
1 – *$135 (tan)* **2** – *$72 (green)*

29

Dedlock Arms (LE-1994)
Charles Dickens' Signature Series
Issued: 1994 • Retired: 1994
#5752-5 • Original Price: $100
Market Value: $130

30

Dickens' Cottages (set/3)
Issued: 1985 • Retired: 1988
#6518-8 • Original Price: $75
Market Value:
1 – *$950 (with Stone Cottage version 1)*
2 – *$860 (with Stone Cottage version 2)*

30a

Version 1   Version 2

Stone Cottage
Issued: 1985 • Retired: 1988
#6518-8 • Original Price: $25
Market Value: **1** – *$450 (tan)* **2** – *$355 (green)*

30b

Thatched Cottage
Issued: 1985 • Retired: 1988
#6518-8 • Original Price: $25
Market Value: $190

Dickens' Village Buildings

	Date Purchased	Price Paid	Value
28c.			
29.			
30.			
30a.			
30b.			
Totals			

Dickens' Village – Buildings

30c

Tudor Cottage
Issued: 1985 • Retired: 1988
#6518-8 • Original Price: $25
Market Value: $380

31

Dickens' Lane Shops (set/3)
Issued: 1986 • Retired: 1989
#6507-2 • Original Price: $80
Market Value: $570

31a

Cottage Toy Shop
Issued: 1986 • Retired: 1989
#6507-2 • Original Price: $27
Market Value: $210

31b

Thomas Kersey Coffee House
Issued: 1986 • Retired: 1989
#6507-2 • Original Price: $27
Market Value: $175

31c

Tuttle's Pub
Issued: 1986 • Retired: 1989
#6507-2 • Original Price: $27
Market Value: $220

Dickens' Village Buildings

	Date Purchased	Price Paid	Value
30c.			
31.			
31a.			
31b.			
31c.			
Totals			

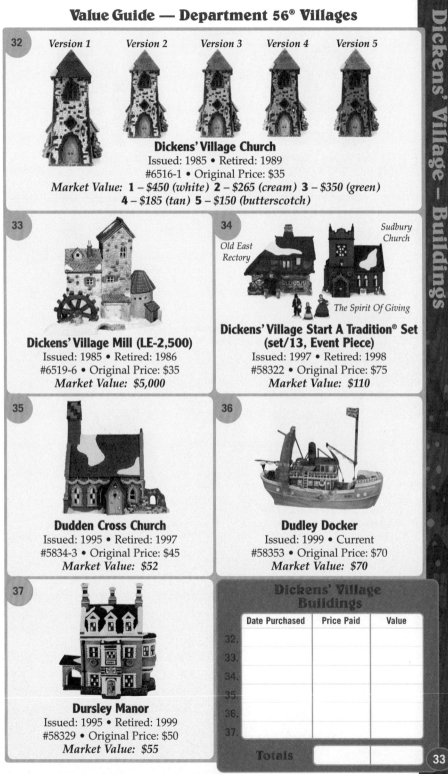

32

Version 1   Version 2   Version 3   Version 4   Version 5

Dickens' Village Church
Issued: 1985 • Retired: 1989
#6516-1 • Original Price: $35
Market Value: **1** – *$450 (white)* **2** – *$265 (cream)* **3** – *$350 (green)*
4 – *$185 (tan)* **5** – *$150 (butterscotch)*

33

Dickens' Village Mill (LE-2,500)
Issued: 1985 • Retired: 1986
#6519-6 • Original Price: $35
Market Value: $5,000

34

Old East Rectory

Sudbury Church

The Spirit Of Giving

Dickens' Village Start A Tradition® Set
(set/13, Event Piece)
Issued: 1997 • Retired: 1998
#58322 • Original Price: $75
Market Value: $110

35

Dudden Cross Church
Issued: 1995 • Retired: 1997
#5834-3 • Original Price: $45
Market Value: $52

36

Dudley Docker
Issued: 1999 • Current
#58353 • Original Price: $70
Market Value: $70

37

Dursley Manor
Issued: 1995 • Retired: 1999
#58329 • Original Price: $50
Market Value: $55

Dickens' Village Buildings

	Date Purchased	Price Paid	Value
32.			
33.			
34.			
35.			
36.			
37.			
Totals			

Dickens' Village – Buildings

38

East Indies Trading Co.
Issued: 1997 • Retired: 1999
#58302 • Original Price: $65
Market Value: N/E

39

Fagin's Hide-A-Way
Issued: 1991 • Retired: 1995
#5552-2 • Original Price: $68
Market Value: $88

40

Version 1

Version 2

The Flat Of Ebenezer Scrooge
Issued: 1989 • Current
#5587-5 • Original Price: $37.50
Market Value: 1 – $37.50 (with panes)
2 – N/E (without panes)

41

Gad's Hill Place (LE-1997)
Charles Dickens' Signature Series
Issued: 1997 • Retired: 1997
#57535 • Original Price: $98
Market Value: $130

42

Giggelswick Mutton & Ham
Issued: 1994 • Retired: 1997
#5822-0 • Original Price: $48
Market Value: $60

Dickens' Village Buildings

	Date Purchased	Price Paid	Value
38.			
39.			
40.			
41.			
42.			
43.			
Totals			

43

The Grapes Inn (LE-1996)
Charles Dickens' Signature Series
Issued: 1996 • Retired: 1996
#57534 • Original Price: $120
Market Value: $145

Dickens' Village – Buildings

44

Great Denton Mill
Issued: 1993 • Retired: 1997
#5812-2 • Original Price: $50
Market Value: $55

45

Great Expectations Satis Manor (set/4, with book)
Literary Classics
Issued: 1998 • Current
#58310 • Original Price: $110
Market Value: $110

46

Green Gate Cottage (LE-22,500)
Issued: 1989 • Retired: 1990
#5586-7 • Original Price: $65
Market Value: $275

47

Hather Harness
Issued: 1994 • Retired: 1997
#5823-8 • Original Price: $48
Market Value: $54

48

Heathmoor Castle (LE-1999)
Issued: 1998 • Retired: 1999
#58313 • Original Price: $90
Market Value: $96

49

Hembleton Pewterer
Issued: 1992 • Retired: 1995
#5800-9 • Original Price: $72
Market Value: $80

50

The Horse And Hounds Pub
Issued: 1998 • Current
#58340 • Original Price: $70
Market Value: $70

Dickens' Village Buildings

	Date Purchased	Price Paid	Value
44.			
45.			
46.			
47.			
48.			
49.			
50.			
Totals			

51

Ivy Glen Church
Issued: 1988 • Retired: 1991
#5927-7 • Original Price: $35
Market Value: $88

52

J. D. Nichols Toy Shop
Issued: 1995 • Retired: 1998
#58328 • Original Price: $48
Market Value: $57

53

Version 1

bottomstamp

Version 2

J. Lytes Coal Merchant
Issued: 1997 • Retired: 1999
#58323 • Original Price: $50
Market Value:
1 – N/E *("V*a*llage" on bottomstamp)*
2 – $55 *("Vi*l*lage" on bottomstamp)*

54

Kenilworth Castle
Issued: 1987 • Retired: 1988
#5916-1 • Original Price: $70
Market Value: $650

55

Version 1

Princess of Whales.
box

Version 2

Kensington Palace (set/23, Event Piece)
Issued: 1998 • Retired: 1998
#58309 • Original Price: $195
Market Value: **1** – N/E *("Princess of W*h*ales" on box)*
2 – $240 *("Princess of W*a*les" on box)*

Dickens' Village Buildings

	Date Purchased	Price Paid	Value
51.			
52.			
53.			
54.			
55.			
Totals			

56

King's Road (set/2)
Issued: 1990 • Retired: 1996
#5568-9 • Original Price: $72
Market Value: $100

56a

C. H. Watt Physician
Issued: 1990 • Retired: 1996
#55691 • Original Price: $36
Market Value: $54

56b

Tutbury Printer
Issued: 1990 • Retired: 1996
#55690 • Original Price: $36
Market Value: $52

57

King's Road Post Office
Issued: 1992 • Retired: 1998
#5801-7 • Original Price: $45
Market Value: $52

58

Kingsford's Brew House
Issued: 1993 • Retired: 1996
#5811-4 • Original Price: $45
Market Value: $60

59

Knottinghill Church
Issued: 1989 • Retired: 1995
#5582-4 • Original Price: $50
Market Value: $73

Dickens' Village Buildings

	Date Purchased	Price Paid	Value
56.			
56a.			
56b.			
57.			
58.			
59.			
Totals			

Dickens' Village – Buildings

Dickens' Village – Buildings

60

Leacock Poulterer
The Christmas Carol Revisited
Issued: 1997 • Retired: 1999
#58303 • Original Price: $48
Market Value: $52

61

New!

Leed's Oyster House
Issued: 1999 • Current
#58446 • Original Price: $68
Market Value: $68

62

Lynton Point Tower
Issued: 1998 • Current
#58315 • Original Price: $80
Market Value: $80

63

The Maltings
Issued: 1995 • Retired: 1998
#5833-5 • Original Price: $50
Market Value: $55

64

Frogmore Chemist   G. Choir's Weights & Scales   Lydby Trunk & Satchel Shop   Custom House

Manchester Square (set/25)
Issued: 1997 • Current
#58301 • Original Price: $250
Market Value: $250

Manchester Square Accessory

65

New!

Margrove Orangery
Issued: 1999 • Current
#58440 • Original Price: $98
Market Value: $98

Dickens' Village Buildings

	Date Purchased	Price Paid	Value
60.			
61.			
62.			
63.			
64.			
65.			
Totals			

66

New!

McShane Cottage (set/2)
Issued: 1999 • Current
#58444 • Original Price: $55
Market Value: $55

67

The Melancholy Tavern
The Christmas Carol Revisited
Issued: 1996 • Retired: 1999
#58347 • Original Price: $45
Market Value: $49

68

a   *b*   *c*   *d*   *e*

Merchant Shops (set/5)
Issued: 1988 • Retired: 1993
#5926-9 • Original Price: $150
Market Value: $260

68a

Geo. Weeton Watchmaker
Issued: 1988 • Retired: 1993
#5926-9 • Original Price: $32.50
Market Value: $53

68b

The Mermaid Fish Shoppe
Issued: 1988 • Retired: 1993
#5926-9 • Original Price: $32.50
Market Value: $78

68c

Poulterer
Issued: 1988 • Retired: 1993
#5926-9 • Original Price: $32.50
Market Value: $62

Dickens' Village Buildings

	Date Purchased	Price Paid	Value
66.			
67.			
68.			
68a.			
68b.			
68c.			
Totals			

Dickens' Village – Buildings

39

Dickens' Village – Buildings

68d

Walpole Tailors
Issued: 1988 • Retired: 1993
#5926-9 • Original Price: $32.50
Market Value: $57

68e

White Horse Bakery
Issued: 1988 • Retired: 1993
#5926-9 • Original Price: $32.50
Market Value: $65

69

Mulberrie Court
Issued: 1996 • Retired: 1999
#58345 • Original Price: $90
Market Value: $95

70

Nephew Fred's Flat
Issued: 1991 • Retired: 1994
#5557-3 • Original Price: $35
Market Value: $84

71

Nettie Quinn Puppets & Marionettes
Issued: 1996 • Current
#58344 • Original Price: $50
Market Value: $50

72

a   *b*

Nicholas Nickleby (set/2)
Issued: 1988 • Retired: 1991
#5925-0 • Original Price: $72
Market Value:
1 – *$192 (with Nickleby Cottage version 1)*
2 – *$168 (with Nickleby Cottage version 2)*

72a

Version 2

Version 1

NICKOLAS NICKLEBY

bottomstamp

Nicholas Nickleby Cottage
Issued: 1988 • Retired: 1991
#5925-0 • Original Price: $36
Market Value:
1 – *$120 ("Nickolas" on bottomstamp)*
2 – *$90 ("Nicholas" on bottomstamp)*

Dickens' Village Buildings

	Date Purchased	Price Paid	Value
68d.			
68e.			
69.			
70.			
71.			
72.			
72a.			
Totals			

72b

Wackford Squeers Boarding School
Issued: 1988 • Retired: 1991
#5925-0 • Original Price: $36
Market Value: $90

73

Norman Church (LE-3,500)
Issued: 1986 • Retired: 1987
#6502-1 • Original Price: $40
Market Value: $3,340

74

North Eastern Sea Fisheries Ltd.
Issued: 1998 • Retired: 1999
#58316 • Original Price: $70
Market Value: $73

75

The Old Curiosity Shop
Issued: 1987 • Retired: 1999
#5905-6 • Original Price: $32
Market Value: $45

76

The Old Globe Theatre
(set/4, LE-1998)
The Historical Landmark Series
Issued: 1997 • Retired: 1998
#58501 • Original Price: $175
Market Value: $190

77

Old Michaelchurch
Issued: 1992 • Retired: 1996
#5562-0 • Original Price: $42
Market Value: $64

Dickens' Village Buildings

	Date Purchased	Price Paid	Value
72b.			
73.			
74.			
75.			
76.			
77.			
Totals			

78

New!

Old Queensbridge Station (set/2)
Issued: 1999 • Current
#58443 • Original Price: $100
Market Value: $100

79

New!

The Old Royal Observatory
(set/2, LE-35,000)
The Historical Landmark Series
Issued: 1999 • Current
#58453 • Original Price: $95
Market Value: $95

80

Version 1

Version 2

The Olde Camden Town Church
The Christmas Carol Revisited
Issued: 1996 • Retired: 1999
#58346 • Original Price: $55
Market Value: **1** – $58 *(general release)* **2** – N/E *(Fortunoff)*

81

a   *b*

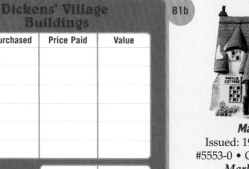

Oliver Twist (set/2)
Issued: 1991 • Retired: 1993
#5553-0 • Original Price: $75
Market Value: $135

81a

Brownlow House
Issued: 1991 • Retired: 1993
#5553-0 • Original Price: $37.50
Market Value: $74

Dickens' Village Buildings

	Date Purchased	Price Paid	Value
78.			
79.			
80.			
81.			
81a.			
81b.			
Totals			

81b

Maylie Cottage
Issued: 1991 • Retired: 1993
#5553-0 • Original Price: $37.50
Market Value: $64

Dickens' Village – Buildings

82

The Original Shops Of Dickens' Village (set/7)
Issued: 1984 • Retired: 1988
#6515-3 • Original Price: $175
Market Value: $1,300

82a

Abel Beesley Butcher
Issued: 1984 • Retired: 1988
#6515-3 • Original Price: $25
Market Value: $134

82b

Bean And Son Smithy Shop
Issued: 1984 • Retired: 1988
#6515-3 • Original Price: $25
Market Value: $195

82c

Candle Shop
Issued: 1984 • Retired: 1988
#6515-3 • Original Price: $25
Market Value: $190

82d

Crowntree Inn
Issued: 1984 • Retired: 1988
#6515-3 • Original Price: $25
Market Value: $300

82e

Golden Swan Baker
Issued: 1984 • Retired: 1988
#6515-3 • Original Price: $25
Market Value: $185

Dickens' Village Buildings

	Date Purchased	Price Paid	Value
82.			
82a.			
82b.			
82c.			
82d.			
82e.			
Totals			

Dickens' Village – Buildings

43

82f

Green Grocer
Issued: 1984 • Retired: 1988
#6515-3 • Original Price: $25
Market Value: $200

82g

Jones & Co. Brush & Basket Shop
Issued: 1984 • Retired: 1988
#6515-3 • Original Price: $25
Market Value: $298

83

The Pied Bull Inn (LE-1993)
Charles Dickens' Signature Series
Issued: 1993 • Retired: 1993
#5751-7 • Original Price: $100
Market Value: $150

84

Portobello Road Thatched Cottages (set/3)
Issued: 1994 • Retired: 1997
#5824-6 • Original Price: $120
Market Value: $130

84a

Browning Cottage
Issued: 1994 • Retired: 1997
#58249 • Original Price: $40
Market Value: $45

84b

Cobb Cottage
Issued: 1994 • Retired: 1997
#58248 • Original Price: $40
Market Value: $45

Dickens' Village Buildings

	Date Purchased	Price Paid	Value
82f.			
82g.			
83.			
84.			
84a.			
84b.			
Totals			

84c

Mr. & Mrs. Pickle
Issued: 1994 • Retired: 1997
#58247 • Original Price: $40
Market Value: $45

85

Pump Lane Shoppes (set/3)
Issued: 1993 • Retired: 1996
#5808-4 • Original Price: $112
Market Value: $142

85a

Bumpstead Nye Cloaks & Canes
Issued: 1993 • Retired: 1996
#58085 • Original Price: $37.50
Market Value: $48

85b

Lomas Ltd. Molasses
Issued: 1993 • Retired: 1996
#58086 • Original Price: $37.50
Market Value: $48

85c

W.M. Wheat Cakes & Puddings
Issued: 1993 • Retired: 1996
#58087 • Original Price: $37.50
Market Value: $48

86

Quilly's Antiques
Issued: 1996 • Retired: 1999
#58348 • Original Price: $46
Market Value: $49

Dickens' Village Buildings

	Date Purchased	Price Paid	Value
84c.			
85.			
85a.			
85b.			
85c.			
86.			
Totals			

Dickens' Village — Buildings

87

Ramsford Palace

Wall Hedge

Corner Wall Topiaries

Palace Fountain   Palace Gate   Palace Guards

Ramsford Palace (set/17, LE-27,500)
Issued: 1996 • Retired: 1996
#58336 • Original Price: $175
Market Value: $530

88

Ruth Marion Scotch Woolens (LE-17,500)
Issued: 1989 • Retired: 1990
#5585-9 • Original Price: $65
Market Value: $380

89

Seton Morris Spice Merchant

Christmas Apples

Seton Morris Spice Merchant (set/10, Event Piece)
Issued: 1998 • Retired: 1998
#58308 • Original Price: $65
Market Value: $75

90

Sir John Falstaff Inn (LE-1995)
The Charles Dickens' Signature Series
Issued: 1995 • Retired: 1995
#5753-3 • Original Price: $100
Market Value: $130

91

New!

The Spider Box Locks
Issued: 1999 • Current
#58448 • Original Price: $60
Market Value: $60

92

New!

Staghorn Lodge
Issued: 1999 • Current
#58445 • Original Price: $72
Market Value: $72

Dickens' Village Buildings

	Date Purchased	Price Paid	Value
87.			
88.			
89.			
90.			
91.			
92.			
Totals			

93

Faversham Lamps & Oil

Town Square Carolers

Morston Steak & Kidney Pie

Town Square Shops (set/2)

Start A Tradition Set (set/13)
Issued: 1995 • Retired: 1996
#5832-7 • Original Price: $85
Market Value: $110

94

Tattyeave Knoll
Issued: 1998 • Retired: 1999
#58311 • Original Price: $55
Market Value: $58

95

Teaman & Crupp China Shop
Issued: 1998 • Current
#58314 • Original Price: $64
Market Value: $64

96

Theatre Royal
Issued: 1989 • Retired: 1992
#5584-0 • Original Price: $45
Market Value: $85

97

Thomas Mudge Timepieces
Issued: 1998 • Current
#58307 • Original Price: $60
Market Value: $60

98

Tower Of London (set/5)
The Historical Landmark Series
Issued: 1997 • Retired: 1997
#58500 • Original Price: $165
Market Value: $365

Dickens' Village Buildings

	Date Purchased	Price Paid	Value
93.			
94.			
95.			
96.			
97.			
98.			
Totals			

99

Victoria Station
Issued: 1989 • Retired: 1998
#5574-3 • Original Price: $100
Market Value: $115

100

Whittlesbourne Church
Issued: 1994 • Retired: 1998
#5821-1 • Original Price: $85
Market Value: $95

101

New!

Wingham Lane Parrot Seller
Issued: 1999 • Current
#58449 • Original Price: $68
Market Value: $68

102

a   b   c

Wrenbury Shops (set/3)
Issued: 1995 • Retired: 1997
#58331 • Original Price: $100
Market Value: $120

102a

The Chop Shop
Issued: 1995 • Retired: 1997
#58333 • Original Price: $35
Market Value: $45

102b

T. Puddlewick Spectacle Shop
Issued: 1995 • Retired: 1998
#58334 • Original Price: $35
Market Value: $45

Dickens' Village Buildings

	Date Purchased	Price Paid	Value
99.			
100.			
101.			
102.			
102a.			
102b.			
102c.			
Totals			

102c

Wrenbury Baker
Issued: 1995 • Retired: 1997
#58332 • Original Price: $35
Market Value: $45

NEW ENGLAND VILLAGE – BUILDINGS

The *New England Village* collection takes collectors into the wonderful world of winter in rural New England. Five new designs were released this year, which brings the total number of buildings in the village to 62. To date, 47 buildings have been honored with retirement.

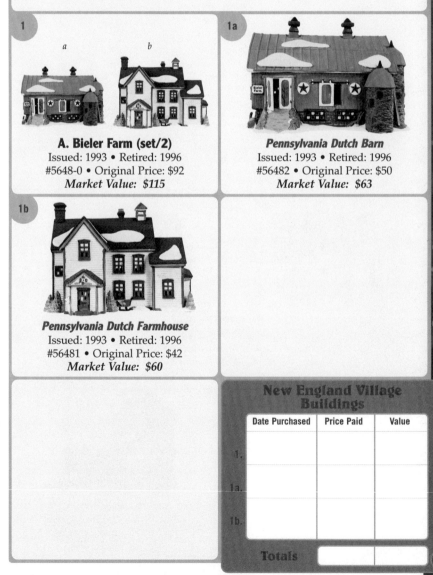

1

a　　　*b*

A. Bieler Farm (set/2)
Issued: 1993 • Retired: 1996
#5648-0 • Original Price: $92
Market Value: $115

1a

Pennsylvania Dutch Barn
Issued: 1993 • Retired: 1996
#56482 • Original Price: $50
Market Value: $63

1b

Pennsylvania Dutch Farmhouse
Issued: 1993 • Retired: 1996
#56481 • Original Price: $42
Market Value: $60

New England Village Buildings

	Date Purchased	Price Paid	Value
1.			
1a.			
1b.			
Totals			

New England Village – Buildings

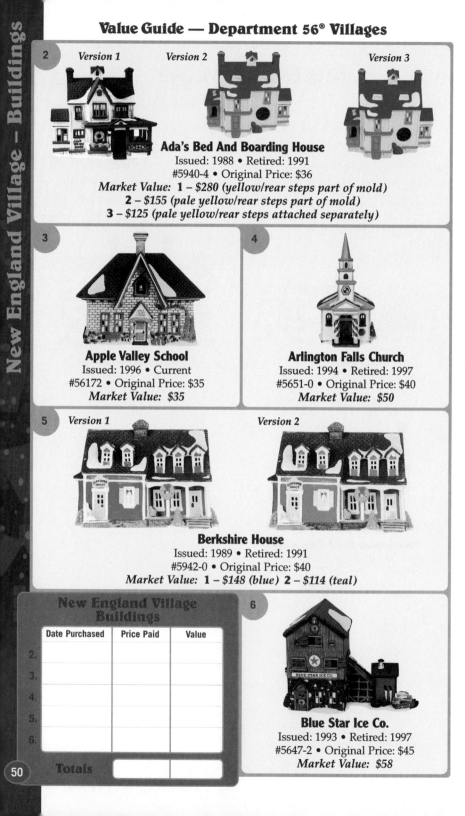

2

Version 1   *Version 2*   *Version 3*

Ada's Bed And Boarding House
Issued: 1988 • Retired: 1991
#5940-4 • Original Price: $36
Market Value: **1** – $280 *(yellow/rear steps part of mold)*
2 – $155 *(pale yellow/rear steps part of mold)*
3 – $125 *(pale yellow/rear steps attached separately)*

3

Apple Valley School
Issued: 1996 • Current
#56172 • Original Price: $35
Market Value: $35

4

Arlington Falls Church
Issued: 1994 • Retired: 1997
#5651-0 • Original Price: $40
Market Value: $50

5

Version 1   *Version 2*

Berkshire House
Issued: 1989 • Retired: 1991
#5942-0 • Original Price: $40
Market Value: **1** – $148 *(blue)* **2** – $114 *(teal)*

New England Village Buildings

	Date Purchased	Price Paid	Value
2.			
3.			
4.			
5.			
6.			
Totals			

6

Blue Star Ice Co.
Issued: 1993 • Retired: 1997
#5647-2 • Original Price: $45
Market Value: $58

Value Guide — Department 56® Villages

7

Bluebird Seed And Bulb
Issued: 1992 • Retired: 1996
#5642-1 • Original Price: $48
Market Value: $57

8

Bobwhite Cottage
Issued: 1996 • Current
#56576 • Original Price: $50
Market Value: $50

9

a *b*

Brewster Bay Cottages (set/2)
Issued: 1995 • Retired: 1997
#5657-0 • Original Price: $90
Market Value: $100

9a

Jeremiah Brewster House
Issued: 1995 • Retired: 1997
#56568 • Original Price: $45
Market Value: $50

9b

Thomas T. Julian House
Issued: 1995 • Retired: 1997
#56569 • Original Price: $45
Market Value: $50

10

Cape Keag Fish Cannery
Issued: 1994 • Retired: 1998
#5652-9 • Original Price: $48
Market Value: $56

11

Captain's Cottage
Issued: 1990 • Retired: 1996
#5947-1 • Original Price: $40
Market Value: $57

New England Village Buildings

	Date Purchased	Price Paid	Value
7.			
8.			
9.			
9a.			
9b.			
10.			
11.			
Totals			

51

New England Village – Buildings

12

a *b* *c*

Cherry Lane Shops (set/3)
Issued: 1988 • Retired: 1990
#5939-0 • Original Price: $80
Market Value: $320

12a

Anne Shaw Toys
Issued: 1988 • Retired: 1990
#5939-0 • Original Price: $27
Market Value: $160

12b

Ben's Barbershop
Issued: 1988 • Retired: 1990
#5939-0 • Original Price: $27
Market Value: $110

12c

Otis Hayes Butcher Shop
Issued: 1988 • Retired: 1990
#5939-0 • Original Price: $27
Market Value: $88

13

Chowder House
Issued: 1995 • Retired: 1998
#56571 • Original Price: $40
Market Value: $50

14

Craggy Cove Lighthouse
Issued: 1987 • Retired: 1994
#5930-7 • Original Price: $35
Market Value: $72

15

Deacon's Way Chapel
Issued: 1998 • Current
#56604 • Original Price: $68
Market Value: $68

New England Village Buildings

	Date Purchased	Price Paid	Value
12.			
12a.			
12b.			
12c.			
13.			
14.			
15.			
Totals			

16

East Willet Pottery
Issued: 1997 • Retired: 1999
#56578 • Original Price: $45
Market Value: $48

17

The Emily Louise (set/2)
Issued: 1998 • Current
#56581 • Original Price: $70
Market Value: $70

18

Franklin Hook & Ladder Co.
Issued: 1998 • Current
#56601 • Original Price: $55
Market Value: $55

19

New!

Hale & Hardy House
Issued: 1999 • Current
#56610 • Original Price: $60
Market Value: $60

20

Harper's Farm
Issued: 1998 • Current
#56605 • Original Price: $65
Market Value: $65

21

New!

Harper's Farmhouse
Issued: 1999 • Current
#56612 • Original Price: $57
Market Value: $57

22

J. Hudson Stoveworks
Issued: 1996 • Retired: 1998
#56574 • Original Price: $60
Market Value: $70

New England Village Buildings

	Date Purchased	Price Paid	Value
16.			
17.			
18.			
19.			
20.			
21.			
22.			
Totals			

New England Village – Buildings

23

Jacob Adams Farmhouse And Barn (set/5)
Issued: 1986 • Retired: 1989
#6538-2 • Original Price: $65
Market Value: $520

24

Jannes Mullet Amish Barn
Issued: 1989 • Retired: 1992
#5944-7 • Original Price: $48
Market Value: $100

25

Jannes Mullet Amish Farm House
Issued: 1989 • Retired: 1992
#5943-9 • Original Price: $32
Market Value: $120

26

***Little Women* The March Residence (set/4, *Literary Classics*, w/book)**
Issued: 1999 • Current
#56606 • Original Price: $90
Market Value: $90

27

McGrebe-Cutters & Sleighs
Issued: 1991 • Retired: 1995
#5640-5 • Original Price: $45
Market Value: $65

28

Moggin Falls General Store
Issued: 1998 • Current
#56602 • Original Price: $60
Market Value: $60

New England Village Buildings

	Date Purchased	Price Paid	Value
23.			
24.			
25.			
26.			
27.			
28.			
29.			
Totals			

29

Navigational Charts & Maps
Issued: 1996 • Retired: 1999
#56575 • Original Price: $48
Market Value: $50

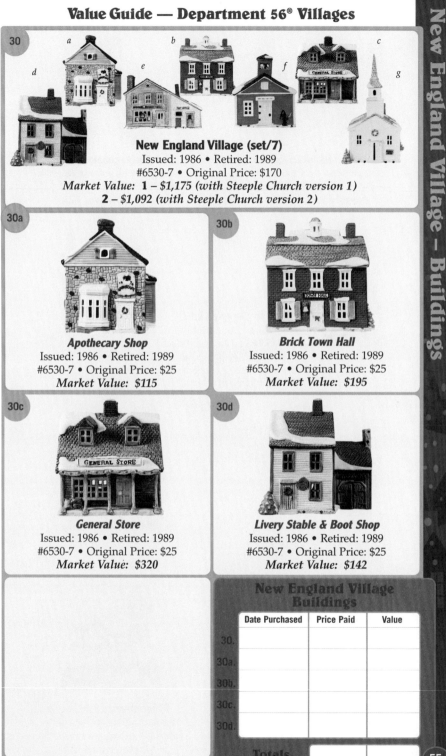

30

d   a   e   b   f   c   g

New England Village (set/7)
Issued: 1986 • Retired: 1989
#6530-7 • Original Price: $170
Market Value: **1** – $1,175 *(with Steeple Church version 1)*
2 – $1,092 *(with Steeple Church version 2)*

30a

Apothecary Shop
Issued: 1986 • Retired: 1989
#6530-7 • Original Price: $25
Market Value: $115

30b

Brick Town Hall
Issued: 1986 • Retired: 1989
#6530-7 • Original Price: $25
Market Value: $195

30c

General Store
Issued: 1986 • Retired: 1989
#6530-7 • Original Price: $25
Market Value: $320

30d

Livery Stable & Boot Shop
Issued: 1986 • Retired: 1989
#6530-7 • Original Price: $25
Market Value: $142

New England Village Buildings

	Date Purchased	Price Paid	Value
30.			
30a.			
30b.			
30c.			
30d.			
Totals			

55

New England Village – Buildings

30e

Nathaniel Bingham Fabrics
Issued: 1986 • Retired: 1989
#6530-7 • Original Price: $25
Market Value: $165

30f

Red Schoolhouse
Issued: 1986 • Retired: 1989
#6530-7 • Original Price: $25
Market Value: $255

30g

Version 1   Version 2

Steeple Church
Issued: 1986 • Retired: 1989
#6530-7 • Original Price: $25
Market Value:
1 – $182 (tree attached with slip)
2 – $100 (tree attached with glue)

31

Old North Church
Issued: 1988 • Retired: 1998
#5932-3 • Original Price: $40
Market Value: $52

32

Pierce Boat Works
Issued: 1995 • Current
#56573 • Original Price: $55
Market Value: $55

New England Village Buildings

	Date Purchased	Price Paid	Value
30e.			
30f.			
30g.			
31.			
32.			
33.			
Totals			

33

Pigeonhead Lighthouse
Issued: 1994 • Retired: 1998
#5653-7 • Original Price: $50
Market Value: $56

34

New!

P. L. Wheeler's Bicycle Shop
Issued: 1999 • Current
#56613 • Original Price: $57
Market Value: $57

35

New!

Platt's Candles & Wax
Issued: 1999 • Current
#56614 • Original Price: $60
Market Value: $60

36

Semple's Smokehouse
Issued: 1997 • Retired: 1999
#56580 • Original Price: $45
Market Value: $49

37

Shingle Creek House
Issued: 1990 • Retired: 1994
#5946-3 • Original Price: $37.50
Market Value: $60

38

b

c

a

Sleepy Hollow (set/3)
Issued: 1990 • Retired: 1993
#5954-4 • Original Price: $96
Market Value: $190

38a

Ichabod Crane's Cottage
Issued: 1990 • Retired: 1993
#5954-4 • Original Price: $32
Market Value: $57

38b

Sleepy Hollow School
Issued: 1990 • Retired: 1993
#5954-4 • Original Price: $32
Market Value: $95

New England Village Buildings

	Date Purchased	Price Paid	Value
34.			
35.			
36.			
37.			
38.			
38a.			
38b.			
Totals			

New England Village – Buildings

38c

Van Tassel Manor
Issued: 1990 • Retired: 1993
#5954-4 • Original Price: $32
Market Value: $60

39

Sleepy Hollow Church
Issued: 1990 • Retired: 1993
#5955-2 • Original Price: $36
Market Value: $65

40

Smythe Woolen Mill (LE-7,500)
Issued: 1987 • Retired: 1988
#6543-9 • Original Price: $42
Market Value: $1,100

41

Steen's Maple House
(with magic smoking element)
Issued: 1997 • Current
#56579 • Original Price: $60
Market Value: $60

42

Steeple Church
Issued: 1986 • Retired: 1990
#6539-0 • Original Price: $30
Market Value: $93

43

Stoney Brook Town Hall
Issued: 1992 • Retired: 1995
#5644-8 • Original Price: $42
Market Value: $55

44

Timber Knoll Log Cabin
Issued: 1987 • Retired: 1990
#6544-7 • Original Price: $28
Market Value: $177

New England Village Buildings

	Date Purchased	Price Paid	Value
38c.			
39.			
40.			
41.			
42.			
43.			
44.			
Totals			

45

New!

Trinity Ledge
Issued: 1999 • Current
#56611 • Original Price: $85
Market Value: $85

46

Van Guilder's Ornamental Ironworks
Issued: 1997 • Retired: 1999
#56577 • Original Price: $50
Market Value: $53

47

Weston Train Station
Issued: 1987 • Retired: 1989
#5931-5 • Original Price: $42
Market Value: $275

48

Woodbridge Post Office
Issued: 1995 • Retired: 1998
#56572 • Original Price: $40
Market Value: $47

49

Yankee Jud Bell Casting
Issued: 1992 • Retired: 1995
#5643-0 • Original Price: $44
Market Value: $60

New England Village Buildings

	Date Purchased	Price Paid	Value
45.			
46.			
47.			
48.			
49.			
Totals			

New England Village – Buildings

ALPINE VILLAGE – BUILDINGS

Brilliantly depicting the holiday season, *Alpine Village* consists of 23 buildings, including two new additions this year, "Glockenspiel" and "The Sound of Music® Wedding Church." Since 1986, many collectors have been charmed by this small European mountain town.

1

Version 1   *Version 2*

Alpine Church
Issued: 1987 • Retired: 1991
#6541-2 • Original Price: $32
Market Value: **1** – *$450 (white trim)* **2** – *$178 (brown trim)*

2

a   *b*

Alpine Shops (set/2)
Issued: 1992 • Retired: 1997
#5618-9 • Original Price: $75
Market Value: $85

2a

Kukuck Uhren
Issued: 1992 • Retired: 1998
#56191 • Original Price: $37.50
Market Value: $40

2b

Metterniche Wurst
Issued: 1992 • Retired: 1997
#56190 • Original Price: $37.50
Market Value: $45

Alpine Village Buildings

	Date Purchased	Price Paid	Value
1.			
2.			
2a.			
2b.			
Totals			

Value Guide — Department 56® Villages

3

Alpine Village (set/5)
Issued: 1986 • Retired: 1996
#6540-4 • Original Price: $150
Market Value: $178

3a

Apotheke
Issued: 1986 • Retired: 1997
#65407 • Original Price: $25
Market Value: $42

3b

Besson Bierkeller
Issued: 1986 • Retired: 1996
#65405 • Original Price: $25
Market Value: $45

3c

E. Staubr Backer
Issued: 1986 • Retired: 1997
#65408 • Original Price: $25
Market Value: $44

3d

Gasthof Eisl
Issued: 1986 • Retired: 1996
#65406 • Original Price: $25
Market Value: $44

3e

Milch-Kase
Issued: 1986 • Retired: 1996
#65409 • Original Price: $25
Market Value: $46

4

Bahnhof
Issued: 1990 • Retired: 1993
#5615-4 • Original Price: $42
Market Value: $85

Alpine Village Buildings

	Date Purchased	Price Paid	Value
3.			
3a.			
3b.			
3c.			
3d.			
3e.			
4.			
Totals			

Alpine Village — Buildings

5

Bakery & Chocolate Shop (Konditorei Schokolade)
Issued: 1994 • Retired: 1998
#5614-6 • Original Price: $37.50
Market Value: $43

6

Bernhardiner Hundchen (St. Bernard Puppies)
Issued: 1997 • Current
#56174 • Original Price: $50
Market Value: $50

7

Danube Music Publisher
Issued: 1996 • Current
#56173 • Original Price: $55
Market Value: $55

8

Federbetten Und Steppdecken
Issued: 1998 • Current
#56176 • Orig. Price: $48
Market Value: $48

9

New!

Glockenspiel (animated, musical)
Issued: 1999 • Current
#56210 • Original Price: $80
Market Value: $80

10

Grist Mill
Issued: 1988 • Retired: 1997
#5953-6 • Original Price: $42
Market Value: $54

11

Heidi's Grandfather's House
Issued: 1998 • Current
#56177 • Original Price: $64
Market Value: $64

Alpine Village Buildings

	Date Purchased	Price Paid	Value
5.			
6.			
7.			
8.			
9.			
10.			
11.			
Totals			

12

Josef Engel Farmhouse
Issued: 1987 • Retired: 1989
#5952-8 • Original Price: $33
Market Value: $980

13

Kamm Haus
Issued: 1995 • Retired: 1999
#56171 • Original Price: $42
Market Value: $45

14

St. Nikolaus Kirche
Issued: 1991 • Retired: 1999
#5617-0 • Original Price: $37.50
Market Value: $43

15

The Sound Of Music®
von Trapp Villa (set/5)
Issued: 1998 • Current
#56178 • Orig. Price: $130
Market Value: $130

16

New!

The Sound Of Music® Wedding Church
Issued: 1999 • Current
#56211 • Original Price: $60
Market Value: $60

17

Spielzeug Laden
Issued: 1997 • Current
#56192 • Original Price: $65
Market Value: $65

18

Sport Laden
Issued: 1993 • Retired: 1998
#5612-0 • Original Price: $50
Market Value: $55

Alpine Village Buildings

	Date Purchased	Price Paid	Value
12.			
13.			
14.			
15.			
16.			
17.			
18.			
Totals			

CHRISTMAS IN THE CITY – BUILDINGS

Experience the true essence of Christmas with *Christmas in the City*. Replicas of urban buildings are decorated for the holidays, while city folk get ready to celebrate the season. Three-story brownstones, corner cafes and churches bring the excitement of the city right into your home.

1

New!

5th Avenue Salon
Issued: 1999 • Current
#58950 • Original Price: $68
Market Value: $68

2

5607 Park Avenue Townhouse
Issued: 1989 • Retired: 1992
#5977-3 • Original Price: $48
Market Value: $94

3

5609 Park Avenue Townhouse
Issued: 1989 • Retired: 1992
#5978-1 • Original Price: $48
Market Value: $94

4

All Saints Corner Church
Issued: 1991 • Retired: 1998
#5542-5 • Original Price: $96
Market Value: $116

5

Arts Academy
Issued: 1991 • Retired: 1993
#5543-3 • Original Price: $45
Market Value: $80

Christmas in the City Buildings

	Date Purchased	Price Paid	Value
1.			
2.			
3.			
4.			
5.			
Totals			

6

Brighton School
Issued: 1995 • Retired: 1998
#58876 • Original Price: $52
Market Value: $65

7

Brokerage House
Issued: 1994 • Retired: 1997
#5881-5 • Original Price: $48
Market Value: $64

8   *a*   *b*

Brownstones On The Square (set/2)
Issued: 1995 • Retired: 1998
#58877 • Original Price: $90
Market Value: N/E

8a

Beekman House
Issued: 1995 • Current
#58878 • Original Price: $45
Market Value: $45

8b

Pickford Place
Issued: 1995 • Retired: 1998
#58879 • Original Price: $45
Market Value: $55

9

Cafe Caprice French Restaurant
Issued: 1996 • Current
#58882 • Original Price: $45
Market Value: $45

10

The Capitol
Issued: 1997 • Retired: 1998
#58887 • Original Price: $110
Market Value: $140

Christmas in the City Buildings

	Date Purchased	Price Paid	Value
6.			
7.			
8.			
8a.			
8b.			
9.			
10.			
Totals			

11

The Cathedral
Issued: 1987 • Retired: 1990
#5962-5 • Original Price: $60
Market Value: $365

12

Cathedral Church Of St. Mark (LE-3,024)
Issued: 1991 • Retired: 1993
#5549-2 • Original Price: $120
Market Value: $2,100

13

Chocolate Shoppe
Issued: 1988 • Retired: 1991
#5968-4 • Original Price: $40
Market Value: $155

14

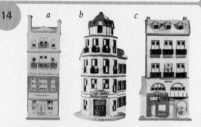

a   b   c

Christmas In The City (set/3)
Issued: 1987 • Retired: 1990
#6512-9 • Original Price: $112
Market Value: $625

14a

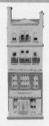

Bakery
Issued: 1987 • Retired: 1990
#6512-9 • Original Price: $37.50
Market Value: $135

14b

Tower Restaurant
Issued: 1987 • Retired: 1990
#6512-9 • Original Price: $37.50
Market Value: $275

Christmas in the City Buildings

	Date Purchased	Price Paid	Value
11.			
12.			
13.			
14.			
14a.			
14b.			
14c.			
Totals			

14c

Toy Shop And Pet Store
Issued: 1987 • Retired: 1990
#6512-9 • Original Price: $37.50
Market Value: $275

15

The City Globe
Issued: 1997 • Current
#58883 • Original Price: $65
Market Value: $65

16

City Hall
Issued: 1988 • Retired: 1991
#5969-2 • Original Price: $65
Market Value: $190

17

New!

Clark Street Automat
Issued: 1999 • Current
#58954 • Original Price: $68
Market Value: $68

18

New!

The Consulate
(set/2, LE-2000)
Issued: 1999 • Current
#58951 • Original Price: $95
Market Value: $95

19

The Doctor's Office
Issued: 1991 • Retired: 1994
#5544-1 • Original Price: $60
Market Value: $87

20

Dorothy's Dress Shop (LE-12,500)
Issued: 1989 • Retired: 1991
#5974-9 • Original Price: $70
Market Value: $385

21

First Metropolitan Bank
Issued: 1994 • Retired: 1997
#5882-3 • Original Price: $60
Market Value: $72

Christmas in the City Buildings

	Date Purchased	Price Paid	Value
15.			
16.			
17.			
18.			
19.			
20.			
21.			
Totals			

22

Grand Central Railway Station
Issued: 1996 • Retired: 1999
#58881 • Original Price: $90
Market Value: $96

23

The Grand Movie Theater
Issued: 1998 • Retired: 1999
#58870 • Original Price: $50
Market Value: $59

24

Hank's Market
Issued: 1988 • Retired: 1992
#5970-6 • Original Price: $40
Market Value: $95

25

Heritage Museum Of Art
Issued: 1994 • Retired: 1998
#5883-1 • Original Price: $96
Market Value: $112

26

Hi-De-Ho Nightclub
Issued: 1997 • Retired: 1999
#58884 • Original Price: $52
Market Value: $60

27

Hollydale's Department Store
Issued: 1991 • Retired: 1997
#5534-4 • Original Price: $75
Market Value: $100

Christmas in the City Buildings

	Date Purchased	Price Paid	Value
22.			
23.			
24.			
25.			
26.			
27.			
Totals			

28

Holy Name Church
Issued: 1995 • Current
#58875 • Original Price: $96
Market Value: $96

29

Ivy Terrace Apartments
Issued: 1995 • Retired: 1997
#5887-4 • Original Price: $60
Market Value: $72

30

Johnson's Grocery & Deli
Issued: 1997 • Current
#58886 • Original Price: $60
Market Value: $60

31

New!

Lafayette's Bakery
Issued: 1999 • Current
#58953 • Original Price: $62
Market Value: $62

32

"Little Italy" Ristorante
Issued: 1991 • Retired: 1995
#5538-7 • Original Price: $50
Market Value: $95

33

New!

Molly O'Brien's Irish Pub
Issued: 1999 • Current
#58952 • Original Price: $62
Market Value: $62

34

Old Trinity Church
Issued: 1998 • Current
#58940 • Original Price: $96
Market Value: $96

Christmas in the City Buildings

	Date Purchased	Price Paid	Value
28.			
29.			
30.			
31.			
32.			
33.			
34.			
Totals			

35

Palace Theatre
Issued: 1987 • Retired: 1989
#5963-3 • Original Price: $45
Market Value: $920

36

Parkview Hospital
Issued: 1999 • Current
#58947 • Original Price: $65
Market Value: $65

37

Precinct 25 Police Station
Issued: 1998 • Current
#58941 • Original Price: $56
Market Value: $56

38

Red Brick Fire Station
Issued: 1990 • Retired: 1995
#5536-0 • Original Price: $55
Market Value: $88

39

Ritz Hotel
Issued: 1989 • Retired: 1994
#5973-0 • Original Price: $55
Market Value: $85

40

Riverside Row Shops
Issued: 1997 • Retired: 1999
#58888 • Original Price: $52
Market Value: $57

Christmas in the City Buildings

	Date Purchased	Price Paid	Value
35.			
36.			
37.			
38.			
39.			
40.			
41.			
Totals			

41

Scottie's Toy Shop

5¢ Pony Rides

Scottie's Toy Shop
(set/10, Event Piece)
Issued: 1998 • Retired: 1998
#58871 • Orig. Price: $65
Market Value: $98

42

Sutton Place Brownstones
Issued: 1987 • Retired: 1989
#5961-7 • Original Price: $80
Market Value: $870

43

The University Club
Issued: 1998 • Current
#58945 • Original Price: $60
Market Value: $60

44

a *b* *c*

Uptown Shoppes (set/3)
Issued: 1992 • Retired: 1996
#5531-0 • Original Price: $150
Market Value: $188

44a

City Clockworks
Issued: 1992 • Retired: 1996
#55313 • Original Price: $56
Market Value: $70

44b

Haberdashery
Issued: 1992 • Retired: 1996
#55311 • Original Price: $40
Market Value: $58

44c

Music Emporium
Issued: 1992 • Retired: 1996
#55312 • Original Price: $54
Market Value: $70

45

Variety Store
Issued: 1988 • Retired: 1990
#5972-2 • Original Price: $45
Market Value: $192

Christmas in the City Buildings

	Date Purchased	Price Paid	Value
42.			
43.			
44.			
44a.			
44b.			
44c.			
45.			
Totals			

46

Washington Street Post Office
Issued: 1996 • Retired: 1998
#58880 • Original Price: $52
Market Value: $64

47

The Wedding Gallery
Issued: 1998 • Current
#58943 • Original Price: $60
Market Value: $60

48

a *b*

West Village Shops (set/2)
Issued: 1993 • Retired: 1996
#5880-7 • Original Price: $90
Market Value: $117

48a

Potter's Tea Seller
Issued: 1993 • Retired: 1996
#58808 • Original Price: $45
Market Value: $60

48b

Spring St. Coffee House
Issued: 1993 • Retired: 1996
#58809 • Original Price: $45
Market Value: $60

49

Wintergarten Cafe
Issued: 1999 • Retired: 1999
#58948 • Original Price: $60
Market Value: $70

Christmas in the City Buildings

	Date Purchased	Price Paid	Value
46.			
47.			
48.			
48a.			
48b.			
49.			
50.			
Totals			

50

Wong's In Chinatown
Issued: 1990 • Retired: 1994
#5537-9 • Original Price: $55
Market Value: $86

NORTH POLE – BUILDINGS

Introduced in 1990, this series vividly portrays Santa's homeland at the North Pole. The village features two new *Elf Land* pieces for 2000, "Cold Care Clinic" and "Mini-Donut Shop." Four additional new buildings – "Elf Mountain Ski Resort," "The Peanut Brittle Factory," "Northern Lights Tinsel Mill" and "Jack In The Box Plant No. 2" – bring the total number of the collection to 46 buildings; 29 of which have been retired.

1 Beard Barber Shop
Issued: 1994 • Retired: 1997
#5634-0 • Original Price: $27.50
Market Value: $42

2 Christmas Bread Bakers
Issued: 1996 • Current
#56393 • Original Price: $55
Market Value: $55

3 New! Cold Care Clinic
Elf Land
Issued: 1999 • Current
#56703 • Original Price: $42
Market Value: $42

4 Custom Stitchers
Elf Land
Issued: 1998 • Current
#56400 • Original Price: $37.50
Market Value: $37.50

5 New! Elf Mountain Ski Resort
Issued: 1999 • Current
#56700 • Original Price: $70
Market Value: $70

North Pole Buildings

	Date Purchased	Price Paid	Value
1.			
2.			
3.			
4.			
5.			
Totals			

73

6

The Elf Spa
Elf Land
Issued: 1998 • Current
#56402 • Original Price: $40
Market Value: $40

7

Elfie's Sleds & Skates
Issued: 1992 • Retired: 1996
#5625-1 • Original Price: $48
Market Value: $64

8

Elfin Forge & Assembly Shop
Issued: 1995 • Retired: 1998
#56384 • Original Price: $65
Market Value: $75

9

Elfin Snow Cone Works
Issued: 1994 • Retired: 1997
#5633-2 • Original Price: $40
Market Value: $54

10

Elsie's Gingerbread (with magic smoking element, LE–1998)
Issued: 1997 • Retired: 1998
#56398 • Original Price: $65
Market Value: $105

11

Elves' Trade School
Issued: 1995 • Retired: 1998
#56387 • Original Price: $50
Market Value: $60

12

The Glacier Gazette
Issued: 1997 • Retired: 1999
#56394 • Original Price: $48
Market Value: $52

North Pole Buildings

	Date Purchased	Price Paid	Value
6.			
7.			
8.			
9.			
10.			
11.			
12.			
Totals			

Value Guide — Department 56® Villages

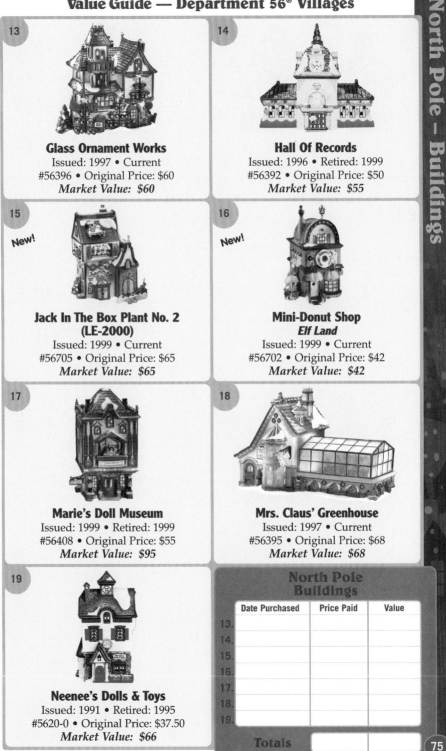

13

Glass Ornament Works
Issued: 1997 • Current
#56396 • Original Price: $60
Market Value: $60

14

Hall Of Records
Issued: 1996 • Retired: 1999
#56392 • Original Price: $50
Market Value: $55

15 New!

**Jack In The Box Plant No. 2
(LE-2000)**
Issued: 1999 • Current
#56705 • Original Price: $65
Market Value: $65

16 New!

Mini-Donut Shop
Elf Land
Issued: 1999 • Current
#56702 • Original Price: $42
Market Value: $42

17

Marie's Doll Museum
Issued: 1999 • Retired: 1999
#56408 • Original Price: $55
Market Value: $95

18

Mrs. Claus' Greenhouse
Issued: 1997 • Current
#56395 • Original Price: $68
Market Value: $68

19

Neenee's Dolls & Toys
Issued: 1991 • Retired: 1995
#5620-0 • Original Price: $37.50
Market Value: $66

North Pole Buildings

	Date Purchased	Price Paid	Value
13.			
14.			
15.			
16.			
17.			
18.			
19.			
Totals			

75

20

a   *b*

North Pole (set/2)
Issued: 1990 • Retired: 1996
#5601-4 • Original Price: $70
Market Value: N/E

20a

Elf Bunkhouse
Issued: 1990 • Retired: 1996
#56016 • Original Price: $35
Market Value: $57

20b

Reindeer Barn
Issued: 1990 • Current
#56015 • Original Price: $35
Market Value: $40

21

North Pole Chapel
Issued: 1993 • Current
#5626-0 • Original Price: $45
Market Value: $45

22

North Pole Dolls   Santa's Bear Works

Entrance

North Pole Dolls & Santa's Bear Works (set/3)
Issued: 1994 • Retired: 1997
#5635-9 • Original Price: $96
Market Value: $120

23

North Pole Express Depot
Issued: 1993 • Retired: 1998
#5627-8 • Original Price: $48
Market Value: $57

North Pole Buildings

	Date Purchased	Price Paid	Value
20.			
20a.			
20b.			
21.			
22.			
23.			
Totals			

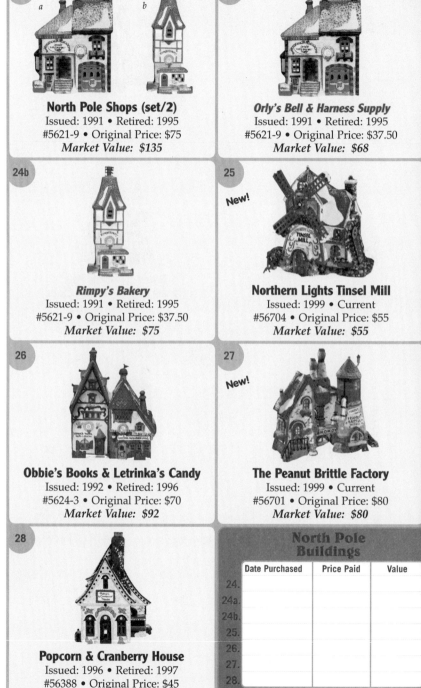

24

a   b

North Pole Shops (set/2)
Issued: 1991 • Retired: 1995
#5621-9 • Original Price: $75
Market Value: $135

24a

Orly's Bell & Harness Supply
Issued: 1991 • Retired: 1995
#5621-9 • Original Price: $37.50
Market Value: $68

24b

Rimpy's Bakery
Issued: 1991 • Retired: 1995
#5621-9 • Original Price: $37.50
Market Value: $75

25

New!

Northern Lights Tinsel Mill
Issued: 1999 • Current
#56704 • Original Price: $55
Market Value: $55

26

Obbie's Books & Letrinka's Candy
Issued: 1992 • Retired: 1996
#5624-3 • Original Price: $70
Market Value: $92

27

New!

The Peanut Brittle Factory
Issued: 1999 • Current
#56701 • Original Price: $80
Market Value: $80

28

Popcorn & Cranberry House
Issued: 1996 • Retired: 1997
#56388 • Original Price: $45
Market Value: $92

North Pole Buildings

	Date Purchased	Price Paid	Value
24.			
24a.			
24b.			
25.			
26.			
27.			
28.			
Totals			

North Pole – Buildings

29

Post Office
Issued: 1992 • Retired: 1999
#5623-5 • Original Price: $45
Market Value: $60

30

Real Plastic Snow Factory
Issued: 1998 • Current
#56403 • Original Price: $80
Market Value: $80

31

Reindeer Flight School
Issued: 1998 • Current
#56404 • Original Price: $55
Market Value: $55

32

Route 1, North Pole, Home Of Mr. & Mrs. Claus
Issued: 1996 • Current
#56391 • Original Price: $110
Market Value: $110

33

Santa's Bell Repair
Issued: 1996 • Retired: 1998
#56389 • Original Price: $45
Market Value: $57

34

Santa's Light Shop
Issued: 1997 • Current
#56397 • Original Price: $52
Market Value: $52

35

Santa's Lookout Tower
Issued: 1993 • Current
#5629-4 • Original Price: $45
Market Value: $48

North Pole Buildings

	Date Purchased	Price Paid	Value
29.			
30.			
31.			
32.			
33.			
34.			
35.			
Totals			

36

Santa's Rooming House
Issued: 1995 • Retired: 1999
#56386 • Original Price: $50
Market Value: $55

37

Santa's Visiting Center (set/6, Event Piece)
Issued: 1999 • Retired: 1999
#56407 • Original Price: $65
Market Value: $95

38

Santa's Woodworks
Issued: 1993 • Retired: 1996
#5628-6 • Original Price: $42
Market Value: $65

39

Santa's Workshop
Issued: 1990 • Retired: 1993
#5600-6 • Original Price: $72
Market Value: $425

40

Gift Wrap & Ribbons

Candy Cane & Peppermint Shop

Candy Cane Lane (set/2)

Candy Cane Elves (set/2)

Start A Tradition (set/12)
Issued: 1996 • Retired: 1996
#56390 • Original Price: $85
Market Value: $108

41

Tassy's Mittens & Hassel's Woolies
Issued: 1991 • Retired: 1995
#5622-7 • Original Price: $50
Market Value: $87

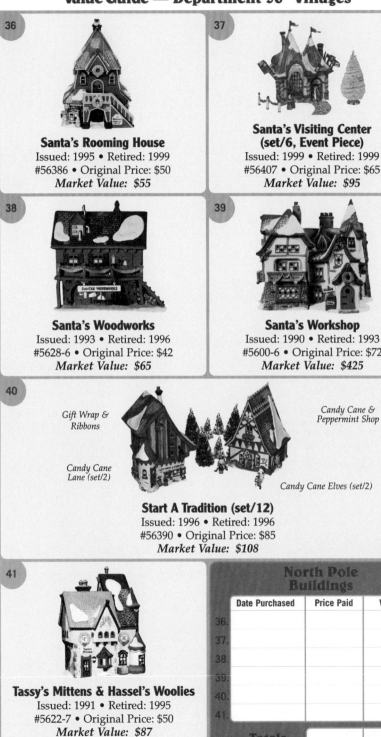

North Pole Buildings

	Date Purchased	Price Paid	Value
36.			
37.			
38.			
39.			
40.			
41.			
Totals			

42

Tillie's Tiny Cup Café
Elf Land
Issued: 1998 • Current
#56401 • Original Price: $37.50
Market Value: $37.50

43

Tin Soldier Shop
Issued: 1995 • Retired: 1997
#5638-3 • Original Price: $42
Market Value: $55

44

Weather & Time Observatory
Issued: 1995 • Retired: 1999
#56385 • Original Price: $50
Market Value: $54

North Pole Buildings

	Date Purchased	Price Paid	Value
42.			
43.			
44.			
Totals			

DISNEY PARK VILLAGE – BUILDINGS

In 1994, Department 56 introduced four Disney theme park buildings – "Disneyland Fire Department #105," "Mickey's Christmas Carol" (set/2) and "Old World Antiques Shops" (set/2). The following year, "Silversmith" and "Tinker Bell's Treasures" were added to the village. The entire collection was retired in 1996, just two years after its release.

1

Disneyland Fire Department #105
Issued: 1994 • Retired: 1996
#5352-0 • Original Price: $45
Market Value: $52

2

Version 1 *Version 2*

Mickey's Christmas Carol (set/2)
Issued: 1994 • Retired: 1996
#5350-3 • Original Price: $144
Market Value:
1 – *$155 (with spires on dormers)*
2 – *$155 (without spires on dormers)*

3
a *b*

Olde World Antiques Shops (set/2)
Issued: 1994 • Retired: 1996
#5351-1 • Original Price: $90
Market Value: $100

3a

Olde World Antiques I
Issued: 1994 • Retired: 1996
#5351-1 • Original Price: $45
Market Value: $55

3b

Olde World Antiques II
Issued: 1994 • Retired: 1996
#5351-1 • Original Price: $45
Market Value: $55

Disney Park Village Buildings

	Date Purchased	Price Paid	Value
1.			
2.			
3.			
3a.			
3b.			
Totals			

4

Silversmith
Issued: 1995 • Retired: 1996
#53521 • Original Price: $50
Market Value: $280

5

Tinker Bell's Treasures
Issued: 1995 • Retired: 1996
#53522 • Original Price: $60
Market Value: $280

Disney Park Village Buildings

	Date Purchased	Price Paid	Value
4.			
5.			
Totals			

LITTLE TOWN OF BETHLEHEM – BUILDINGS

Originally released as a complete set, "Little Town Of Bethlehem" (set/12) was available from 1987 until its retirement in 1999. For 2000, "Gatekeeper's Dwelling," "Innkeeper's Caravansary" and "Nativity" (set/2) made their debut into the Department 56 collectible line.

1 New!

Gatekeeper's Dwelling
Issued: 1999 • Current
#59797 • Original Price: $55
Market Value: $55

2 New!

Innkeeper's Caravansary
Issued: 1999 • Current
#59795 • Original Price: $70
Market Value: $70

3

Little Town Of Bethlehem (set/12)
Issued: 1987 • Retired: 1999
#5975-7 • Original Price: $150
Market Value: N/E

4 New!

Nativity (set/2)
Issued: 1999 • Current
#59796 • Original Price: $55
Market Value: $55

Little Town of Bethlehem Buildings		
Date Purchased	Price Paid	Value
1.		
2.		
3.		
4.		
Totals		

HERITAGE VILLAGE – ACCESSORIES

Just as a piece of jewelry can make an outfit, accessory pieces add a personal touch to displays. The following pieces are not specific to a particular village and can be mixed and matched with all Department 56 villages.

1

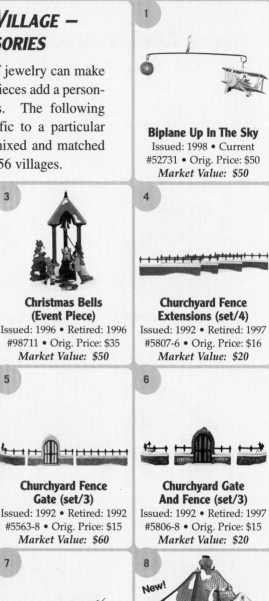

Biplane Up In The Sky
Issued: 1998 • Current
#52731 • Orig. Price: $50
Market Value: $50

2

Christmas At The Park (set/3)
Issued: 1993 • Current
#5866-1 • Orig. Price: $27.50
Market Value: $27.50

3

Christmas Bells (Event Piece)
Issued: 1996 • Retired: 1996
#98711 • Orig. Price: $35
Market Value: $50

4

Churchyard Fence Extensions (set/4)
Issued: 1992 • Retired: 1997
#5807-6 • Orig. Price: $16
Market Value: $20

5

Churchyard Fence Gate (set/3)
Issued: 1992 • Retired: 1992
#5563-8 • Orig. Price: $15
Market Value: $60

6

Churchyard Gate And Fence (set/3)
Issued: 1992 • Retired: 1997
#5806-8 • Orig. Price: $15
Market Value: $20

7

Dashing Through The Snow
Issued: 1993 • Current
#5820-3 • Orig. Price: $32.50
Market Value: $32.50

8

New!

Dorothy's Skate Rental
Issued: 1999 • Current
#55515 • Orig. Price: $35
Market Value: $35

Heritage Village Accessories

	Date Purchased	Price Paid	Value
1.			
2.			
3.			
4.			
5.			
6.			
7.			
8.			

Totals

Value Guide — Department 56® Villages

9

New!

Family Winter Outing (set/3, animated)
Issued: 1999 • Current
#55033 • Orig. Price: $10
Market Value: $10

10

Gate House (Event Piece)
Issued: 1992 • Retired: 1992
#5530-1 • Orig. Price: $22.50
Market Value: $53

11

New!

Hear Ye, Hear Ye
Issued: 1999 • Current
#55523 • Orig. Price: $13.50
Market Value: $13.50

12

Heritage Village Promotional Sign
Issued: 1989 • Retired: 1990
#9953-8 • Orig. Price: $5
Market Value: $30

13

The Holly & The Ivy (set/2, Event Piece)
Issued: 1997 • Retired: 1997
#56100 • Orig. Price: $17.50
Market Value: $33

14

Lighted Tree w/Children And Ladder (set/3)
Issued: 1986 • Retired: 1989
#6510-2 • Orig. Price: $35
Market Value: $300

15

One Horse Open Sleigh
Issued: 1988 • Retired: 1993
#5982-0 • Orig. Price: $20
Market Value: $42

16

Painting Our Own Village Sign
Issued: 1998 • Current
#55501 • Orig. Price: $12.50
Market Value: $12.50

Heritage Village Accessories

	Date Purchased	Price Paid	Value
9.			
10.			
11.			
12.			
13.			
14.			
15.			
16.			
Totals			

Heritage Village – Accessories

17

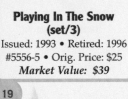

Playing In The Snow (set/3)
Issued: 1993 • Retired: 1996
#5556-5 • Orig. Price: $25
Market Value: $39

18

Version 1   *Version 2*

Poinsettia Delivery Truck
Issued: 1997 • Retired: 1999
#59000 • Orig. Price: $32.50
Market Value:
1 – $37 (general release) **2** – $45 (William Glen)

19

Porcelain Trees (set/2)
Issued: 1986 • Retired: 1992
#6537-4 • Orig. Price: $14
Market Value: $40

20

Skating Party (set/3)
Issued: 1991 • Current
#5523-9 • Orig. Price: $27.50
Market Value: $27.50

21

Skating Pond
Issued: 1987 • Retired: 1990
#6545-5 • Orig. Price: $24
Market Value: $82

22

Ski Slope
Issued: 1998 • Current
#52733 • Orig. Price: $75
Market Value: $75

23

Snow Children (set/3)
Issued: 1988 • Retired: 1994
#5938-2 • Orig. Price: $15
Market Value: $37

Heritage Village Accessories

	Date Purchased	Price Paid	Value
17.			
18.			
19.			
20.			
21.			
22.			
23.			
Totals			

Value Guide — Department 56® Villages

24

**Stars And Stripes Forever
(Event Piece, music box)**
Issued: 1998 • Retired: 1999
#55502 • Orig. Price: $50
Market Value: $53

25

New!

**Through The Woods
(set/4)**
Issued: 1999 • Current
#52791 • Orig. Price: $75
Market Value: $75

26

Town Square Gazebo
Issued: 1989 • Retired: 1997
#5513-1 • Orig. Price: $19
Market Value: $26

27

Town Tree (set/5)
Issued: 1993 • Current
#5565-4 • Orig. Price: $45
Market Value: $45

28

**Town Tree Trimmers
(set/4)**
Issued: 1993 • Current
#5566-2 • Orig. Price: $32.50
Market Value: $32.50

29

Two Rivers Bridge
Issued: 1994 • Retired: 1997
#5656-1 • Orig. Price: $35
Market Value: $45

30

Up, Up & Away Witch
Issued: 1998 • Current
#52711 • Orig. Price: $50
Market Value: $50

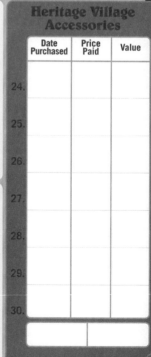

Heritage Village Accessories

	Date Purchased	Price Paid	Value
24.			
25.			
26.			
27.			
28.			
29.			
30.			

Totals

Heritage Village – Accessories

31

Village Animated Accessory Track
Issued: 1996 • Current
#52642 • Orig. Price: $65
Market Value: $40

32

Village Animated All Around The Park (set/18)
Issued: 1994 • Retired: 1996
#5247-7 • Orig. Price: $95
Market Value: $115

33

Village Animated Skating Pond (set/15)
Issued: 1993 • Current
#5229-9 • Orig. Price: $60
Market Value: $60

34

Village Animated Ski Mountain
Issued: 1996 • Retired: 1998
#52641 • Orig. Price: $75
Market Value: N/E

35

Village Animated Sledding Hill
Issued: 1997 • Current
#52645 • Orig. Price: $65
Market Value: $65

36

Village Express Electric Train Set (set/24)
Issued: 1998 • Current
#52710 • Orig. Price: $270
Market Value: $270

37

Village Express Train (set/22, manufactured by Bachman Trains)
Issued: 1988 • Retired: 1996
#5980-3 • Orig. Price: $95
Market Value: $125

38

Village Express Train (set/22, manufactured by Tyco)
Issued: 1987 • Retired: 1988
#5997-8 • Orig. Price: $90
Market Value: $300

Heritage Village Accessories

	Date Purchased	Price Paid	Value
31.			
32.			
33.			
34.			
35.			
36.			
37.			
38.			

Totals

39

Village Express Van
Issued: 1992 • Retired: 1996
#5865-3 • Orig. Price: $25
Market Value: $40
(green, general release)

"Village Express Van" Versions

Black – $120
Gold – $850
Bachman's – $88
Bronner's – $58
The Christmas Dove – $60
European Imports – $56
Fortunoff – $115
Incredible Xmas Place – $70
Lemon Tree – $50

The Limited Edition – $102
Lock, Stock & Barrel – $110
North Pole City – $60
Parkwest – $515
Robert's – $58
St. Nick's – $65
Stats – $58
William Glen – $60
The Windsor Shoppe – $58

40

New!

Village Monuments (set/3)
Issued: 1999 • Current
#55524 • Orig. Price: $25
Market Value: $25

41

Village Porcelain Pine, Large
Issued: 1992 • Retired: 1997
#5218-3 • Orig. Price: $12.50
Market Value: $14

42

Village Porcelain Pine, Small
Issued: 1992 • Retired: 1997
#5219-1 • Orig. Price: $10
Market Value: $13

43

Village Porcelain Pine Trees (set/2)
Issued: 1994 • Retired: 1997
#5251-5 • Orig. Price: $15
Market Value: $18

44

Village Sign With Snowman
Issued: 1989 • Retired: 1994
#5572-7 • Orig. Price: $10
Market Value: $18

45

Village Streetcar (set/10)
Issued: 1994 • Retired: 1998
#5240-0 • Orig. Price: $65
Market Value: $70

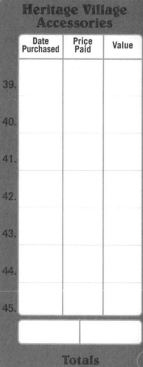

	Heritage Village Accessories		
	Date Purchased	Price Paid	Value
39.			
40.			
41.			
42.			
43.			
44.			
45.			
Totals			

Heritage Village – Accessories

46

Village Train Trestle
Issued: 1988 • Retired: 1990
#5981-1 • Orig. Price: $17
Market Value: $70

47

Village Up, Up & Away, Animated Sleigh
Issued: 1995 • Current
#52593 • Orig. Price: $40
Market Value: $40

48

Village Waterfall
Issued: 1996 • Current
#52644 • Orig. Price: $65
Market Value: $40

DICKENS' VILLAGE – ACCESSORIES

Introduced in 1984, *Dickens' Village* accessories add life to this Victorian-era village. With 11 new pieces introduced in 1999, the total number of accessories for *Dickens' Village* now totals 101.

1

New!

The 12 Days Of Dickens' Village Sign
Issued: 1999 • Current
#58467 • Orig. Price: $20
Market Value: $20

2

Ale Mates (set/2)
Issued: 1998 • Current
#58417 • Orig. Price: $25
Market Value: $25

3

Ashley Pond Skating Party (set/6)
Issued: 1997 • Retired: 1999
#58405 • Orig. Price: $70
Market Value: $73

4

The Bird Seller (set/3)
Issued: 1992 • Retired: 1995
#5803-3 • Orig. Price: $25
Market Value: $37

Heritage Village Accessories

	Date Purchased	Price Paid	Value
46.			
47.			
48.			

Dickens' Village Accessories

1.			
2.			
3.			
4.			

Totals

5

Blacksmith (set/3)
Issued: 1987 • Retired: 1990
#5934-0 • Orig. Price: $20
Market Value: $85

6

Bringing Fleeces To The Mill (set/2)
Issued: 1993 • Retired: 1998
#5819-0 • Orig. Price: $35
Market Value: $42

7

Bringing Home The Yule Log (set/3)
Issued: 1991 • Retired: 1998
#5558-1 • Orig. Price: $27.50
Market Value: $33

8

Brixton Road Watchman (set/2)
Issued: 1995 • Retired: 1999
#58390 • Orig. Price: $25
Market Value: $29

9

New!

Busy Railway Station (set/3)
Issued: 1999 • Current
#58464 • Orig. Price: $27.50
Market Value: $27.50

10

C. Bradford, Wheelwright & Son (set/2)
Issued: 1993 • Retired: 1996
#5818-1 • Orig. Price: $24
Market Value: $38

11

Version 1   Version 2   Version 3

Carolers (set/3)
Issued: 1984 • Retired: 1990
#6526-9 • Orig. Price: $10
Market Value: **1** – *$125 (white lamppost)*
2 – *$43 (black lamppost, tan viola)*
3 – *N/E (black lamppost, brown/tan viola)*

12

Carolers On The Doorstep (set/4)
Issued: 1990 • Retired: 1993
#5570-0 • Orig. Price: $25
Market Value: $44

13

Caroling With The Cratchit Family (set/3)
Christmas Carol Revisited
Issued: 1996 • Current
#58396 • Orig. Price: $37.50
Market Value: $37.50

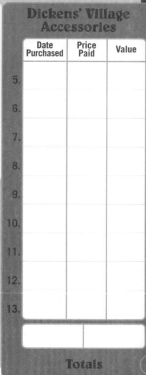

Dickens' Village Accessories

	Date Purchased	Price Paid	Value
5.			
6.			
7.			
8.			
9.			
10.			
11.			
12.			
13.			

Totals

Dickens' Village – Accessories

14

Chelsea Lane Shoppers (set/4)
Issued: 1993 • Retired: 1999
#5816-5 • Orig. Price: $30
Market Value: $33

15

Chelsea Market Curiosities Monger & Cart (set/2)
Issued: 1994 • Retired: 1998
#5827-0 • Orig. Price: $27.50
Market Value: $34

16

Chelsea Market Fish Monger & Cart (set/2)
Issued: 1993 • Retired: 1997
#5814-9 • Orig. Price: $25
Market Value: $36

17

Version 1

Version 2

Chelsea Market Flower Monger & Cart (set/2)
Issued: 1993 • Current
#5815-7 • Orig. Price: $27.50
Market Value: **1** – *$27.50 (general release)*
2 – *N/E (Lord & Taylor)*

18

Chelsea Market Fruit Monger & Cart (set/2)
Issued: 1993 • Retired: 1997
#5813-0 • Orig. Price: $25
Market Value: $36

19

Chelsea Market Hat Monger & Cart (set/2)
Issued: 1995 • Current
#58392 • Orig. Price: $27.50
Market Value: $27.50

20

Chelsea Market Mistletoe Monger & Cart (set/2)
Issued: 1994 • Retired: 1998
#5826-2 • Orig. Price: $25
Market Value: $36

21

Child's Play (set/2)
Issued: 1998 • Current
#58415 • Orig. Price: $25
Market Value: $25

22

Childe Pond & Skaters (set/4)
Issued: 1988 • Retired: 1991
#5903-0 • Orig. Price: $30
Market Value: $87

Dickens' Village Accessories

	Date Purchased	Price Paid	Value
14.			
15.			
16.			
17.			
18.			
19.			
20.			
21.			
22.			

Totals

23

Christmas Carol Christmas Morning Figures (set/3)
Issued: 1989 • Current
#5588-3 • Orig. Price: $18
Market Value: $18

24

Christmas Carol Christmas Spirits Figures (set/4)
Issued: 1989 • Current
#5589-1 • Orig. Price: $27.50
Market Value: $27.50

25

Christmas Carol Figures (set/3)
Issued: 1986 • Retired: 1990
#6501-3 • Orig. Price: $12.50
Market Value: $87

26

Christmas Carol Holiday Trimming Set (set/21)
Issued: 1994 • Retired: 1997
#5831-9 • Orig. Price: $65
Market Value: $78

27

"A Christmas Carol" Reading By Charles Dickens (set/4)
Issued: 1996 • Current
#58403 • Orig. Price: $45
Market Value: $45

28

"A Christmas Carol" Reading By Charles Dickens (set/7, LE-42,500)
Charles Dickens' Signature Series
Issued: 1996 • Retired: 1997
#58404 • Orig. Price: $75
Market Value: $147

29

Christmas Pudding Costermonger (set/3)
Issued: 1997 • Current
#58408 • Orig. Price: $32.50
Market Value: $32.50

30

Cobbler & Clock Peddler (set/2)
Issued: 1995 • Retired: 1997
#58394 • Orig. Price: $25
Market Value: $32

31

Come Into The Inn (set/3)
Issued: 1991 • Retired: 1994
#5560-3 • Orig. Price: $22
Market Value: $38

32

Constables (set/3)
Issued: 1989 • Retired: 1991
#5579-4 • Orig. Price: $17.50
Market Value: $70

Dickens' Village Accessories

	Date Purchased	Price Paid	Value
23.			
24.			
25.			
26.			
27.			
28.			
29.			
30.			
31.			
32.			

Totals

Dickens' Village – Accessories

33

David Copperfield Characters (set/5)
Issued: 1989 • Retired: 1992
#5551-4 • Orig. Price: $32.50
Market Value: $48

34

Delivering Coal For The Hearth (set/2)
Issued: 1997 • Retired: 1999
#58326 • Orig. Price: $32.50
Market Value: $36

35

Dickens' Village Sign
Issued: 1987 • Retired: 1993
#6569-2 • Orig. Price: $6
Market Value: $20

36

Version 1   *Version 2*   *Version 3*

Dover Coach
Issued: 1987 • Retired: 1990
#6590-0 • Orig. Price: $18
Market Value: **1** *– $100 (without mustache)*
2 *– $67 (with mustache, tight reins)*
3 *– $65 (with mustache, loose reins)*

37

Eight Maids A-Milking (set/2)
#VIII, The 12 Days Of Dickens' Village
Issued: 1996 • Current
#58384 • Orig. Price: $25
Market Value: $25

38

Eleven Lords A-Leaping
#XI, The 12 Days Of Dickens' Village
Issued: 1998 • Current
#58413 • Orig. Price: $27.50
Market Value: $27.50

39

English Post Box
Issued: 1992 • Current
#58050 • Orig. Price: $4.50
Market Value: $4.50

40

Farm People & Animals (set/5)
Issued: 1987 • Retired: 1989
#5901-3 • Orig. Price: $24
Market Value: $100

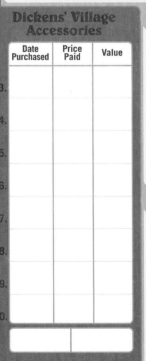

Dickens' Village Accessories

	Date Purchased	Price Paid	Value
33.			
34.			
35.			
36.			
37.			
38.			
39.			
40.			
Totals			

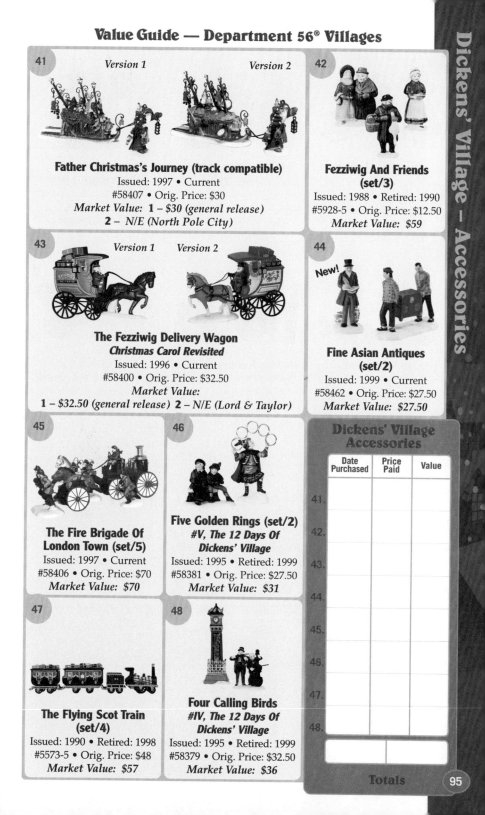

41 Version 1   Version 2

Father Christmas's Journey (track compatible)
Issued: 1997 • Current
#58407 • Orig. Price: $30
Market Value: **1** – $30 *(general release)*
2 – N/E *(North Pole City)*

42

Fezziwig And Friends (set/3)
Issued: 1988 • Retired: 1990
#5928-5 • Orig. Price: $12.50
Market Value: $59

43 Version 1   Version 2

The Fezziwig Delivery Wagon
Christmas Carol Revisited
Issued: 1996 • Current
#58400 • Orig. Price: $32.50
Market Value:
1 – $32.50 *(general release)* **2** – N/E *(Lord & Taylor)*

44

New!

Fine Asian Antiques (set/2)
Issued: 1999 • Current
#58462 • Orig. Price: $27.50
Market Value: $27.50

45

The Fire Brigade Of London Town (set/5)
Issued: 1997 • Current
#58406 • Orig. Price: $70
Market Value: $70

46

Five Golden Rings (set/2)
#V, The 12 Days Of Dickens' Village
Issued: 1995 • Retired: 1999
#58381 • Orig. Price: $27.50
Market Value: $31

47

The Flying Scot Train (set/4)
Issued: 1990 • Retired: 1998
#5573-5 • Orig. Price: $48
Market Value: $57

48

Four Calling Birds
#IV, The 12 Days Of Dickens' Village
Issued: 1995 • Retired: 1999
#58379 • Orig. Price: $32.50
Market Value: $36

Dickens' Village Accessories

	Date Purchased	Price Paid	Value
41.			
42.			
43.			
44.			
45.			
46.			
47.			
48.			
Totals			

49

Gingerbread Vendor (set/2)
Issued: 1996 • Current
#58402 • Orig. Price: $22.50
Market Value: $22.50

50

A Good Day's Catch (set/2)
Issued: 1999 • Current
#58420 • Orig. Price: $27.50
Market Value: $27.50

51

Here We Come A-Wassailing (set/5)
Issued: 1998 • Current
#58410 • Orig. Price: $45
Market Value: $45

52

Holiday Coach
Issued: 1991 • Retired: 1998
#5561-1 • Orig. Price: $68
Market Value: $80

53

Holiday Travelers (set/3)
Issued: 1990 • Retired: 1999
#5571-9 • Orig. Price: $22.50
Market Value: $27

54

King's Road Cab
Issued: 1989 • Retired: 1998
#5581-6 • Orig. Price: $30
Market Value: $37

Dickens' Village Accessories

	Date Purchased	Price Paid	Value
49.			
50.			
51.			
52.			
53.			
54.			
55.			
56.			
57.			

55
New!

Kings' Road Market Cross
Issued: 1999 • Current
#58456 • Orig. Price: $25
Market Value: $25

56

Lamplighter w/Lamp (set/2)
Issued: 1989 • Current
#5577-8 • Orig. Price: $9
Market Value: $10

57

Lionhead Bridge
Issued: 1992 • Retired: 1997
#5864-5 • Orig. Price: $22
Market Value: $34

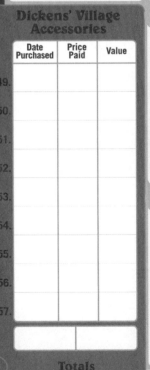

58

New!

The Locomotive Shed & Water Tower
Issued: 1999 • Current
#58465 • Orig. Price: $32.50
Market Value: $32.50

59

New!

Master Gardeners (set/2)
Issued: 1999 • Current
#58458 • Orig. Price: $30
Market Value: $30

60

New!

Meeting Family At The Railroad Station (set/4)
Issued: 1999 • Current
#58457 • Orig. Price: $32.50
Market Value: $32.50

61

New!

Members Of Parliament (set/2)
Issued: 1999 • Current
#58455 • Orig. Price: $19
Market Value: $19

62

Nicholas Nickleby Characters (set/4)
Issued: 1988 • Retired: 1991
#5929-3 • Orig. Price: $20
Market Value: $40

63

Nine Ladies Dancing (set/2)
#IX, The 12 Days Of Dickens' Village
Issued: 1997 • Current
#58385 • Orig. Price: $30
Market Value: $30

64

The Old Puppeteer (set/3)
Issued: 1992 • Retired: 1995
#5802-5 • Orig. Price: $32
Market Value: $43

65

Oliver Twist Characters (set/3)
Issued: 1991 • Retired: 1993
#5554-9 • Orig. Price: $35
Market Value: $45

66

Version 1   *Version 2*

Ox Sled
Issued: 1987 • Retired: 1989
#5951-0 • Orig. Price: $20
Market Value: 1 – $235 (tan pants/green seat)
2 – $138 (blue pants/black seat)

Dickens' Village Accessories

	Date Purchased	Price Paid	Value
58.			
59.			
60.			
61.			
62.			
63.			
64.			
65.			
66.			

Totals

67

A Partridge In A Pear Tree
#I, The 12 Days Of Dickens' Village
Issued: 1995 • Retired: 1999
#5835-1 • Orig. Price: $35
Market Value: $38

68

A Peaceful Glow On Christmas Eve (set/3)
Issued: 1994 • Current
#5830-0 • Orig. Price: $30
Market Value: $30

69

Portobello Road Peddlers (set/3)
Issued: 1994 • Retired: 1998
#5828-9 • Orig. Price: $27.50
Market Value: $35

70

Postern
(*Dickens' Village* Ten Year Anniversary Piece)
Issued: 1994 • Retired: 1994
#9871-0 • Orig. Price: $17.50
Market Value: $32

71

Poultry Market (set/3)
Issued: 1991 • Retired: 1995
#5559-0 • Orig. Price: $30
Market Value: $46

72

New!

The Queen's Parliamentary Coach (LE-2000)
Issued: 1999 • Current
#58454 • Orig. Price: $60
Market Value: $60

73

Red Christmas Sulky
Issued: 1996 • Current
#58401 • Orig. Price: $30
Market Value: $30

74

Royal Coach
Issued: 1989 • Retired: 1992
#5578-6 • Orig. Price: $55
Market Value: $85

75

Seven Swans A-Swimming (set/4)
#VII, The 12 Days Of Dickens' Village
Issued: 1996 • Current
#58383 • Orig. Price: $27.50
Market Value: $27.50

76

Shopkeepers (set/4)
Issued: 1987 • Retired: 1988
#5966-8 • Orig. Price: $15
Market Value: $40

Dickens' Village Accessories

	Date Purchased	Price Paid	Value
67.			
68.			
69.			
70.			
71.			
72.			
73.			
74.			
75.			
76.			
Totals			

77

Silo & Hay Shed (set/2)
Issued: 1987 • Retired: 1989
#5950-1 • Orig. Price: $18
Market Value: $170

78

Sitting In Camden Park (set/4)
Issued: 1998 • Current
#58411 • Orig. Price: $35
Market Value: $35

79

Six Geese A-Laying (set/2)
#VI, The 12 Days Of Dickens' Village
Issued: 1995 • Retired: 1999
#58382 • Orig. Price: $30
Market Value: $35

80

Stone Bridge
Issued: 1987 • Retired: 1990
#6546-3 • Orig. Price: $12
Market Value: $80

81

"Tallyho!" (set/5)
Issued: 1995 • Retired: 1998
#58391 • Orig. Price: $50
Market Value: $60

82

Ten Pipers Piping (set/3)
#X, The 12 Days Of Dickens' Village
Issued: 1997 • Current
#58386 • Orig. Price: $30
Market Value: $30

83

Tending The Cold Frame (set/3)
Issued: 1998 • Retired: 1999
#58416 • Orig. Price: $32.50
Market Value: $36

84

Tending The New Calves (set/3)
Issued: 1996 • Retired: 1999
#58395 • Orig. Price: $30
Market Value: $34

85

Thatchers (set/3)
Issued: 1994 • Retired: 1997
#5829-7 • Orig. Price: $35
Market Value: $38

86

Three French Hens (set/3)
#III, The 12 Days Of Dickens' Village
Issued: 1995 • Retired: 1999
#58378 • Orig. Price: $32.50
Market Value: $34

Dickens' Village Accessories

	Date Purchased	Price Paid	Value
77.			
78.			
79.			
80.			
81.			
82.			
83.			
84.			
85.			
86.			
Totals			

87

Town Crier & Chimney Sweep (set/2)
Issued: 1990 • Current
#5569-7 • Orig. Price: $15
Market Value: $16

88

New!

A Treasure From The Sea (set/2)
Issued: 1999 • Current
#58461 • Orig. Price: $22.50
Market Value: $22.50

89

Twelve Drummers Drumming
#XII, The 12 Days Of Dickens' Village
Issued: 1999 • Current
#58387 • Orig. Price: $65
Market Value: $65

90

Two Turtle Doves (set/4)
#II, The 12 Days Of Dickens' Village
Issued: 1995 • Retired: 1999
#5836-0 • Orig. Price: $32.50
Market Value: $34

91

New!

Under The Bumbershoot
Issued: 1999 • Current
#58460 • Orig. Price: $20
Market Value: $20

92

Until We Meet Again (set/2)
Issued: 1998 • Current
#58414 • Orig. Price: $27.50
Market Value: $27.50

93

Victoria Station Train Platform
Issued: 1990 • Retired: 1999
#5575-1 • Orig. Price: $20
Market Value: $26

94

Village Street Peddlers (set/2)
Issued: 1992 • Retired: 1994
#5804-1 • Orig. Price: $16
Market Value: $29

95

Village Train (set/3)
Issued: 1985 • Retired: 1986
#6527-7 • Orig. Price: $12
Market Value: $430

Dickens' Village Accessories

	Date Purchased	Price Paid	Value
87.			
88.			
89.			
90.			
91.			
92.			
93.			
94.			
95.			

Totals

96

Village Well & Holy Cross (set/2)
Issued: 1987 • Retired: 1989
#6547-1 • Orig. Price: $13
Market Value: $154

97

Violet Vendor/Carolers/ Chestnut Vendor (set/3)
Issued: 1989 • Retired: 1992
#5580-8 • Orig. Price: $23
Market Value: $42

98

Vision Of A Christmas Past (set/3)
Issued: 1993 • Retired: 1996
#5817-3 • Orig. Price: $27.50
Market Value: $40

99

Winter Sleighride
Issued: 1994 • Current
#5825-4 • Orig. Price: $18
Market Value: $18

100

"Ye Olde Lamplighter" Dickens' Village Sign
Issued: 1995 • Current
#58393 • Orig. Price: $20
Market Value: $20

101

Yeomen Of The Guard (set/5)
Issued: 1996 • Retired: 1997
#58397 • Orig. Price: $30
Market Value: $63

NEW ENGLAND VILLAGE – ACCESSORIES

New England Village accessories were introduced in 1986. There are eight new accessories this year, bringing the total released to 46. The most valuable is "Maple Sugaring Shed," (set/3) which is worth $255.

1

Amish Buggy
Issued: 1990 • Retired: 1992
#5949-8 • Orig. Price: $22
Market Value: $65

Dickens' Village Accessories

	Date Purchased	Price Paid	Value
96.			
97.			
98.			
99.			
100.			
101.			

New England Village Accessories

1.		

Totals

2

Version 1   Version 2

Amish Family (set/3)
Issued: 1990 • Retired: 1992
#5948-0 • Orig. Price: $20
Market Value: **1** – *$50 (with mustache)*
2 – *$38 (without mustache)*

3

An Artist's Touch
Issued: 1998 • Current
#56638 • Orig. Price: $17
Market Value: $17

4

Blue Star Ice Harvesters (set/2)
Issued: 1993 • Retired: 1997
#5650-2 • Orig. Price: $27.50
Market Value: $30

5

Christmas Bazaar . . . Flapjacks & Hot Cider (set/2)
Issued: 1997 • Retired: 1999
#56596 • Orig. Price: $27.50
Market Value: $29

6

Christmas Bazaar . . . Handmade Quilts (set/2)
Issued: 1996 • Retired: 1999
#56594 • Orig. Price: $25
Market Value: $27

7

Christmas Bazaar . . . Sign (set/2)
Issued: 1997 • Retired: 1999
#56598 • Orig. Price: $16
Market Value: $17

8

Christmas Bazaar . . . Toy Vendor & Cart (set/2)
Issued: 1997 • Retired: 1999
#56597 • Orig. Price: $27.50
Market Value: $29

9

Christmas Bazaar . . . Woolens & Preserves (set/2)
Issued: 1996 • Retired: 1999
#56595 • Orig. Price: $25
Market Value: $27

10

Covered Wooden Bridge
Issued: 1986 • Retired: 1990
#6531-5 • Orig. Price: $10
Market Value: $44

New England Village Accessories

	Date Purchased	Price Paid	Value
2.			
3.			
4.			
5.			
6.			
7.			
8.			
9.			
10.			

Totals

Value Guide — Department 56® Villages

11

New!

Dairy Delivery Sleigh
Issued: 1999 • Current
#56622 • Orig. Price: $37.50
Market Value: $37.50

12

New!

Doctor's House Call (set/2)
Issued: 1999 • Current
#56616 • Orig. Price: $27.50
Market Value: $27.50

13

Farm Animals (set/4)
Issued: 1989 • Retired: 1991
#5945-5 • Orig. Price: $15
Market Value: $47

14

Farm Animals (set/8)
Issued: 1995 • Current
#56588 • Orig. Price: $32.50
Market Value: $32.50

15

Farmer's Market (set/2)
Issued: 1998 • Current
#56637 • Orig. Price: $55
Market Value: $55

16

Fly-casting In The Brook
Issued: 1998 • Current
#56633 • Orig. Price: $15
Market Value: $15

17

"Fresh Paint" New England Village Sign
Issued: 1995 • Current
#56592 • Orig. Price: $20
Market Value: $20

18

Harvest Pumpkin Wagon
Issued: 1995 • Retired: 1999
#56591 • Orig. Price: $45
Market Value: $48

19

Harvest Seed Cart (set/3)
Issued: 1992 • Retired: 1995
#5645-6 • Orig. Price: $27.50
Market Value: $39

20

It's Almost Thanksgiving (set/4)
Issued: 1999 • Current
#56639 • Orig. Price: $60
Market Value: $60

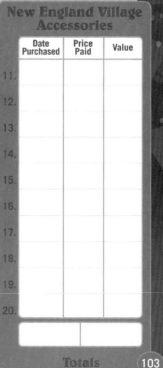

	Date Purchased	Price Paid	Value
11.			
12.			
13.			
14.			
15.			
16.			
17.			
18.			
19.			
20.			
Totals			

New England Village Accessories

103

21

Knife Grinder (set/2)
Issued: 1993 • Retired: 1996
#5649-9 • Orig. Price: $22.50
Market Value: $30

22

New!

Let's Go One More Time (set/3)
Issued: 1999 • Current
#56621 • Orig. Price: $30
Market Value: $30

23

Load Up The Wagon (set/2)
Issued: 1998 • Current
#56630 • Orig. Price: $40
Market Value: $40

24

Lobster Trappers (set/4)
Issued: 1995 • Current
#56589 • Orig. Price: $35
Market Value: $35

25

Lumberjacks (set/2)
Issued: 1995 • Retired: 1998
#56590 • Orig. Price: $30
Market Value: $38

26

New!

Making The Christmas Candles (set/2)
Issued: 1999 • Current
#56620 • Orig. Price: $25
Market Value: $25

27

Maple Sugaring Shed (set/3)
Issued: 1987 • Retired: 1989
#6589-7 • Orig. Price: $19
Market Value: $255

28

Market Day (set/3)
Issued: 1991 • Retired: 1993
#5641-3 • Orig. Price: $35
Market Value: $47

29

New!

Mill Creek Crossing
Issued: 1999 • Current
#56623 • Orig. Price: $32.50
Market Value: $32.50

New England Village Accessories

	Date Purchased	Price Paid	Value
21.			
22.			
23.			
24.			
25.			
26.			
27.			
28.			
29.			

Totals

Value Guide — Department 56® Villages

30

New England Village Sign
Issued: 1987 • Retired: 1993
#6570-6 • Orig. Price: $6
Market Value: $22

31

**New England
Winter Set (set/5)**
Issued: 1986 • Retired: 1990
#6532-3 • Orig. Price: $18
Market Value: $50

32

**A New Potbellied Stove
For Christmas (set/2)**
Issued: 1996 • Retired: 1998
#56593 • Orig. Price: $35
Market Value: $43

33

**The Old Man And
The Sea (set/3)**
Issued: 1994 • Retired: 1998
#5655-3 • Orig. Price: $25
Market Value: $35

34

**Over The River And
Through The Woods**
Issued: 1994 • Retired: 1998
#5654-5 • Orig. Price: $35
Market Value: $44

35

New!

Pennyfarthing Pedaling
Issued: 1999 • Current
#56615 • Orig. Price: $13.50
Market Value: $13.50

36

Red Covered Bridge
Issued: 1988 • Retired: 1994
#5987-0 • Orig. Price: $15
Market Value: $33

37

New!

The Sailors' Knot
Issued: 1999 • Current
#56617 • Orig. Price: 27.50
Market Value: $27.50

38

**Sea Captain & His Mates
(set/4)**
Issued: 1998 • Current
#56587 • Orig. Price: $32.50
Market Value: $32.50

39

**Sleepy Hollow Characters
(set/3)**
Issued: 1990 • Retired: 1992
#5956-0 • Orig. Price: $27.50
Market Value: $48

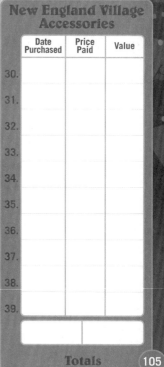

New England Village Accessories

	Date Purchased	Price Paid	Value
30.			
31.			
32.			
33.			
34.			
35.			
36.			
37.			
38.			
39.			

Totals

40

Version 1 *Version 2*

Sleighride (also known as "Dickens' Sleighride")
Issued: 1986 • Retired: 1990
#6511-0 • Orig. Price: $19.50
Market Value: **1** *– $55 (thin scarf)* **2** *– $52 (thick scarf)*

41

Tapping The Maples (set/7)
Issued: 1997 • Current
#56599 • Orig. Price: $75
Market Value: $75

42

Town Tinker (set/2)
Issued: 1992 • Retired: 1995
#5646-4 • Orig. Price: $24
Market Value: $35

43

Under The Mistletoe
Issued: 1998 • Current
#56631 • Orig. Price: $16.50
Market Value: $16.50

44

Village Harvest People (set/4)
Issued: 1988 • Retired: 1991
#5941-2 • Orig. Price: $27.50
Market Value: $55

New England Village Accessories

	Date Purchased	Price Paid	Value
40.			
41.			
42.			
43.			
44.			
45.			
46.			
47.			
Totals			

45

Volunteer Firefighters (set/2)
Issued: 1998 • Current
#56635 • Orig. Price: $37.50
Market Value: $37.50

46

Woodcutter And Son (set/2)
Issued: 1988 • Retired: 1990
#5986-2 • Orig. Price: $10
Market Value: $50

47 New!

The Woodworker
Issued: 1999 • Current
#56619 • Orig. Price: $35
Market Value: $35

ALPINE VILLAGE – ACCESSORIES

From the new "Sisters Of The Abbey" to "The Sound Of Music® Gazebo," all 17 accessories of *Alpine Village* promise to enhance your collection. The most valuable is the 1986 version of "Alpine Villagers (set/3)."

1

"Alpen Horn Player"
Alpine Village Sign
Issued: 1995 • Current
#56182 • Orig. Price: $20
Market Value: $20

2

Alpine Village Sign
Issued: 1987 • Retired: 1993
#6571-4 • Orig. Price: $6
Market Value: $22

3

Alpine Villagers (set/3)
Issued: 1986 • Retired: 1992
#6542-0 • Orig. Price: $13
Market Value: $39

4

New!

Alpine Villagers (set/5)
Issued: 1999 • Current
#56215 • Orig. Price: $32.50
Market Value: $32.50

5

Buying Bakers Bread
(set/2)
Issued: 1992 • Retired: 1995
#5619-7 • Orig. Price: $20
Market Value: $37

6

Climb Every Mountain
(set/4)
Issued: 1993 • Current
#5613-8 • Orig. Price: $27.50
Market Value: $27.50

7

Heidi & Her Goats (set/4)
Issued: 1997 • Current
#56201 • Orig. Price: $30
Market Value: $30

8

New!

Leading The Bavarian Cow
Issued: 1999 • Current
#56214 • Orig. Price: $20
Market Value: $20

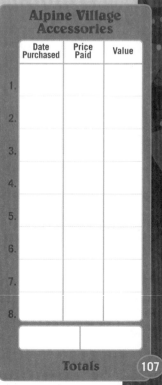

	Alpine Village Accessories		
	Date Purchased	Price Paid	Value
1.			
2.			
3.			
4.			
5.			
6.			
7.			
8.			
	Totals		

Alpine Village – Accessories

9

A New Batch Of Christmas Friends (set/3)
Issued: 1997 • Current
#56175 • Orig. Price: $27.50
Market Value: $27.50

10

Nutcracker Vendor & Cart
Issued: 1996 • Current
#56183 • Orig. Price: $25
Market Value: $25

11

Polka Fest (set/3)
Issued: 1994 • Retired: 1999
#5607-3 • Orig. Price: $30
Market Value: $34

12

St. Nicholas
Issued: 1998 • Current
#56203 • Orig. Price: $12
Market Value: $12

13

Silent Night (music box)
Issued: 1995 • Retired: 1999
#56180 • Orig. Price: $32.50
Market Value: $34

14
New!

Sisters Of The Abbey (set/2)
Issued: 1999 • Current
#56213 • Orig. Price: $20
Market Value: $20

15
New!

The Sound Of Music® Gazebo (music box)
Issued: 1999 • Current
#56212 • Orig. Price: $40
Market Value: $40

16

The Toy Peddler (set/3)
Issued: 1990 • Retired: 1998
#5616-2 • Orig. Price: $22
Market Value: $32

17

Trekking In The Snow (set/3)
Issued: 1998 • Current
#56202 • Orig. Price: $27.50
Market Value: $27.50

Alpine Village Accessories

	Date Purchased	Price Paid	Value
9.			
10.			
11.			
12.			
13.			
14.			
15.			
16.			
17.			
Totals			

CHRISTMAS IN THE CITY – ACCESSORIES

Available since 1987, there are now 52 *Christmas in the City* accessories. The "Salvation Army Band" (set/6) is currently the most valuable on the secondary market.

1

1919 Ford® Model-T
Issued: 1998 • Current
#58906 • Orig. Price: $20
Market Value: $20

2

All Around The Town (set/2)
Issued: 1991 • Retired: 1993
#5545-0 • Orig. Price: $18
Market Value: $32

3

New!

All In Together Girls
Issued: 1999 • Current
#58960 • Orig. Price: $23.50
Market Value: $23.50

4

Automobiles (set/3)
Issued: 1987 • Retired: 1996
#5964-1 • Orig. Price: $15
Market Value: $28

5

Big Smile For The Camera (set/2)
Issued: 1997 • Retired: 1999
#58900 • Orig. Price: $27.50
Market Value: $30

6

Boulevard (set/14)
Issued: 1989 • Retired: 1992
#5516-6 • Orig. Price: $25
Market Value: $55

7

Bringing Home The Baby (set/2)
Issued: 1999 • Current
#58909 • Orig. Price: $27.50
Market Value: $27.50

8

New!

Busy City Sidewalks (set/4)
Issued: 1999 • Current
#58955 • Orig. Price: $32.50
Market Value: $32.50

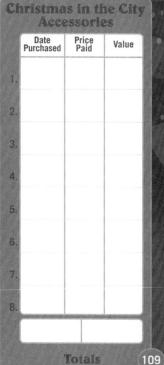

Christmas in the City Accessories

	Date Purchased	Price Paid	Value
1.			
2.			
3.			
4.			
5.			
6.			
7.			
8.			
Totals			

Christmas in the City – Accessories

9

Busy Sidewalks (set/4)
Issued: 1990 • Retired: 1992
#5535-2 • Orig. Price: $28
Market Value: $56

10

Caroling Thru The City (set/3)
Issued: 1991 • Retired: 1998
#5548-4 • Orig. Price: $27.50
Market Value: $32

11

A Carriage Ride For The Bride (track compatible)
Issued: 1998 • Current
#58901 • Orig. Price: $40
Market Value: $40

12

Central Park Carriage
Issued: 1989 • Current
#5979-0 • Orig. Price: $30
Market Value: $30

13

Chamber Orchestra (set/4)
Issued: 1994 • Retired: 1998
#5884-0 • Orig. Price: $37.50
Market Value: $43

14

Choirboys All-In-A-Row
Issued: 1995 • Retired: 1998
#58892 • Orig. Price: $20
Market Value: $30

15

Christmas In The City Sign
Issued: 1987 • Retired: 1993
#5960-9 • Orig. Price: $6
Market Value: $23

16

The City Ambulance
Issued: 1999 • Current
#58910 • Orig. Price: $15
Market Value: $15

17

City Bus & Milk Truck (set/2)
Issued: 1988 • Retired: 1991
#5983-8 • Orig. Price: $15
Market Value: $41

18

"City Fire Dept.," Fire Truck (set/3)
Issued: 1991 • Retired: 1995
#5547-6 • Orig. Price: $18
Market Value: $39

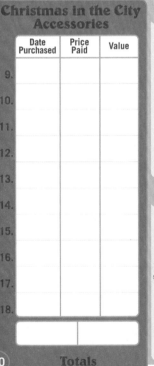

Christmas in the City Accessories

	Date Purchased	Price Paid	Value
9.			
10.			
11.			
12.			
13.			
14.			
15.			
16.			
17.			
18.			
Totals			

19

City Newsstand (set/4)
Issued: 1988 • Retired: 1991
#5971-4 • Orig. Price: $25
Market Value: $80

20

City People (set/5)
Issued: 1987 • Retired: 1990
#5965-0 • Orig. Price: $27.50
Market Value: $59

21

City Police Car
Issued: 1998 • Current
#58903 • Orig. Price: $16.50
Market Value: $16.50

22

City Taxi
Issued: 1996 • Current
#58894 • Orig. Price: $12.50
Market Value: $12.50

23

City Workers (set/4)
Issued: 1987 • Retired: 1988
#5967-6 • Orig. Price: $15
Market Value: $45

24

**Don't Drop The
Presents! (set/2)**
Issued: 1992 • Retired: 1995
#5532-8 • Orig. Price: $25
Market Value: $37

25

New!

Excellent Taste (set/2)
Issued: 1999 • Current
#58958 • Orig. Price: $22
Market Value: $22

26

The Family Tree
Issued: 1996 • Current
#58895 • Orig. Price: $18
Market Value: $18

27

The Fire Brigade (set/2)
Issued: 1991 • Retired: 1995
#5546-8 • Orig. Price: $20
Market Value: $38

28

New!

**Fresh Flowers For Sale
(set/2)**
Issued: 1999 • Current
#58957 • Orig. Price: $30
Market Value: $30

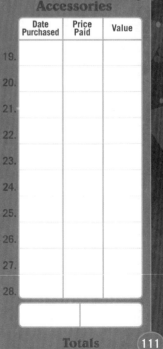

Christmas in the City Accessories

	Date Purchased	Price Paid	Value
19.			
20.			
21.			
22.			
23.			
24.			
25.			
26.			
27.			
28.			

Totals

Christmas in the City – Accessories

29

Going Home For The Holidays (set/3)
Issued: 1996 • Retired: 1999
#58896 • Orig. Price: $27.50
Market Value: $30

30

Holiday Field Trip (set/3)
Issued: 1994 • Retired: 1998
#5885-8 • Orig. Price: $27.50
Market Value: $33

31

Hot Dog Vendor (set/3)
Issued: 1994 • Retired: 1997
#5886-6 • Orig. Price: $27.50
Market Value: $31

32

Version 1   Version 2

Johnson's Grocery . . . Holiday Deliveries (track compatible)
Issued: 1997 • Current
#58897 • Orig. Price: $18
Market Value: 1 – $18 (general release)
2 – N/E (William Glen)

33

"A Key To The City" Christmas In The City Sign
Issued: 1995 • Current
#58893 • Orig. Price: $20
Market Value: $20

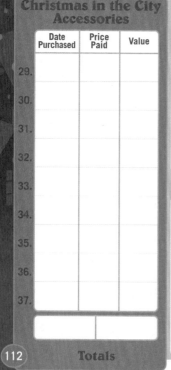

Christmas in the City Accessories

	Date Purchased	Price Paid	Value
29.			
30.			
31.			
32.			
33.			
34.			
35.			
36.			
37.			

Totals

34

Let's Go Shopping In The City (set/3)
Issued: 1997 • Retired: 1999
#58899 • Orig. Price: $35
Market Value: $39

35

Mailbox & Fire Hydrant (set/2)
Issued: 1989 • Retired: 1990
#5517-4 • Orig. Price: $6
Market Value: $25

36

Mailbox & Fire Hydrant (set/2)
Issued: 1990 • Retired: 1998
#5214-0 • Orig. Price: $5
Market Value: N/E

37

One-Man Band And The Dancing Dog (set/2)
Issued: 1995 • Retired: 1998
#58891 • Orig. Price: $17.50
Market Value: $29

38

Organ Grinder (set/3)
Issued: 1989 • Retired: 1991
#5957-9 • Orig. Price: $21
Market Value: $39

39

New!

Picking Out The Christmas Tree (set/3)
Issued: 1999 • Current
#58959 • Orig. Price: $37.50
Market Value: $37.50

40

Popcorn Vendor (set/3)
Issued: 1989 • Retired: 1992
#5958-7 • Orig. Price: $22
Market Value: $40

41

Ready For The Road
Issued: 1998 • Current
#58907 • Orig. Price: $20
Market Value: $20

42

Rest Ye Merry Gentlemen
Issued: 1990 • Current
#5540-9 • Orig. Price: $12.50
Market Value: $13

43

River Street Ice House Cart
Issued: 1989 • Retired: 1991
#5959-5 • Orig. Price: $20
Market Value: $57

44

Salvation Army Band (set/6)
Issued: 1988 • Retired: 1991
#5985-4 • Orig. Price: $24
Market Value: $90

45

Spirit Of The Season
Issued: 1997 • Retired: 1999
#58898 • Orig. Price: $20
Market Value: $20

46

Steppin' Out On The Town (set/5)
Issued: 1997 • Retired: 1999
#58885 • Orig. Price: $35
Market Value: $37

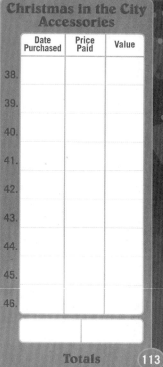

Christmas in the City Accessories

	Date Purchased	Price Paid	Value
38.			
39.			
40.			
41.			
42.			
43.			
44.			
45.			
46.			
Totals			

47

Street Musicians (set/3)
Issued: 1993 • Retired: 1997
#5564-6 • Orig. Price: $25
Market Value: $34

48

'Tis The Season
Issued: 1990 • Retired: 1994
#5539-5 • Orig. Price: $12.50
Market Value: $26

49

To Protect And To Serve (set/3)
Issued: 1998 • Current
#58902 • Orig. Price: $32.50
Market Value: $32.50

50

New!

Visiting The Nativity (set/3)
Issued: 1999 • Current
#58956 • Orig. Price: $37.50
Market Value: $37.50

51

Welcome Home (set/3)
Issued: 1992 • Retired: 1995
#5533-6 • Orig. Price: $27.50
Market Value: $35

52

"Yes, Virginia . . . " (set/2)
Issued: 1995 • Current
#58890 • Orig. Price: $12.50
Market Value: $12.50

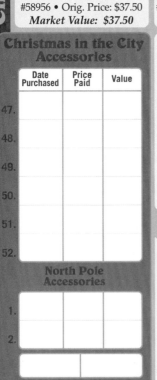

Christmas in the City Accessories

	Date Purchased	Price Paid	Value
47.			
48.			
49.			
50.			
51.			
52.			

North Pole Accessories

1.			
2.			

Totals

NORTH POLE – ACCESSORIES

Accessories for the *North Pole* were first introduced in 1990. The collection now totals 46, with twelve new pieces introduced in 1999, including two animated pieces.

1

Baker Elves (set/3)
Issued: 1991 • Retired: 1995
#5603-0 • Orig. Price: $27.50
Market Value: $43

2

"A Busy Elf" North Pole Sign
Issued: 1995 • Retired: 1999
#56366 • Orig. Price: $20
Market Value: $27

3

Candy Cane Lampposts (set/4)
Issued: 1996 • Current
#52621 • Orig. Price: $13
Market Value: $13

4

New!

Canine Courier
Issued: 1999 • Current
#56709 • Orig. Price: $32.50
Market Value: $32.50

5

Charting Santa's Course (set/2)
Issued: 1995 • Retired: 1997
#56364 • Orig. Price: $25
Market Value: $32

6

New!

Check This Out
Issued: 1999 • Current
#56711 • Orig. Price: $13.50
Market Value: $13.50

7

Christmas Fun Run (set/6)
Issued: 1998 • Current
#56434 • Orig. Price: $35
Market Value: $35

8

Dash Away Delivery
Issued: 1998 • Current
#56438 • Orig. Price: $40
Market Value: $40

9

Delivering Real Plastic Snow
Issued: 1998 • Current
#56435 • Orig. Price: $17
Market Value: $17

10

Delivering The Christmas Greens (set/2)
Issued: 1997 • Current
#56373 • Orig. Price: $27.50
Market Value: $27.50

11

Don't Break The Ornaments (set/2)
Issued: 1997 • Current
#56372 • Orig. Price: $27.50
Market Value: $27.50

12

New!

Downhill Daredevils (set/2)
Issued: 1999 • Current
#56707 • Orig. Price: $16.50
Market Value: $16.50

North Pole Accessories

	Date Purchased	Price Paid	Value
3.			
4.			
5.			
6.			
7.			
8.			
9.			
10.			
11.			
12.			

Totals

North Pole – Accessories

13

Downhill Elves (set/2)
Issued: 1998 • Current
#56439 • Orig. Price: $9
Market Value: $9

14

Early Rising Elves (set/5)
Issued: 1996 • Retired: 1999
#56369 • Orig. Price: $32.50
Market Value: $34

15

Elves On Ice (set/4)
Issued: 1996 • Current
#52298 • Orig. Price: $7.50
Market Value: $9

16

New!

Elves On Track (set/3, track compatible)
Issued: 1999 • Current
#56714 • Orig. Price: $10
Market Value: $10

17

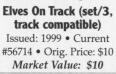

End Of The Line (set/2)
Issued: 1996 • Retired: 1999
#56370 • Orig. Price: $28
Market Value: $30

18

New!

A Happy Harley® Day
Issued: 1999 • Current
#56706 • Orig. Price: $17
Market Value: $17

North Pole Accessories		
Date Purchased	**Price Paid**	**Value**
13.		
14.		
15.		
16.		
17.		
18.		
19.		
20.		
21.		
22.		
Totals		

19

Happy New Year!
Issued: 1999 • Current
#56443 • Orig. Price: $17.50
Market Value: $17.50

20

Have A Seat (set/6)
Issued: 1998 • Current
#56437 • Orig. Price: $30
Market Value: $30

21

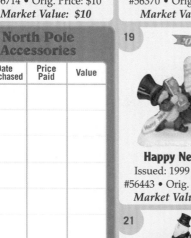

Holiday Deliveries
Issued: 1996 • Current
#56371 • Orig. Price: $16.50
Market Value: $16.50

22

I'll Need More Toys (set/2)
Issued: 1995 • Retired: 1998
#56365 • Orig. Price: $25
Market Value: $30

Value Guide — Department 56® Villages

23

Last Minute Delivery
Issued: 1994 • Retired: 1998
#5636-7 • Orig. Price: $35
Market Value: $37

24

Letters For Santa (set/3)
Issued: 1992 • Retired: 1994
#5604-9 • Orig. Price: $30
Market Value: $66

25

Loading The Sleigh (set/6)
Issued: 1998 • Current
#52732 • Orig. Price: $125
Market Value: $125

26

New!

Marshmallows Around The Campfire (set/3)
Issued: 1999 • Current
#56712 • Orig. Price: $30
Market Value: $30

27

North Pole Express (set/3)
Issued: 1996 • Retired: 1999
#56368 • Orig. Price: $37.50
Market Value: $39

28

North Pole Gate
Issued: 1993 • Retired: 1998
#5632-4 • Orig. Price: $32.50
Market Value: $42

29

New!

Open Wide!
Issued: 1999 • Current
#56713 • Orig. Price: $13
Market Value: $13

30

Peppermint Skating Party (set/6)
Issued: 1998 • Current
#56363 • Orig. Price: $64
Market Value: $64

31

New!

Photo With Santa (set/3, track compatible)
Issued: 1999 • Current
#56444 • Orig. Price: $7.50
Market Value: $7.50

32

Reindeer Training Camp (set/2)
Issued: 1998 • Current
#56436 • Orig. Price: $27.50
Market Value: $27.50

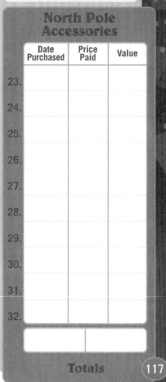

North Pole Accessories

	Date Purchased	Price Paid	Value
23.			
24.			
25.			
26.			
27.			
28.			
29.			
30.			
31.			
32.			
Totals			

North Pole – Accessories

33

Santa & Mrs. Claus (set/2)
Issued: 1990 • Current
#5609-0 • Orig. Price: $15
Market Value: $15

34

Santa's Little Helpers (set/3)
Issued: 1990 • Retired: 1993
#5610-3 • Orig. Price: $28
Market Value: $65

35

Sing A Song For Santa (set/3)
Issued: 1993 • Retired: 1998
#5631-6 • Orig. Price: $28
Market Value: $33

36
New!

Ski Bums
Issued: 1999 • Current
#56710 • Orig. Price: $22.50
Market Value: $22.50

37

Sleigh & Eight Tiny Reindeer (set/5)
Issued: 1990 • Current
#5611-1 • Orig. Price: $40
Market Value: $42

38

Snow Cone Elves (set/4)
Issued: 1994 • Retired: 1997
#5637-5 • Orig. Price: $30
Market Value: $36

39
New!

Tangled In Tinsel
Issued: 1999 • Current
#56708 • Orig. Price: $25
Market Value: $25

40

Tee Time Elves (set/2)
Issued: 1999 • Current
#56442 • Orig. Price: $27.50
Market Value: $27.50

41

Testing The Toys (set/2)
Issued: 1992 • Retired: 1999
#5605-7 • Orig. Price: $16.50
Market Value: $20

42

Toymaker Elves (set/3)
Issued: 1991 • Retired: 1995
#5602-2 • Orig. Price: $27.50
Market Value: $42

North Pole Accessories

	Date Purchased	Price Paid	Value
33.			
34.			
35.			
36.			
37.			
38.			
39.			
40.			
41.			
42.			
Totals			

Value Guide — Department 56® Villages

43

Trimming The North Pole
Issued: 1990 • Retired: 1993
#5608-1 • Orig. Price: $10
Market Value: $40

44

Untangle The Christmas Lights
Issued: 1997 • Current
#56374 • Orig. Price: $35
Market Value: $35

45

Welcome To Elf Land
Elf Land
Issued: 1998 • Current
#56431 • Orig. Price: $35
Market Value: $35

46

Woodsmen Elves (set/3)
Issued: 1993 • Retired: 1995
#5630-8 • Orig. Price: $30
Market Value: $62

DISNEY PARKS VILLAGE – ACCESSORIES

Released in just two years, the entire *Disney Park Villages* accessories collection contains only four pieces. The smallest collection to date, all pieces retired in 1996.

1

Balloon Seller (set/2)
Issued: 1995 • Retired: 1996
#53539 • Orig. Price: $25
Market Value: $54

2

Disney Parks Family (set/3)
Issued: 1994 • Retired: 1996
#5354-6 • Orig. Price: $32.50
Market Value: $39

3

Mickey & Minnie (set/2)
Issued: 1994 • Retired: 1996
#5353-8 • Orig. Price: $22.50
Market Value: $35

4

Olde World Antiques Gate
Issued: 1994 • Retired: 1996
#5355-4 • Orig. Price: $15
Market Value: $20

North Pole Accessories		
Date Purchased	Price Paid	Value
43.		
44.		
45.		
46.		

Disney Parks Village Accessories		
1.		
2.		
3.		
4.		

Totals

119

LITTLE TOWN OF BETHLEHEM – ACCESSORIES

New for 2000 are five *Little Town of Bethlehem* pieces that are sure to be the perfect additions to the newly released nativity buildings.

1

New!

The Good Shepherd & His Animals (set/6)
Issued: 1999 • Current
#59791 • Orig. Price: $25
Market Value: $25

2

New!

Heralding Angels (set/3)
Issued: 1999 • Current
#59759 • Orig. Price: $20
Market Value: $20

3

New!

Town Gate (set/2)
Issued: 1999 • Current
#59794 • Orig. Price: $25
Market Value: $25

4

New!

Town Well & Palm Trees (set/3)
Issued: 1999 • Current
#59793 • Orig. Price: $45
Market Value: $45

5

New!

Wise Men From The East (set/2)
Issued: 1999 • Current
#59792 • Orig. Price: $25
Market Value: $25

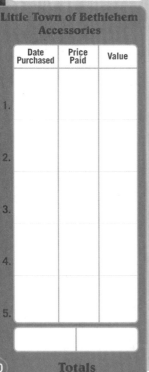

Little Town of Bethlehem Accessories

	Date Purchased	Price Paid	Value
1.			
2.			
3.			
4.			
5.			
Totals			

Value Guide — Department 56® Villages

HERITAGE VILLAGE – HINGED BOXES

Pieces from both *Dickens' Village* and *North Pole* are represented in these nine beautiful Department 56 hinged boxes.

1

Bah Humbug
Issued: 1997 • Current
#58430 • Orig. Price: $15
Market Value: $15

2

Chimney Sweep
Issued: 1998 • Current
#58434 • Orig. Price: $15
Market Value: $15

3

God Bless Us Every One
Issued: 1997 • Current
#58432 • Orig. Price: $13
Market Value: $15

4

Royal Coach
Issued: 1998 • Current
#57501 • Orig. Price: $25
Market Value: $25

5

Sleighride
Issued: 1998 • Current
#57502 • Orig. Price: $20
Market Value: $20

6

The Spirit Of Christmas
Issued: 1997 • Current
#58431 • Orig. Price: $15
Market Value: $15

7

Town Crier
Issued: 1998 • Current
#58433 • Orig. Price: $15
Market Value: $15

8

Caroling Elf
Issued: 1998 • Current
#57506 • Orig. Price: $15
Market Value: $15

9

Elf On A Sled
Issued: 1998 • Current
#57505 • Orig. Price: $15
Market Value: $15

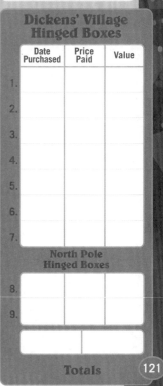

Dickens' Village Hinged Boxes

	Date Purchased	Price Paid	Value
1.			
2.			
3.			
4.			
5.			
6.			
7.			

North Pole Hinged Boxes

8.			
9.			

Totals

121

HERITAGE VILLAGE – ORNAMENTS

There are now a total of 32 ornaments in the *Heritage Village* ornament collection.

1

Fezziwig's Warehouse

The Cottage Of Bob Cratchit & Tiny Tim

Scrooge & Marley Counting House

Christmas Carol Cottages (set/3)
Classic Ornament Series
Issued: 1998 • Current
#98745 • Orig. Price: $50
Market Value: $50

2

Crown & Cricket Inn Ornament (LE-1996)
Issued: 1996 • Retired: 1996
#98730 • Orig. Price: $15
Market Value: $26

3

Dedlock Arms Ornament (LE-1994)
Issued: 1994 • Retired: 1994
#9872-8 • Orig. Price: $12.50
Market Value: $26

4

Dickens' Village Church
Classic Ornament Series
Issued: 1997 • Retired: 1998
#98737 • Orig. Price: $15
Market Value: $16

5

Dickens' Village Church
Classic Ornament Series
Issued: 1998 • Current
#98767 • Orig. Price: $20
Market Value: $20

Dickens' Village Ornaments

	Date Purchased	Price Paid	Value
1.			
2.			
3.			
4.			
5.			
6.			
7.			
8.			
9.			

6

Dickens' Village Mill
Classic Ornament Series
Issued: 1997 • Retired: 1998
#98733 • Orig. Price: $15
Market Value: $17

7

Dickens' Village Mill
Classic Ornament Series
Issued: 1998 • Current
#98766 • Orig. Price: $22.50
Market Value: $22.50

8

Gad's Hill Place Ornament (LE-1997)
Issued: 1997 • Retired: 1997
#98732 • Orig. Price: $15
Market Value: $25

9

The Grapes Inn Ornament (LE-1996)
Issued: 1996 • Retired: 1996
#98729 • Orig. Price: $15
Market Value: $26

Totals

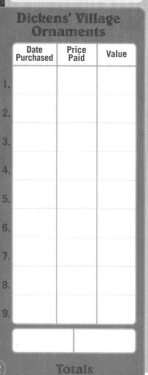

10

Old Curiosity Shop
Classic Ornament Series
Issued: 1997 • Retired: 1998
#98738 • Orig. Price: $15
Market Value: $17

11

The Old Curiosity Shop
Classic Ornament Series
Issued: 1998 • Current
#98768 • Orig. Price: $20
Market Value: $20

12

The Pied Bull Inn
Ornament (LE-1996)
Issued: 1996 • Retired: 1996
#98731 • Orig. Price: $15
Market Value: $30

13

Sir John Falstaff Inn
Ornament (LE-1995)
Issued: 1995 • Retired: 1995
#9870-1 • Orig. Price: $15
Market Value: $29

14

New!

Victoria Station
Classic Ornament Series
Issued: 1999 • Current
#98780 • Orig. Price: $22.50
Market Value: $22.50

15

Captain's Cottage
Classic Ornament Series
Issued: 1998 • Current
#98756 • Orig. Price: $20
Market Value: $20

16

Craggy Cove Lighthouse
Classic Ornament Series
Issued: 1997 • Retired: 1998
#98739 • Orig. Price: $15
Market Value: $20

17

Craggy Cove Lighthouse
Classic Ornament Series
Issued: 1998 • Current
#98769 • Orig. Price: $20
Market Value: $20

18

Steeple Church
Classic Ornament Series
Issued: 1998 • Current
#98757 • Orig. Price: $20
Market Value: $20

19

Cathedral Church Of
St. Mark
Classic Ornament Series
Issued: 1998 • Current
#98759 • Orig. Price: $22.50
Market Value: $22.50

Dickens' Village Ornaments

	Date Purchased	Price Paid	Value
10.			
11.			
12.			
13.			
14.			

New England Village Ornaments

15.			
16.			
17.			
18.			

Christmas in the City Ornaments

19.			

Totals

Heritage Village – Ornaments

20

City Hall
Classic Ornament Series
Issued: 1997 • Retired: 1998
#98741 • Orig. Price: $15
Market Value: $19

21

City Hall
Classic Ornament Series
Issued: 1998 • Current
#98771 • Orig. Price: $20
Market Value: $20

22

Dorothy's Dress Shop
Classic Ornament Series
Issued: 1997 • Retired: 1998
#98740 • Orig. Price: $15
Market Value: $18

23

Dorothy's Dress Shop
Classic Ornament Series
Issued: 1998 • Retired: 1999
#98770 • Orig. Price: $20
Market Value: $22

24
New!

Hollydale's Department Store
Classic Ornament Series
Issued: 1999 • Current
#98782 • Orig. Price: $20
Market Value: $20

25

Red Brick Fire Station
Classic Ornament Series
Issued: 1998 • Current
#98758 • Orig. Price: $20
Market Value: $20

26

Elf Bunkhouse
Classic Ornament Series
Issued: 1998 • Current
#98763 • Orig. Price: $20
Market Value: $20

27

North Pole Santa's Workshop
Classic Ornament Series
Issued: 1997 • Retired: 1998
#98734 • Orig. Price: $18
Market Value: $20

28
New!

Real Plastic Snow Factory
Issued: 1999 • Current
#98781 • Orig. Price: $22.50
Market Value: $22.50

29

Reindeer Barn
Classic Ornament Series
Issued: 1998 • Current
#98762 • Orig. Price: $20
Market Value: $20

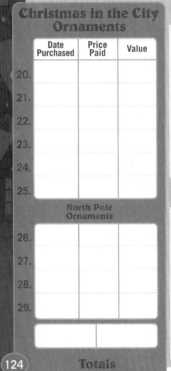

Christmas in the City Ornaments

	Date Purchased	Price Paid	Value
20.			
21.			
22.			
23.			
24.			
25.			
North Pole Ornaments			
26.			
27.			
28.			
29.			
Totals			

30

Santa's Lookout Tower
Classic Ornament Series
Issued: 1997 • Retired: 1998
#98742 • Orig. Price: $15
Market Value: $17

31

Santa's Lookout Tower
Classic Ornament Series
Issued: 1998 • Current
#98773 • Orig. Price: $20
Market Value: $20

32

Santa's Workshop
Classic Ornament Series
Issued: 1998 • Current
#98772 • Orig. Price: $22
Market Value: $22

North Pole Ornaments

	Date Purchased	Price Paid	Value
30.			
31.			
32.			
Totals			

Future Releases

Use this page to record future Heritage Village releases.

Heritage Village	Original Price	Status	Date Purch.	Price Paid	Value

Page Total:	Price Paid	Value

Total Value Of My Collection

Add the "Page Totals" together to find the "Grand Total."

Heritage Village – Buildings		
Page Number	Price Paid	Value
Page 25		
Page 26		
Page 27		
Page 28		
Page 29		
Page 30		
Page 31		
Page 32		
Page 33		
Page 34		
Page 35		
Page 36		
Page 37		
Page 38		
Page 39		
Page 40		
Page 41		
Page 42		
Page 43		
Page 44		
Page 45		
Page 46		
Page 47		
Page 48		
Page 49		
Page 50		
Page 51		
Page 52		
Page 53		
Subtotal:		

Heritage Village – Buildings		
Page Number	Price Paid	Value
Page 54		
Page 55		
Page 56		
Page 57		
Page 58		
Page 59		
Page 60		
Page 61		
Page 62		
Page 63		
Page 64		
Page 65		
Page 66		
Page 67		
Page 68		
Page 69		
Page 70		
Page 71		
Page 72		
Page 73		
Page 74		
Page 75		
Page 76		
Page 77		
Page 78		
Page 79		
Page 80		
Page 81		
Page 82		
Page 83		
Subtotal:		

Page Total:	Price Paid	Value

Heritage Village – Accessories

Page Number	Price Paid	Value
Page 84		
Page 85		
Page 86		
Page 87		
Page 88		
Page 89		
Page 90		
Page 91		
Page 92		
Page 93		
Page 94		
Page 95		
Page 96		
Page 97		
Page 98		
Page 99		
Page 100		
Page 101		
Page 102		
Page 103		
Page 104		
Page 105		
Page 106		
Page 107		
Subtotal:		

Heritage Village – Accessories

Page Number	Price Paid	Value
Page 108		
Page 109		
Page 110		
Page 111		
Page 112		
Page 113		
Page 114		
Page 115		
Page 116		
Page 117		
Page 118		
Page 119		
Page 120		
Subtotal:		

Heritage Village – Hinged Boxes & Ornaments

Page Number	Price Paid	Value
Page 121		
Page 122		
Page 123		
Page 124		
Page 125		
Subtotal:		

Page Total:	Price Paid	Value

GRAND TOTAL:	Price Paid	Value

The Original Snow Village® Overview

*T*he Original Snow Village was introduced by Department 56 with the release of six miniature, ceramic, lighted buildings in 1976 – all priced between $15 and $25. These simply designed pieces reflected a time when kids played in the streets, front doors stayed unlocked and everyone knew each other by name.

The nostalgic buildings of The Original Snow Village collection prompted collectors to reminisce about and recapture their past by collecting pieces of this tiny town. A shiny, glazed finish and an attached snow-laden evergreen tree were both features of the original buildings, as well as future releases. The collection was designed to be one large grouping rather than separate villages, as in The Heritage Village Collection, which was introduced eight years later. Two churches were included in the original six, depicting the variety of churches present in any given small town.

Four new buildings were introduced in 1978, while an additional 11 pieces were added the following year. In 1979, the first accessory, "Carolers" (set/4), was added to the growing collection and the first retirement occurred in the village, permanently securing its position as a collectible. During the 1980s, increasingly elaborate pieces made their way into stores, with more detail and special touches given to both the buildings and accessories.

An Architectural Tribute

In 1990, Department 56 released the first two pieces in the *American Architecture Series*, which celebrates famous American architecture across the country. To date, several styles have been celebrated, including "Prairie House," a style made popular by architect Frank Lloyd Wright; and

"Queen Anne Victorian," which is characterized by bay windows and a wrap-around porch.

For A Limited Time Only

The Original Snow Village collection has featured only a handful of pieces that are limited editions. In 1993, the original 1978 design of the "Nantucket" house underwent several changes, including the addition of a garage, a few new evergreen trees and some Christmas wreaths. This new piece was released as "Nantucket Renovation" and was limited to production during the year 1993.

As we all know, Santa comes to town each year and Department 56 has made sure that Snow Village is at the top of his list of places to stop. Introduced in 1994, "Santa Comes To Town, 1995" brings the jolly old man into the village as an accessory piece that collectors can look forward to year after year.

"Rock Around The Clock . . . "

In a nod to the fabulous 1950s, a number of Snow Village buildings are reminiscent of the poodle skirt and bobby socks era, although the village is said to span from the mid-to-late-20th century. These reminders of the past include "Cinema 56," "Dinah's Drive-In," "The Honeymooner Motel," and "Rockabilly Records." Accessories such as "Woody Station Wagon," "Classic Cars" (set/3) and "Christmas Cadillac" help authenticate the character of an Original Snow Village 1950s-era display.

Sign Of The Times

As the years roll by, Department 56 keeps up with the times by adding more modern facilities. "Peppermint Porch Day Care" was available in 1995 for the working moms in Snow Village and ". . . *Another Man's Treasure* Garage" (set/22) was released in 1998 to reflect the popularity of the street-side tag, yard and garage sales that have become popular Saturday morning pastimes.

What's New For The Original Snow Village®

*T*his section highlights the 11 Snow Village buildings and 20 Snow Village accessories that were introduced on December 10, 1999.

SNOW VILLAGE BUILDINGS

CEDAR POINT CABIN ... There's nothing like spending a snowy evening in a toasty warm log cabin. The lights are bright inside inviting in family and friends who are tired after a day in the great outdoors.

CHAMPSFIELD STADIUM (set/24) ... Why not spend a day watching a game at the brand new sports stadium? There are plenty of spectators in attendance already and the team hasn't even kicked off yet!

GRIMSLY MANOR ... This Gothic home is painted a soft blue color with white trim. The architecture of "Grimsly Manor" is exquisite with slender windows and a large porch.

HOLY SPIRIT CHURCH (set/2) ... This stone building with its beautiful stained glass windows is perfectly decorated for the holidays with festive displays of wreaths and garland.

A HOME IN THE MAKING (set/5) ... Even in the middle of winter, the village is growing. Here, construction workers are busy at work putting up the roof and siding for this beautiful home.

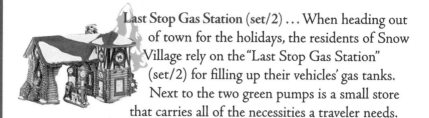

Last Stop Gas Station (set/2) ... When heading out of town for the holidays, the residents of Snow Village rely on the "Last Stop Gas Station" (set/2) for filling up their vehicles' gas tanks. Next to the two green pumps is a small store that carries all of the necessities a traveler needs.

LUCKY DRAGON RESTAURANT ... A taste of Japan can be found here at the "Lucky Dragon Restaurant." Its detailed features, such as a curved roof and strong pillars, are typical of Japanese architecture.

SHELLY'S DINER (set/2) ... The bright red sign in the front of "Shelly's Diner" (set/2) alerts customers that the restaurant is always open, while green and red Christmas decorations enhance the appearance of this shiny silver building.

SUPER SUDS LAUNDROMAT ... The folks in Snow Village can spend time in the "Cozy Cafe" or the "Book Nook" while their clothes are spinning in the dryer next door. "Super Suds Laundromat" is easy to spot with its yellow walls and wide white sign.

VILLAGE BANK & TRUST ... Who better to watch over the villagers' savings than the people at the "Village Bank & Trust?" This large brick building is festively decorated with wreaths and garland.

WSNO RADIO ... The most popular radio station in Snow Village is "WSNO Radio." Behind-the-scenes antics that occur during the broadcasts can be viewed through a large window in the front of the two-story building.

SNOW VILLAGE ACCESSORIES

Snow Village is filled with excitement on Christmas Day when "Santa Comes To Town, 2000." And during your Christmas break, you can look "Through The Woods" (set/4, animated), to spot "Santa's Little Helpers" who are making their dog look just like a reindeer. While enjoying your trek through the woods, be careful as you come upon the "Backwoods Outhouse," as two children are hidden in the snow drifts making "Angels In The Snow" (set/2). Once it's time to head to town, you can spend the afternoon enjoying the sites. "Is That Frosty?" a delivery man who works for "Gifts On The Go" (set/2) shouts at the neighborhood children. Just after the Christmas festivities end, the next celebration in Snow Village is "The Dragon Parade." Once the parade is over, it's time for the annual "Family Winter Outing" (set/3, animated). After the family spends time skiing, they take a break and have fun "Finding The Bird's Song" (set/2).

As the family returns from their outing, it's time to celebrate Mom's birthday! "Send In The Clown!" shout the children. Before the party, the children set out to find the perfect gift for mom and bump into a man on his "Laundry Day." While shopping, the children spot a couple giving their newborn a warm "Welcome To The Congregation" and they see some football players warming up "Before The Big Game" (set/4). A boy carrying his money to the bank to make his "First Deposit" and across the street, some girls are "On The Way To Ballet Class" (set/3). The children are starting to feel cold and begin to miss the warmer weather, like during Halloween when at every house there are "Treats For The Kids" (set/3). They also miss the summer months when they get to spend time on "The Backyard Patio" (set/2) and hear the ice-cream truck signaling "It's Time For An Icy Treat" (set/2). Finally, they decide on a fabulous gift for mom, the "Holy Spirit Baptistery" (music box).

The Snow Village ornaments released this year from the *Classic Ornament Series* are "Street Car," "Queen Anne Victorian" and "Jingle Belle Houseboat."

Recent Retirements

*D*epartment 56 announced the following Snow Village retirements on November 5, 1999. Each year, the retirements are made public in *USA Today*, as well as on the Department 56 web site (*www.department56.com*). Collectors can also pre-register to receive an E-mail directly from the company on the morning of the announcement.

SNOW VILLAGE BUILDINGS

- ❏ 2000 Holly Lane (1999, set/11)
- ❏ Birch Run Ski Chalet (1996)
- ❏ The Brandon Bungalow (1997)
- ❏ Christmas Barn Dance (1997)
- ❏ Christmas Lake High School (1996)
- ❏ Fisherman's Nook Cabins (1994, set/2)
- ❏ Fisherman's Nook Resort (1994)
- ❏ McDonald's® (1997)
- ❏ Nick's Tree Farm (1996, set/10)
- ❏ Rollerama Roller Rink (1997)
- ❏ Rosita's Cantina (1996)
- ❏ Shingle Victorian (1996)

SNOW VILLAGE ACCESSORIES

- ❏ At The Barn Dance, It's Allemande Left (1997, set/2)
- ❏ Caroling Through The Snow (1996)
- ❏ Christmas Kids (1997, set/5)
- ❏ Everybody Goes Skating At Rollerama (1997, set/2)
- ❏ Firewood Delivery Truck (1995)
- ❏ Flag Pole (1989)
- ❏ A Harley-Davidson® Holiday (1996, set/2)

SNOW VILLAGE ACCESSORIES, CONT.

- ❏ He Led Them Down The Streets Of Town (1997, set/3)
- ❏ Hitch-Up The Buckboard (1997)
- ❏ Holiday Hoops (1996, set/3)
- ❏ Kids, Candy Canes . . . & Ronald McDonald® (1997, set/3)
- ❏ McDonald's® . . . Lights Up The Night (1997)
- ❏ Santa Comes To Town, 1999 (LE-1999)
- ❏ Terry's Towing (1996, set/2)
- ❏ Tree Lot (1988)
- ❏ The Whole Family Goes Shopping (1997, set/3)

The Original Snow Village® Top Ten

*T*his section lists the ten most valuable Snow Village pieces as established by their value on the secondary market. Our market meter shows the percentage increase of each piece's value over the issue price.

Cathedral Church
#5067-4
Issued: 1980 ✦ Retired: 1981
Issue Price: $36 ✦ Value: **$3,000**
Market Meter: +8,234%

Adobe House
#5066-6
Issued: 1979 ✦ Retired: 1980
Issue Price: $18 ✦ Value: $2,700
Market Meter: +14,900%

Mobile Home
#5063-3
Issued: 1979 ✦ Retired: 1980
Issue Price: $18 ✦ Value: **$1,900**
Market Meter: +10,456%

Mission Church
#5062-5
Issued: 1979 ✦ Retired: 1980
Issue Price: $30 ✦ Value: $1,500
Market Meter: +4,900%

Skating Rink/Duck Pond Set
#5015-3
Issued: 1978 ✦ Retired: 1979
Issue Price: $16 ✦ Value: **$1,000**
Market Meter: +6,150%

Stone Church
#5059-1
Issued: 1979 • Retired: 1980
Issue Price: $32 • Value: $960
Market Meter: +2,900%

Congregational Church
#5034-2
Issued: 1984 • Retired: 1985
Issue Price: $28 • Value: $650
Market Meter: +2,222%

Diner
#5078-4
Issued: 1986 • Retired: 1987
Issue Price: $22 • Value: $640
Market Meter: +2,810%

Bank
#5024-5
Issued: 1982 • Retired: 1983
Issue Price: $32 • Value: $630
Market Meter: +1,869%

Stone Church
#5009-6
Issued: 1977 • Retired: 1979
Issue Price: $35 • Value: $620
Market Meter: +1,672%

How To Use Your Collector's Value Guide™

1. Locate your piece in the Snow Village Value Guide. The Original Snow Village buildings are listed first, followed by Snow Village accessories. Pieces are listed alphabetically within each section. To help you locate your pieces we have provided easy-to-use numerical and alphabetical indexes in the back of the book (beginning on page 251).

56 Flavors Ice Cream Parlor
Issued: 1990 • Retired: 1992
#5151-9 • Original Price: $42
Market Value: $177

2. Find the market value of your piece. If there is a variation with a secondary market value, you will also find that value noted. (Store exclusives are also listed in the same manner.) If no market value has been established for a piece, it is listed as "N/E" (not established). Pieces currently available at stores reflect the retail price.

3. Record the year your piece was purchased, the retail price you paid and its secondary market value in the corresponding boxes at the bottom of the page.

Snow Village Buildings

Date Purchased	Price Paid	Value
5/25/91	$42	$177
2.		
3.		
4.		
5.		
Totals		

4. Calculate the value for the page by adding all of the boxes in each column. Please be sure to use a pencil so you can change the totals in the book as your collection grows.

5. Transfer the totals from each page to the "Total Value Of My Collection" worksheets for Snow Village, which you can find on page 200.

6. Add all of the totals together to determine the overall value of your collection.

SNOW VILLAGE – BUILDINGS

Depicting a small American town, Snow Village is a magical place that captures the essence of culture in the United States. The largest village in the Department 56 collection, with a total of 240 buildings from which to choose. To date, the most valuable piece on the secondary market is "Cathedral Church" (#5067-4) with a value of $3,000.

1
56 Flavors Ice Cream Parlor
Issued: 1990 • Retired: 1992
#5151-9 • Original Price: $42
Market Value: $177

2
2000 Holly Lane
(set/11, Event Piece)
Issued: 1999 • Retired: 1999
#54977 • Original Price: $65
Market Value: $65

3
2101 Maple
Issued: 1986 • Retired: 1986
#5043-1 • Original Price: $32
Market Value: $330

4
Adobe House
Issued: 1979 • Retired: 1980
#5066-6 • Original Price: $18
Market Value: $2,700

5
Airport
Issued: 1992 • Retired: 1996
#5439-9 • Original Price: $60
Market Value: $90

Snow Village Buildings

	Date Purchased	Price Paid	Value
1.			
2.			
3.			
4.			
5.			
Totals			

Snow Village – Buildings

6

Al's TV Shop
Issued: 1992 • Retired: 1995
#5423-2 • Original Price: $40
Market Value: $66

7

All Saints Church
Issued: 1986 • Retired: 1997
#5070-9 • Original Price: $38
Market Value: $62

8

. . . *Another Man's Treasure* Garage (set/22)
Issued: 1998 • Current
#54945 • Original Price: $60
Market Value: $60

9

Apothecary
Issued: 1986 • Retired: 1990
#5076-8 • Original Price: $34
Market Value: $105

10

Bakery
Issued: 1981 • Retired: 1983
#5077-6 • Original Price: $30
Market Value: $270

11

Bakery
Issued: 1986 • Retired: 1991
#5077-6 • Original Price: $35
Market Value: $88

12

Bank
Issued: 1982 • Retired: 1983
#5024-5 • Original Price: $32
Market Value: $630

Snow Village Buildings

	Date Purchased	Price Paid	Value
6.			
7.			
8.			
9.			
10.			
11.			
12.			
Totals			

13

Barn
Issued: 1981 • Retired: 1984
#5074-1 • Original Price: $32
Market Value: $440

14

Bayport
Issued: 1984 • Retired: 1986
#5015-6 • Original Price: $30
Market Value: $230

15

Beacon Hill House
Issued: 1986 • Retired: 1988
#5065-2 • Original Price: $31
Market Value: $180

16

Beacon Hill Victorian
Issued: 1995 • Retired: 1998
#54857 • Original Price: $60
Market Value: $80

17

Birch Run Ski Chalet
Issued: 1996 • Retired: 1999
#54882 • Original Price: $60
Market Value: $68

18

Boulder Springs House
Issued: 1996 • Retired: 1997
#54873 • Original Price: $60
Market Value: $78

19

Bowling Alley
Issued: 1995 • Retired: 1998
#54858 • Original Price: $42
Market Value: $60

Snow Village Buildings

	Date Purchased	Price Paid	Value
13.			
14.			
15.			
16.			
17.			
18.			
19.			
Totals			

Snow Village – Buildings

20

The Brandon Bungalow
Issued: 1997 • Retired: 1999
#54918 • Original Price: $55
Market Value: $58

21

Brownstone
Issued: 1979 • Retired: 1981
#5056-7 • Original Price: $36
Market Value: $580

22

Cape Cod
Issued: 1978 • Retired: 1980
#5013-8 • Original Price: $20
Market Value: $385

23

Carmel Cottage
Issued: 1994 • Retired: 1997
#5466-6 • Original Price: $48
Market Value: $60

24

The Carnival Carousel
(animated, musical)
Issued: 1998 • Current
#54933 • Original Price: $150
Market Value: $150

25

Carriage House
Issued: 1982 • Retired: 1984
#5021-0 • Original Price: $28
Market Value: $325

26

Carriage House
Issued: 1986 • Retired: 1988
#5071-7 • Original Price: $29
Market Value: $112

Snow Village Buildings

	Date Purchased	Price Paid	Value
20.			
21.			
22.			
23.			
24.			
25.			
26.			
Totals			

Value Guide — Department 56® Villages

27

Cathedral Church
Issued: 1980 • Retired: 1981
#5067-4 • Original Price: $36
Market Value: $3,000

28

Cathedral Church
Issued: 1987 • Retired: 1990
#5019-9 • Original Price: $50
Market Value: $108

29

New!

Cedar Point Cabin
Issued: 1999 • Current
#55009 • Original Price: $66
Market Value: $66

30

Centennial House
Issued: 1982 • Retired: 1984
#5020-2 • Original Price: $32
Market Value: $335

31

Center For The Arts
Issued: 1998 • Current
#54940 • Original Price: $64
Market Value: $64

32

New!

Champsfield Stadium (set/24)
Issued: 1999 • Current
#55001 • Original Price: $195
Market Value: $195

33

Chateau
Issued: 1983 • Retired: 1984
#5084-9 • Original Price: $35
Market Value: $445

Snow Village Buildings

	Date Purchased	Price Paid	Value
27.			
28.			
29.			
30.			
31.			
32.			
33.			
Totals			

143

Snow Village – Buildings

34

Christmas Barn Dance
Issued: 1997 • Retired: 1999
#54910 • Original Price: $65
Market Value: $69

35

Christmas Cove Lighthouse
Issued: 1995 • Current
#5483-6 • Original Price: $60
Market Value: $60

36

Christmas Lake High School
Issued: 1996 • Retired: 1999
#54881 • Original Price: $52
Market Value: $56

37

The Christmas Shop
Issued: 1991 • Retired: 1996
#5097-0 • Original Price: $37.50
Market Value: $64

38

Church Of The Open Door
Issued: 1985 • Retired: 1988
#5048-2 • Original Price: $34
Market Value: $150

39

Cinema 56
Issued: 1999 • Current
#54978 • Original Price: $85
Market Value: $85

40

Cobblestone Antique Shop
Issued: 1988 • Retired: 1992
#5123-3 • Original Price: $36
Market Value: $77

Snow Village Buildings

	Date Purchased	Price Paid	Value
34.			
35.			
36.			
37.			
38.			
39.			
40.			
Totals			

41

Coca-Cola® Brand Bottling Plant
Issued: 1994 • Retired: 1997
#5469-0 • Original Price: $65
Market Value: $88

42

Coca-Cola® Brand Corner Drugstore
Issued: 1995 • Retired: 1998
#5484-4 • Original Price: $55
Market Value: $86

43

Colonial Church
Issued: 1989 • Retired: 1992
#5119-5 • Original Price: $60
Market Value: $86

44

Colonial Farm House
Issued: 1980 • Retired: 1982
#5070-9 • Original Price: $30
Market Value: $310

45

Congregational Church
Issued: 1984 • Retired: 1985
#5034-2 • Original Price: $28
Market Value: $650

46

Corner Cafe
Issued: 1988 • Retired: 1991
#5124-1 • Original Price: $37
Market Value: $100

47

Corner Store
Issued: 1981 • Retired: 1983
#5076-8 • Original Price: $30
Market Value: $245

Snow Village Buildings

	Date Purchased	Price Paid	Value
41.			
42.			
43.			
44.			
45.			
46.			
47.			
Totals			

Snow Village – Buildings

48

Country Church
Issued: 1976 • Retired: 1979
#5004-7 • Original Price: $18
Market Value: $380

49

Countryside Church
Issued: 1979 • Retired: 1984
#5058-3 • Original Price: $27.50
Market Value: $270

50

Courthouse
Issued: 1989 • Retired: 1993
#5144-6 • Original Price: $65
Market Value: $195

51

Craftsman Cottage
American Architecture Series
Issued: 1992 • Retired: 1995
#5437-2 • Original Price: $55
Market Value: $77

52

Cumberland House
Issued: 1987 • Retired: 1995
#5024-5 • Original Price: $42
Market Value: $75

53

Dairy Barn
Issued: 1993 • Retired: 1997
#5446-1 • Original Price: $55
Market Value: $78

Snow Village Buildings

	Date Purchased	Price Paid	Value
48.			
49.			
50.			
51.			
52.			
53.			
Totals			

54

Delta House
Issued: 1984 • Retired: 1986
#5012-1 • Original Price: $32
Market Value: $300

55

Depot & Train With Two Train Cars (set/2)
Issued: 1985 • Retired: 1988
#5051-2 • Original Price: $65
Market Value: $155

56

Dinah's Drive-In
Issued: 1993 • Retired: 1996
#5447-0 • Original Price: $45
Market Value: $120

57

Diner
Issued: 1986 • Retired: 1987
#5078-4 • Original Price: $22
Market Value: $640

58

Doctor's House
Issued: 1989 • Retired: 1992
#5143-8 • Original Price: $56
Market Value: $105

59

Double Bungalow
Issued: 1991 • Retired: 1994
#5407-0 • Original Price: $45
Market Value: $67

60

Duplex
Issued: 1985 • Retired: 1987
#5050-4 • Original Price: $35
Market Value: $155

Snow Village Buildings

	Date Purchased	Price Paid	Value
54.			
55.			
56.			
57.			
58.			
59.			
60.			
Totals			

147

61

Dutch Colonial
American Architecture Series
Issued: 1995 • Retired: 1996
#54856 • Original Price: $45
Market Value: $70

62

English Church
Issued: 1981 • Retired: 1982
#5078-4 • Original Price: $30
Market Value: $390

63

English Cottage
Issued: 1981 • Retired: 1982
#5073-3 • Original Price: $25
Market Value: $300

64

English Tudor
Issued: 1983 • Retired: 1985
#5033-4 • Original Price: $30
Market Value: $280

65

Farm House
Issued: 1987 • Retired: 1992
#5089-0 • Original Price: $40
Market Value: $77

66

Farm House
Issued: 1997 • Current
#54912 • Original Price: $50
Market Value: $50

Snow Village Buildings

	Date Purchased	Price Paid	Value
61.			
62.			
63.			
64.			
65.			
66.			
67.			
Totals			

67

The Farmer's Co-op Granary
Issued: 1998 • Current
#54946 • Original Price: $64
Market Value: $64

68

Federal House
American Architecture Series
Issued: 1994 • Retired: 1997
#5465-8 • Original Price: $50
Market Value: $75

69

Finklea's Finery: Costume Shop
Issued: 1991 • Retired: 1993
#5405-4 • Original Price: $45
Market Value: $69

70

Fire Station
Issued: 1983 • Retired: 1984
#5032-6 • Original Price: $32
Market Value: $585

71

Fire Station No. 2
Issued: 1987 • Retired: 1989
#5091-1 • Original Price: $40
Market Value: $210

72

Fire Station #3
Issued: 1998 • Current
#54942 • Original Price: $70
Market Value: $70

73

Bass   Trout

Fisherman's Nook Cabins (set/2)
Issued: 1994 • Retired: 1999
#5461-5 • Original Price: $50
Market Value: $58

74

Fisherman's Nook Resort
Issued: 1994 • Retired: 1999
#5460-7 • Original Price: $75
Market Value: $81

Snow Village Buildings

	Date Purchased	Price Paid	Value
68.			
69.			
70.			
71.			
72.			
73.			
74.			
Totals			

Snow Village – Buildings

75

Flower Shop
Issued: 1982 • Retired: 1983
#5082-2 • Original Price: $25
Market Value: $475

76

Gabled Cottage
Issued: 1976 • Retired: 1979
#5002-1 • Original Price: $20
Market Value: $385

77

Gabled House
Issued: 1982 • Retired: 1983
#5081-4 • Original Price: $30
Market Value: $425

78

Galena House
Issued: 1984 • Retired: 1985
#5009-1 • Original Price: $32
Market Value: $380

79

Version 1   *Version 2*   *Version 3*

General Store
Issued: 1978 • Retired: 1980
#5012-0 • Original Price: $25
Market Value: **1** – *$480 (white)* **2** – *$600 (tan)* **3** – *$545 (gold)*

Snow Village Buildings

	Date Purchased	Price Paid	Value
75.			
76.			
77.			
78.			
79.			
80.			
Totals			

80

Giant Trees
Issued: 1979 • Retired: 1982
#5065-8 • Original Price: $20
Market Value: $300

81

Version 1

Version 2

Gingerbread House
Issued: 1983 • Retired: 1984
#5025-3 • Original Price: $24
Market Value: **1** – *$370 (coin bank)*
2 – *$370 (lit house)*

82

Glenhaven House
Issued: 1994 • Retired: 1997
#5468-2 • Original Price: $45
Market Value: $68

83

Good Shepherd Chapel
& Church School (set/2)
Issued: 1992 • Retired: 1996
#5424-0 • Original Price: $72
Market Value: $90

84

Gothic Church
Issued: 1983 • Retired: 1986
#5028-8 • Original Price: $36
Market Value: $275

85

Gothic Farmhouse
American Architecture Series
Issued: 1991 • Retired: 1997
#5404-6 • Original Price: $48
Market Value: $68

86

Governor's Mansion
Issued: 1983 • Retired: 1985
#5003-2 • Original Price: $32
Market Value: $320

Snow Village Buildings

	Date Purchased	Price Paid	Value
81.			
82.			
83.			
84.			
85.			
86.			
Totals			

Snow Village – Buildings

87

Gracie's Dry Goods & General Store (set/2)
Issued: 1997 • Current
#54915 • Original Price: $70
Market Value: $70

88

Grandma's Cottage
Issued: 1992 • Retired: 1996
#5420-8 • Original Price: $42
Market Value: $73

89

New!

Grimsly Manor
Issued: 1999 • Current
#55004 • Original Price: $120
Market Value: $120

90

Grocery
Issued: 1983 • Retired: 1985
#5001-6 • Original Price: $35
Market Value: $350

91

Harley-Davidson® Manufacturing (set/3)
Issued: 1998 • Current
#54948 • Original Price: $80
Market Value: $80

92

Harley-Davidson® Motorcycle Shop
Issued: 1996 • Current
#54886 • Original Price: $65
Market Value: $65

93

Hartford House
Issued: 1992 • Retired: 1995
#5426-7 • Original Price: $55
Market Value: $82

Snow Village Buildings

	Date Purchased	Price Paid	Value
87.			
88.			
89.			
90.			
91.			
92.			
93.			
Totals			

94

Haunted Mansion (animated)
Issued: 1998 • Current
#54935 • Original Price: $110
Market Value: $110

95

Haversham House
Issued: 1984 • Retired: 1987
#5008-3 • Original Price: $37
Market Value: $285

96

Hershey's™ Chocolate Shop
Issued: 1997 • Current
#54913 • Original Price: $55
Market Value: $55

97

Hidden Ponds House
Issued: 1998 • Current
#54944 • Original Price: $50
Market Value: $50

98

Highland Park House
Issued: 1986 • Retired: 1988
#5063-6 • Original Price: $35
Market Value: $155

99

Holly Brothers Garage
Issued: 1995 • Retired: 1998
#54854 • Original Price: $48
Market Value: $70

100

New!

Holy Spirit Church (set/2)
Issued: 1999 • Current
#55003 • Original Price: $70
Market Value: $70

Snow Village Buildings

	Date Purchased	Price Paid	Value
94.			
95.			
96.			
97.			
98.			
99.			
100.			
Totals			

Snow Village – Buildings

101

New!

**A Home In The Making
(set/5, Early Release)**
Issued: 1999 • Current
#54979 • Original Price: $95
Market Value: $95

102

**Home Sweet Home/
House & Windmill (set/2)**
Issued: 1988 • Retired: 1991
#5126-8 • Original Price: $60
Market Value: $120

103

Homestead
Issued: 1978 • Retired: 1984
#5011-2 • Original Price: $30
Market Value: $260

104

The Honeymooner Motel
Issued: 1991 • Retired: 1993
#5401-1 • Original Price: $42
Market Value: $90

105

Hunting Lodge
Issued: 1993 • Retired: 1996
#5445-3 • Original Price: $50
Market Value: $150

106

The Inn
Issued: 1976 • Retired: 1979
#5003-9 • Original Price: $20
Market Value: $480

Snow Village Buildings

	Date Purchased	Price Paid	Value
101.			
102.			
103.			
104.			
105.			
106.			
Totals			

Value Guide — Department 56® Villages

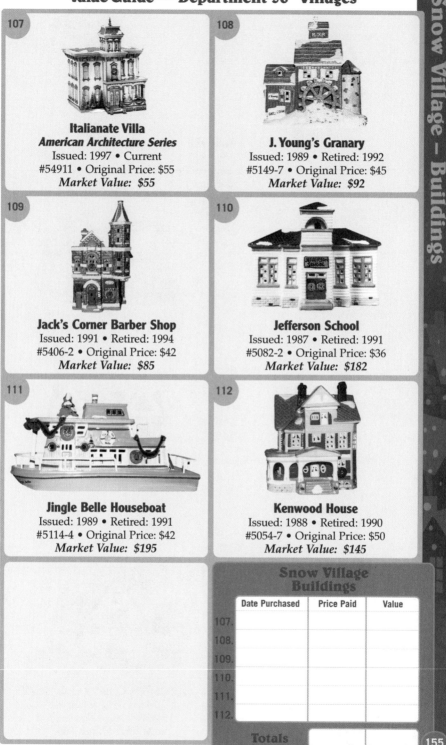

107

Italianate Villa
American Architecture Series
Issued: 1997 • Current
#54911 • Original Price: $55
Market Value: $55

108

J. Young's Granary
Issued: 1989 • Retired: 1992
#5149-7 • Original Price: $45
Market Value: $92

109

Jack's Corner Barber Shop
Issued: 1991 • Retired: 1994
#5406-2 • Original Price: $42
Market Value: $85

110

Jefferson School
Issued: 1987 • Retired: 1991
#5082-2 • Original Price: $36
Market Value: $182

111

Jingle Belle Houseboat
Issued: 1989 • Retired: 1991
#5114-4 • Original Price: $42
Market Value: $195

112

Kenwood House
Issued: 1988 • Retired: 1990
#5054-7 • Original Price: $50
Market Value: $145

Snow Village Buildings

	Date Purchased	Price Paid	Value
107.			
108.			
109.			
110.			
111.			
112.			
Totals			

113

Version 1   *Version 2*

Knob Hill
Issued: 1979 • Retired: 1981
#5055-9 • Original Price: $30
Market Value: **1** – $360 *(gray)* **2** – $350 *(yellow)*

114

Large Single Tree
Issued: 1981 • Retired: 1989
#5080-6 • Original Price: $17
Market Value: $58

115

New!

Last Stop Gas Station (set/2)
Issued: 1999 • Current
#55012 • Original Price: $72
Market Value: $72

116

Lighthouse
Issued: 1987 • Retired: 1988
#5030-0 • Original Price: $36
Market Value: $580

117

Lincoln Park Duplex
Issued: 1986 • Retired: 1988
#5060-1 • Original Price: $33
Market Value: $140

Snow Village Buildings

	Date Purchased	Price Paid	Value
113.			
114.			
115.			
116.			
117.			
118.			
Totals			

118

Linden Hills Country Club (set/2)
Issued: 1997 • Current
#54917 • Original Price: $60
Market Value: $60

Value Guide — Department 56® Villages

119

Version 1   *Version 2*

Lionel® Electric Train Shop
Issued: 1998 • Current
#54947 • Original Price: $55
Market Value: **1** *– N/E (Allied Model Trains)* **2** *– $55 (general release)*

120

Log Cabin
Issued: 1979 • Retired: 1981
#5057-5 • Original Price: $22
Market Value: $500

121

New!

Lucky Dragon Restaurant
Issued: 1999 • Current
#55011 • Original Price: $75
Market Value: $75

122

Main Street House
Issued: 1984 • Retired: 1986
#5005-9 • Original Price: $27
Market Value: $245

123

Mainstreet Gift Shop
(GCC Piece)
Issued: 1997 • Retired: 1997
#54887 • Original Price: $50
Market Value: $90

Snow Village Buildings

	Date Purchased	Price Paid	Value
119.			
120.			
121.			
122.			
123.			
Totals			

124

Mainstreet Hardware Store
Issued: 1990 • Retired: 1993
#5153-5 • Original Price: $42
Market Value: $87

125

Mansion
Issued: 1977 • Retired: 1979
#5008-8 • Original Price: $30
Market Value: $520

126

Maple Ridge Inn
Issued: 1988 • Retired: 1990
#5121-7 • Original Price: $55
Market Value: $83

127

Marvel's Beauty Salon
Issued: 1994 • Retired: 1997
#5470-4 • Original Price: $37.50
Market Value: $57

128

McDonald's®
Issued: 1997 • Retired: 1999
#54914 • Original Price: $65
Market Value: $68

129

Mission Church
Issued: 1979 • Retired: 1980
#5062-5 • Original Price: $30
Market Value: $1,500

Snow Village Buildings

	Date Purchased	Price Paid	Value
124.			
125.			
126.			
127.			
128.			
129.			
130.			
Totals			

130

Mobile Home
Issued: 1979 • Retired: 1980
#5063-3 • Original Price: $18
Market Value: $1,900

Value Guide — Department 56® Villages

131

Morningside House
Issued: 1990 • Retired: 1992
#5152-7 • Original Price: $45
Market Value: $70

132

Mount Olivet Church
Issued: 1993 • Retired: 1996
#5442-9 • Original Price: $65
Market Value: $74

133

Mountain Lodge
Issued: 1976 • Retired: 1979
#5001-3 • Original Price: $20
Market Value: $385

134

Nantucket
Issued: 1978 • Retired: 1986
#5014-6 • Original Price: $25
Market Value: $265

135

Nantucket Renovation (LE-1993)
Issued: 1993 • Retired: 1993
#5441-0 • Original Price: $55
Market Value: $75

136

New Hope Church
Issued: 1997 • Retired: 1998
#54904 • Original Price: $60
Market Value: $75

137

New School House
Issued: 1984 • Retired: 1986
#5037-7 • Original Price: $35
Market Value: $260

Snow Village Buildings

	Date Purchased	Price Paid	Value
131.			
132.			
133.			
134.			
135.			
136.			
137.			
Totals			

Snow Village – Buildings

138

New Stone Church
Issued: 1982 • Retired: 1984
#5083-0 • Original Price: $32
Market Value: $372

139

Nick The Tree Farmer   *Nick's Tree Farm*

Nick's Tree Farm (set/10)
Issued: 1996 • Retired: 1999
#54871 • Original Price: $40
Market Value: $44

140

North Creek Cottage
Issued: 1989 • Retired: 1992
#5120-9 • Original Price: $45
Market Value: $70

141

Oak Grove Tudor
Issued: 1991 • Retired: 1994
#5400-3 • Original Price: $42
Market Value: $63

142

Old Chelsea Mansion (with book)
Issued: 1997 • Retired: 1998
#54903 • Original Price: $85
Market Value: $102

143

Kringle's Toy Shop   *Nikki's Cocoa Shop*

Saturday Morning Downtown

The Original Snow Village Start A Tradition Set (set/8)
Issued: 1997 • Retired: 1998
#54902 • Original Price: $75
Market Value: $100

144

Pacific Heights House
Issued: 1986 • Retired: 1988
#5066-0 • Original Price: $33
Market Value: $110

Snow Village Buildings

	Date Purchased	Price Paid	Value
138.			
139.			
140.			
141.			
142.			
143.			
144.			
Totals			

Value Guide — Department 56® Villages

145

Palos Verdes
Issued: 1988 • Retired: 1990
#5141-1 • Original Price: $37.50
Market Value: $82

146

Paramount Theater
Issued: 1989 • Retired: 1993
#5142-0 • Original Price: $42
Market Value: $190

147

Parish Church
Issued: 1984 • Retired: 1986
#5039-3 • Original Price: $32
Market Value: $327

148

Parsonage
Issued: 1983 • Retired: 1985
#5029-6 • Original Price: $35
Market Value: $350

149

Peppermint Porch Day Care
Issued: 1995 • Retired: 1997
#5485-2 • Original Price: $45
Market Value: $65

150

Pinewood Log Cabin
Issued: 1989 • Retired: 1995
#5150-0 • Original Price: $37.50
Market Value: $68

151

Pioneer Church
Issued: 1982 • Retired: 1984
#5022-9 • Original Price: $30
Market Value: $332

Snow Village Buildings

	Date Purchased	Price Paid	Value
145.			
146.			
147.			
148.			
149.			
150.			
151.			
Totals			

152

Pisa Pizza
Issued: 1995 • Retired: 1998
#54851 • Original Price: $35
Market Value: $52

153

Plantation House
Issued: 1985 • Retired: 1987
#5047-4 • Original Price: $37
Market Value: $110

154

Prairie House
American Architecture Series
Issued: 1990 • Retired: 1993
#5156-0 • Original Price: $42
Market Value: $75

155

Print Shop & Village News
Issued: 1992 • Retired: 1994
#5425-9 • Original Price: $37.50
Market Value: $75

156

Queen Anne Victorian
American Architecture Series
Issued: 1990 • Retired: 1996
#5157-8 • Original Price: $48
Market Value: $78

157

Ramsey Hill House
Issued: 1986 • Retired: 1989
#5067-9 • Original Price: $36
Market Value: $110

158

Red Barn
Issued: 1987 • Retired: 1992
#5081-4 • Original Price: $38
Market Value: $108

Snow Village Buildings

	Date Purchased	Price Paid	Value
152.			
153.			
154.			
155.			
156.			
157.			
158.			
Totals			

159

Redeemer Church
Issued: 1988 • Retired: 1992
#5127-6 • Original Price: $42
Market Value: $75

160

Reindeer Bus Depot
Issued: 1996 • Retired: 1997
#54874 • Original Price: $42
Market Value: $62

161

Ridgewood
Issued: 1985 • Retired: 1987
#5052-0 • Original Price: $35
Market Value: $160

162

River Road House
Issued: 1984 • Retired: 1987
#5010-5 • Original Price: $36
Market Value: $220

163

Rock Creek Mill
Issued: 1998 • Retired: 1998
#54932 • Original Price: $64
Market Value: $110

164

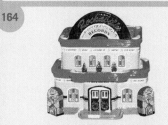

Rockabilly Records
Issued: 1996 • Retired: 1998
#54880 • Original Price: $45
Market Value: $57

165

Rollerama Roller Rink
Issued: 1997 • Retired: 1999
#54916 • Original Price: $56
Market Value: $58

Snow Village Buildings

	Date Purchased	Price Paid	Value
159.			
160.			
161.			
162.			
163.			
164.			
165.			
Totals			

166

Rosita's Cantina
Issued: 1996 • Retired: 1999
#54883 • Original Price: $50
Market Value: $52

167

Ryman Auditorium®
Issued: 1995 • Retired: 1997
#54855 • Original Price: $75
Market Value: $100

168

St. Anthony Hotel & Post Office
Issued: 1987 • Retired: 1989
#5006-7 • Original Price: $40
Market Value: $110

169

Saint James Church
Issued: 1986 • Retired: 1988
#5068-7 • Original Price: $37
Market Value: $172

170

St. Luke's Church
Issued: 1992 • Retired: 1994
#5421-6 • Original Price: $45
Market Value: $70

171

School House
Issued: 1979 • Retired: 1982
#5060-9 • Original Price: $30
Market Value: $382

172

The Secret Garden Florist
Issued: 1996 • Current
#54885 • Original Price: $50
Market Value: $50

Snow Village Buildings

	Date Purchased	Price Paid	Value
166.			
167.			
168.			
169.			
170.			
171.			
172.			
Totals			

Value Guide — Department 56® Villages

173

The Secret Garden Greenhouse
Issued: 1998 • Current
#54949 • Original Price: $60
Market Value: $60

174

Service Station
Issued: 1988 • Retired: 1991
#5128-4 • Original Price: $37.50
Market Value: $268

175

New!

Shelly's Diner (set/2)
Issued: 1999 • Current
#55008 • Original Price: $110
Market Value: $110

176

Shingle Victorian
American Architecture Series
Issued: 1996 • Retired: 1999
#54884 • Original Price: $55
Market Value: $57

177

Single Car Garage
Issued: 1988 • Retired: 1990
#5125-0 • Original Price: $22
Market Value: $58

178

Skate & Ski Shop
Issued: 1994 • Retired: 1998
#5467-4 • Original Price: $50
Market Value: $60

179

Skating Pond
Issued: 1982 • Retired: 1984
#5017-2 • Original Price: $25
Market Value: $370

Snow Village Buildings

	Date Purchased	Price Paid	Value
173.			
174.			
175.			
176.			
177.			
178.			
179.			
Totals			

Snow Village – Buildings

180

Skating Rink/Duck Pond Set
Issued: 1978 • Retired: 1979
#5015-3 • Original Price: $16
Market Value: $1,000

181

Small Chalet
Issued: 1976 • Retired: 1979
#5006-2 • Original Price: $15
Market Value: $450

182

Version 1   Version 2

Small Double Trees
Issued: 1978 • Retired: 1989
#5016-1 • Original Price: $13.50
Market Value: 1 – $185 (blue birds) 2 – $58 (red birds)

183

Smokey Mountain Retreat
(with magic smoking element)
Issued: 1996 • Current
#54872 • Original Price: $65
Market Value: $65

184

Snow Carnival Ice Palace (set/2)
Issued: 1995 • Retired: 1998
#54850 • Original Price: $95
Market Value: $115

Snow Village Buildings

	Date Purchased	Price Paid	Value
180.			
181.			
182.			
183.			
184.			
185.			
Totals			

185

Snow Village Factory
Issued: 1987 • Retired: 1989
#5013-0 • Original Price: $45
Market Value: $135

Value Guide — Department 56® Villages

186

Snow Village Resort Lodge
Issued: 1987 • Retired: 1989
#5092-0 • Original Price: $55
Market Value: $140

187

Sunday School Serenade

Shady Oak Church

Snow Village Starter Set (set/6)
Issued: 1994 • Retired: 1996
#5462-3 • Original Price: $50
Market Value: $78

188

Snowy Hills Hospital
Issued: 1993 • Retired: 1996
#5448-8 • Original Price: $48
Market Value: $92

189

Decorate The Tree

Snowy Pines Inn

Snowy Pines Inn (set/9, Event Piece)
Issued: 1998 • Retired: 1998
#54934 • Original Price: $65
Market Value: $85

190

Sonoma House
Issued: 1986 • Retired: 1988
#5062-8 • Original Price: $33
Market Value: $150

191

Southern Colonial
American Architecture Series
Issued: 1991 • Retired: 1994
#5403-8 • Original Price: $50
Market Value: $85

192

Spanish Mission Church
Issued: 1990 • Retired: 1992
#5155-1 • Original Price: $42
Market Value: $84

Snow Village Buildings

	Date Purchased	Price Paid	Value
186.			
187.			
188.			
189.			
190.			
191.			
192.			
Totals			

193

Springfield House
Issued: 1987 • Retired: 1990
#5027-0 • Original Price: $40
Market Value: $82

194

Spruce Place
Issued: 1985 • Retired: 1987
#5049-0 • Original Price: $33
Market Value: $260

195

Starbucks® Coffee
Issued: 1995 • Current
#54859 • Original Price: $48
Market Value: $48

196

Steepled Church
Issued: 1976 • Retired: 1979
#5005-4 • Original Price: $25
Market Value: $600

197

Stick Style House
American Architecture Series
Issued: 1998 • Current
#54943 • Original Price: $60
Market Value: $60

198

Stone Church
Issued: 1977 • Retired: 1979
#5009-6 • Original Price: $35
Market Value: $620

199

Stone Church
Issued: 1979 • Retired: 1980
#5059-1 • Original Price: $32
Market Value: $960

Snow Village Buildings

	Date Purchased	Price Paid	Value
193.			
194.			
195.			
196.			
197.			
198.			
199.			
Totals			

200

Stone Mill House
Issued: 1980 • Retired: 1982
#5068-2 • Original Price: $30
Market Value: $520

201

Stonehurst House
Issued: 1988 • Retired: 1994
#5140-3 • Original Price: $37.50
Market Value: $65

202

Stratford House
Issued: 1984 • Retired: 1986
#5007-5 • Original Price: $28
Market Value: $178

203

Street Car
Issued: 1982 • Retired: 1984
#5019-9 • Original Price: $16
Market Value: $350

204

Stucco Bungalow
Issued: 1985 • Retired: 1986
#5045-8 • Original Price: $30
Market Value: $375

205

Summit House
Issued: 1984 • Retired: 1985
#5036-9 • Original Price: $28
Market Value: $370

206

New!

Super Suds Laundromat
Issued: 1999 • Current
#55006 • Original Price: $60
Market Value: $60

Snow Village Buildings

	Date Purchased	Price Paid	Value
200.			
201.			
202.			
203.			
204.			
205.			
206.			
Totals			

Snow Village – Buildings

207

Swiss Chalet
Issued: 1982 • Retired: 1984
#5023-7 • Original Price: $28
Market Value: $438

208

Town Church
Issued: 1980 • Retired: 1982
#5071-7 • Original Price: $33
Market Value: $340

209

Town Hall
Issued: 1983 • Retired: 1984
#5000-8 • Original Price: $32
Market Value: $345

210

Toy Shop
Issued: 1986 • Retired: 1990
#5073-3 • Original Price: $36
Market Value: $97

211

Version 1   *Version 2*

Train Station With 3 Train Cars (set/4)
Issued: 1980 • Retired: 1985
#5085-6 • Original Price: $100
Market Value: **1** *– $400 (6 window panes/1 round window in door)*
2 *– $360 (8 window panes/2 square windows in door)*

Snow Village Buildings

	Date Purchased	Price Paid	Value
207.			
208.			
209.			
210.			
211.			
212.			
Totals			

212

Trinity Church
Issued: 1984 • Retired: 1986
#5035-0 • Original Price: $32
Market Value: $300

Value Guide — Department 56® Villages

213

Tudor House
Issued: 1979 • Retired: 1981
#5061-7 • Original Price: $25
Market Value: $320

214

Turn Of The Century
Issued: 1983 • Retired: 1986
#5004-0 • Original Price: $36
Market Value: $240

215

Twin Peaks
Issued: 1986 • Retired: 1986
#5042-3 • Original Price: $32
Market Value: $440

216

Uptown Motors Ford® (set/3)
Issued: 1998 • Current
#54941 • Original Price: $95
Market Value: $95

217

Victorian
Issued: 1979 • Retired: 1982
#5054-2 • Original Price: $30
Market Value: $360

218

Victorian Cottage
Issued: 1983 • Retired: 1984
#5002-4 • Original Price: $35
Market Value: $360

219

Victorian House
Issued: 1977 • Retired: 1979
#5007-0 • Original Price: $30
Market Value: $460

Snow Village Buildings

	Date Purchased	Price Paid	Value
213.			
214.			
215.			
216.			
217.			
218.			
218.			
Totals			

Snow Village – Buildings

220

New!

Village Bank & Trust
Issued: 1999 • Current
#55002 • Original Price: $75
Market Value: $75

221

Village Church
Issued: 1983 • Retired: 1984
#5026-1 • Original Price: $30
Market Value: $425

222

Village Greenhouse
Issued: 1991 • Retired: 1995
#5402-0 • Original Price: $35
Market Value: $64

223

Village Market
Issued: 1988 • Retired: 1991
#5044-0 • Original Price: $39
Market Value: $87

224

Village Police Station
Issued: 1995 • Retired: 1998
#54853 • Original Price: $48
Market Value: $60

225

Village Post Office
Issued: 1992 • Retired: 1995
#5422-4 • Original Price: $35
Market Value: $75

Snow Village Buildings

	Date Purchased	Price Paid	Value
220.			
221.			
222.			
223.			
224.			
225.			
226.			
Totals			

226

Village Public Library
Issued: 1993 • Retired: 1997
#5443-7 • Original Price: $55
Market Value: $68

Value Guide — Department 56® Villages

227

Village Realty
Issued: 1990 • Retired: 1993
#5154-3 • Original Price: $42
Market Value: $77

228

Village Station
Issued: 1992 • Retired: 1997
#5438-0 • Original Price: $65
Market Value: $75

229

Village Station And Train (set/2)
Issued: 1988 • Retired: 1992
#5122-5 • Original Price: $65
Market Value: $110

230

Village Vet And Pet Shop
Issued: 1992 • Retired: 1995
#5427-5 • Original Price: $32
Market Value: $78

231

Village Warming House
Issued: 1989 • Retired: 1992
#5145-4 • Original Price: $42
Market Value: $80

232

Waverly Place
Issued: 1986 • Retired: 1986
#5041-5 • Original Price: $35
Market Value: $305

233

Wedding Chapel
Issued: 1994 • Current
#5464-0 • Original Price: $55
Market Value: $55

Snow Village Buildings

	Date Purchased	Price Paid	Value
227.			
228.			
229.			
230.			
231.			
232.			
233.			
Totals			

234

Williamsburg House
Issued: 1985 • Retired: 1988
#5046-6 • Original Price: $37
Market Value: $145

235

Woodbury House
Issued: 1993 • Retired: 1996
#5444-5 • Original Price: $45
Market Value: $67

236

Wooden Church
Issued: 1983 • Retired: 1985
#5031-8 • Original Price: $30
Market Value: $350

237

Wooden Clapboard
Issued: 1981 • Retired: 1984
#5072-5 • Original Price: $32
Market Value: $248

238

New!

WSNO Radio
Issued: 1999 • Current
#55010 • Original Price: $75
Market Value: $75

Snow Village Buildings

	Date Purchased	Price Paid	Value
234.			
235.			
236.			
237.			
238.			
Totals			

SNOW VILLAGE – ACCESSORIES

Since 1979, collectors have had the option of adding accessories to their *Snow Village* collection. Twenty new pieces were introduced for 2000, including two animated pieces.

3 Nuns With Songbooks
Issued: 1987 • Retired: 1988
#5102-0 • Orig. Price: $6
Market Value: $135

1955 Ford® Automobiles (6 assorted)
Issued: 1998 • Current
#54950 • Orig. Price: $10 (ea.)
Market Value: $10 (ea.)

1964½ Ford® Mustang (3 assorted)
Issued: 1998 • Current
#54951 • Orig. Price: $10 (ea.)
Market Value: $10 (ea.)

New!

Angels In The Snow (set/2)
Issued: 1999 • Current
#55024 • Orig. Price: $30
Market Value: $30

. . . Another Man's Treasure Accessories (set/3)
Issued: 1998 • Current
#54976 • Orig. Price: $27.50
Market Value: $27.50

Apple Girl/Newspaper Boy (set/2)
Issued: 1988 • Retired: 1990
#5129-2 • Orig. Price: $11
Market Value: $28

Snow Village Accessories

	Date Purchased	Price Paid	Value
1.			
2.			
3.			
4.			
5.			
6.			
7.			
Totals			

At The Barn Dance, It's Allemande Left (set/2)
Issued: 1997 • Retired: 1999
#54929 • Orig. Price: $30
Market Value: $34

8

Version 1   Version 2

Auto With Tree
Issued: 1985 • Current
#5055-5 • Orig. Price: $5
Market Value: 1 – $85 (short/flat) 2 – $6.50 (tall/round)

9

New!

Backwoods Outhouse
Issued: 1999 • Current
#55036 • Orig. Price: $20
Market Value: $20

10

New!

The Backyard Patio (set/2)
Issued: 1999 • Current
#52836 • Orig. Price: $40
Market Value: $40

11

New!

Before The Big Game (set/4)
Issued: 1999 • Current
#55019 • Orig. Price: $37.50
Market Value: $37.50

12

Biplane Up In The Sky
Issued: 1998 • Current
#52731 • Orig. Price: $50
Market Value: $50

13

Bringing Home The Tree
Issued: 1989 • Retired: 1992
#5169-1 • Orig. Price: $15
Market Value: $30

14

Calling All Cars (set/2)
Issued: 1989 • Retired: 1991
#5174-8 • Orig. Price: $15
Market Value: $72

15

Carnival Tickets & Cotton Candy
Issued: 1998 • Current
#54938 • Orig. Price: $30
Market Value: $30

16

Carolers (set/4)
Issued: 1979 • Retired: 1986
#5064-1 • Orig. Price: $12
Market Value: $122

Snow Village Accessories

	Date Purchased	Price Paid	Value
8.			
9.			
10.			
11.			
12.			
13.			
14.			
15.			
16.			
	Totals		

Snow Village – Accessories

17

Caroling At The Farm
Issued: 1994 • Current
#5463-1 • Orig. Price: $35
Market Value: $35

18

Caroling Family (set/3)
Issued: 1987 • Retired: 1990
#5105-5 • Orig. Price: $20
Market Value: $32

19

**Caroling Through
The Snow**
Issued: 1996 • Retired: 1999
#54896 • Orig. Price: $15
Market Value: N/E

20

The Catch Of The Day
Issued: 1998 • Current
#54956 • Orig. Price: $30
Market Value: $30

21

Ceramic Car
Issued: 1980 • Retired: 1986
#5069-0 • Orig. Price: $5
Market Value: $58

22

Ceramic Sleigh
Issued: 1981 • Retired: 1986
#5079-2 • Orig. Price: $5
Market Value: $63

23

**Check It Out
Bookmobile (set/3)**
Issued: 1993 • Retired: 1995
#5451-8 • Orig. Price: $25
Market Value: $37

24

Children In Band
Issued: 1987 • Retired: 1989
#5104-7 • Orig. Price: $15
Market Value: $33

25

Choir Kids
Issued: 1989 • Retired: 1992
#5147-0 • Orig. Price: $15
Market Value: $36

26

Chopping Firewood (set/2)
Issued: 1995 • Current
#54863 • Orig. Price: $16.50
Market Value: $16.50

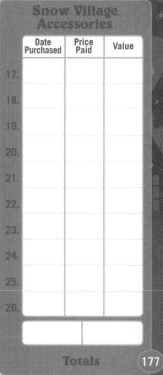

**Snow Village
Accessories**

	Date Purchased	Price Paid	Value
17.			
18.			
19.			
20.			
21.			
22.			
23.			
24.			
25.			
26.			

Totals

Snow Village – Accessories

27

Christmas At The Farm (set/2)
Issued: 1993 • Retired: 1996
#5450-0 • Orig. Price: $16
Market Value: $28

28

Christmas Cadillac
Issued: 1991 • Retired: 1994
#5413-5 • Orig. Price: $9
Market Value: $25

29

Christmas Children (set/4)
Issued: 1987 • Retired: 1990
#5107-1 • Orig. Price: $20
Market Value: $35

30

Christmas Kids (set/5)
Issued: 1997 • Retired: 1999
#54922 • Orig. Price: $27.50
Market Value: $29

31

Christmas Puppies (set/2)
Issued: 1992 • Retired: 1996
#5432-1 • Orig. Price: $27.50
Market Value: $37

32

Christmas Trash Cans (set/2)
Issued: 1990 • Retired: 1998
#5209-4 • Orig. Price: $6.50
Market Value: $17

33

Christmas Visit To The Florist (set/3)
Issued: 1998 • Current
#54957 • Orig. Price: $30
Market Value: $30

34

Classic Cars (set/3)
Issued: 1993 • Retired: 1998
#5457-7 • Orig. Price: $22.50
Market Value: $32

35

Coca-Cola® Brand Billboard
Issued: 1994 • Retired: 1997
#5481-0 • Orig. Price: $18
Market Value: $30

Snow Village Accessories

	Date Purchased	Price Paid	Value
27.			
28.			
29.			
30.			
31.			
32.			
33.			
34.			
35.			

Totals

Value Guide — Department 56® Villages

36

Coca-Cola® Brand Delivery Men (set/2)
Issued: 1994 • Retired: 1998
#5480-1 • Orig. Price: $25
Market Value: $34

37

Coca-Cola® Brand Delivery Truck
Issued: 1994 • Retired: 1998
#5479-8 • Orig. Price: $15
Market Value: $26

38

Cold Weather Sports (set/4)
Issued: 1991 • Retired: 1994
#5410-0 • Orig. Price: $27.50
Market Value: $50

39

Come Join The Parade
Issued: 1991 • Retired: 1992
#5411-9 • Orig. Price: $12.50
Market Value: $23

40

Costumes For Sale (set/2)
Issued: 1998 • Current
#54973 • Orig. Price: $60
Market Value: $60

41

Couldn't Wait Until Christmas
Issued: 1998 • Current
#54972 • Orig. Price: $17
Market Value: $17

42

Country Harvest
Issued: 1991 • Retired: 1993
#5415-1 • Orig. Price: $13
Market Value: $30

43

Crack The Whip (set/3)
Issued: 1989 • Retired: 1996
#5171-3 • Orig. Price: $25
Market Value: $32

44

Doghouse/Cat In Garbage Can (set/2)
Issued: 1988 • Retired: 1992
#5131-4 • Orig. Price: $15
Market Value: $30

45

Down The Chimney He Goes
Issued: 1990 • Retired: 1993
#5158-6 • Orig. Price: $6.50
Market Value: $16

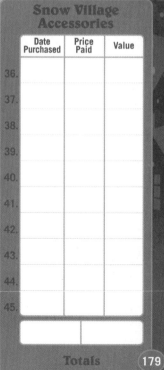

Snow Village Accessories

	Date Purchased	Price Paid	Value
36.			
37.			
38.			
39.			
40.			
41.			
42.			
43.			
44.			
45.			

Totals

Snow Village – Accessories

46 New!

The Dragon Parade
Issued: 1999 • Current
#55032 • Orig. Price: $35
Market Value: $35

47

Early Morning Delivery (set/3)
Issued: 1992 • Retired: 1995
#5431-3 • Orig. Price: $27.50
Market Value: $38

48

Everybody Goes Skating At Rollerama (set/2)
Issued: 1997 • Retired: 1999
#54928 • Orig. Price: $25
Market Value: $27

49

Family Mom/Kids, Goose/Girl (set/2)
Issued: 1985 • Retired: 1988
#5057-1 • Orig. Price: $11
Market Value: 1 – $55 (large) 2 – $47 (small)

50 New!

Family Winter Outing (set/3)
Issued: 1999 • Current
#55033 • Orig. Price: $10
Market Value: $10

51

Farm Accessory Set (set/35)
Issued: 1997 • Current
#54931 • Orig. Price: $75
Market Value: $75

52

Farmer's Flatbed
Issued: 1998 • Current
#54955 • Orig. Price: $17.50
Market Value: $17.50

53

Feeding The Birds (set/3)
Issued: 1994 • Retired: 1997
#5473-9 • Orig. Price: $25
Market Value: $33

54 New!

Finding The Bird's Song (set/2)
Issued: 1999 • Current
#55020 • Orig. Price: $25
Market Value: $25

Snow Village Accessories

	Date Purchased	Price Paid	Value
46.			
47.			
48.			
49.			
50.			
51.			
52.			
53.			
54.			
Totals			

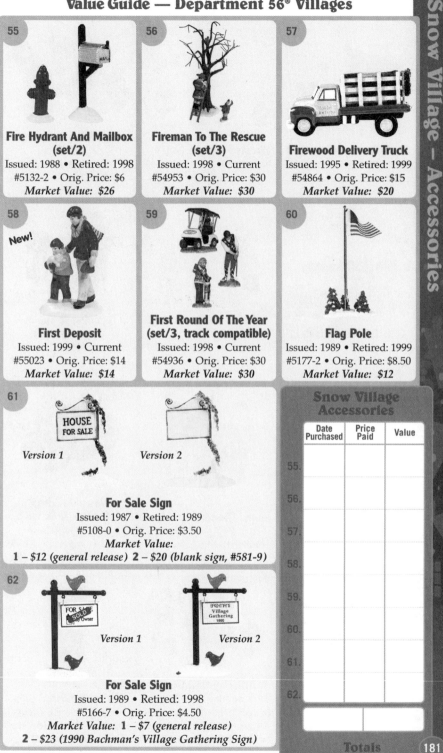

55

Fire Hydrant And Mailbox (set/2)
Issued: 1988 • Retired: 1998
#5132-2 • Orig. Price: $6
Market Value: $26

56

Fireman To The Rescue (set/3)
Issued: 1998 • Current
#54953 • Orig. Price: $30
Market Value: $30

57

Firewood Delivery Truck
Issued: 1995 • Retired: 1999
#54864 • Orig. Price: $15
Market Value: $20

58

New!

First Deposit
Issued: 1999 • Current
#55023 • Orig. Price: $14
Market Value: $14

59

First Round Of The Year (set/3, track compatible)
Issued: 1998 • Current
#54936 • Orig. Price: $30
Market Value: $30

60

Flag Pole
Issued: 1989 • Retired: 1999
#5177-2 • Orig. Price: $8.50
Market Value: $12

61

HOUSE FOR SALE

Version 1

Version 2

For Sale Sign
Issued: 1987 • Retired: 1989
#5108-0 • Orig. Price: $3.50
Market Value:
1 – $12 *(general release)* **2** – $20 *(blank sign, #581-9)*

62

FOR SALE by Owner

Village Gathering 1990

Version 1

Version 2

For Sale Sign
Issued: 1989 • Retired: 1998
#5166-7 • Orig. Price: $4.50
Market Value: **1** – $7 *(general release)*
2 – $23 *(1990 Bachman's Village Gathering Sign)*

Snow Village Accessories

	Date Purchased	Price Paid	Value
55.			
56.			
57.			
58.			
59.			
60.			
61.			
62.			
Totals			

Snow Village – Accessories

63

Fresh Frozen Fish (set/2)
Issued: 1990 • Retired: 1993
#5163-2 • Orig. Price: $20
Market Value: $45

64

Frosty Playtime (set/3)
Issued: 1995 • Retired: 1997
#54860 • Orig. Price: $30
Market Value: $42

65

Fun At The Firehouse (set/2)
Issued: 1998 • Current
#54954 • Orig. Price: $27.50
Market Value: $27.50

66

New!

Gifts On The Go (set/2)
Issued: 1999 • Current
#55035 • Orig. Price: $30
Market Value: $30

67

Girl/Snowman, Boy (set/2)
Issued: 1986 • Retired: 1987
#5095-4 • Orig. Price: $11
Market Value: $70

68

Going To The Chapel (set/2)
Issued: 1994 • Current
#5476-3 • Orig. Price: $20
Market Value: $20

Snow Village Accessories

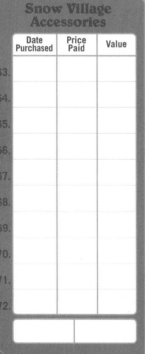

	Date Purchased	Price Paid	Value
63.			
64.			
65.			
66.			
67.			
68.			
69.			
70.			
71.			
72.			

Totals

69

Grand Ole Opry Carolers
Issued: 1995 • Retired: 1997
#54867 • Orig. Price: $25
Market Value: $33

70

Harley-Davidson® Fat Boy & Softail
Issued: 1996 • Current
#54900 • Orig. Price: $16.50
Market Value: $17.50

71

A Harley-Davidson® Holiday (set/2)
Issued: 1996 • Retired: 1999
#54898 • Orig. Price: $22.50
Market Value: $27

72

Harley-Davidson® Sign
Issued: 1996 • Current
#54901 • Orig. Price: $18
Market Value: $18

73

Harley-Davidson® Water Tower
Issued: 1998 • Current
#54975 • Orig. Price: $32.50
Market Value: $32.50

74

Hayride
Issued: 1988 • Retired: 1990
#5117-9 • Orig. Price: $30
Market Value: $66

75

He Led Them Down The Streets Of Town (set/3)
Issued: 1997 • Retired: 1999
#54927 • Orig. Price: $30
Market Value: $33

76

Heading For The Hills (2 assorted)
Issued: 1996 • Current
#54897 • Orig. Price: $8.50 (ea.)
Market Value: $8.50 (ea.)

77

A Heavy Snowfall (set/2)
Issued: 1992 • Current
#5434-8 • Orig. Price: $16
Market Value: $16

78

A Herd Of Holiday Heifers (set/3)
Issued: 1993 • Retired: 1997
#5455-0 • Orig. Price: $18
Market Value: $28

79

Here Comes Santa (LE-1996)
Issued: 1996 • Retired: 1996
Various • Orig. Price: $25
*Market Value:
all exclusives – $42
(Fortunoff – $80)*

"Here Comes Santa" Versions
Bachman's (#07744), Bronner's (#07745), Broughton (#07748), Cabbage Rose (#07752), Calabash (#07753), Calico Butterfly (#07751), Carson Pirie Scott (#07763), Christmas Loft (#07755), Dickens Gift Shop (#07750), European Imports (#07762), Fibber Magee's (#07747), Fortunoff (#07741), Gustaf's (#07759), Ingle's Nook (#07754), Limited Edition (#07746), North Pole City (#07742), Pine Cone (#07740), Royal Dutch (#07760), Russ Country Gardens (#07756), St. Nick's (#07757), Seventh Avenue (#07758), Stats (#07749), William Glen (#07743), Young's Ltd. (#07761).

80

Here We Come A Caroling (set/3)
Issued: 1990 • Retired: 1992
#5161-6 • Orig. Price: $18
Market Value: $32

81

Hitch Up The Buckboard (track compatible)
Issued: 1997 • Retired: 1999
#54930 • Orig. Price: $40
Market Value: $43

	Snow Village Accessories		
	Date Purchased	Price Paid	Value
73.			
74.			
75.			
76.			
77.			
78.			
79.			
80.			
81.			
Totals			

82

Holiday Hoops (set/3)
Issued: 1996 • Retired: 1999
#54893 • Orig. Price: $20
Market Value: $23

83

A Holiday Sleigh Ride Together (track compatible)
Issued: 1997 • Current
#54921 • Orig. Price: $32.50
Market Value: $32.50

84

New!

Holy Spirit Baptistery (music box)
Issued: 1999 • Current
#55022 • Orig. Price: $37.50
Market Value: $37.50

85

Home Delivery (set/2)
Issued: 1990 • Retired: 1992
#5162-4 • Orig. Price: $16
Market Value: $31

86

A Home For The Holidays
Issued: 1990 • Retired: 1996
#5165-9 • Orig. Price: $6.50
Market Value: $17

87

New!

Is That Frosty?
Issued: 1999 • Current
#55030 • Orig. Price: $22.50
Market Value: $22.50

88

New!

It's Time For An Icy Treat (set/2)
Issued: 1999 • Current
#55013 • Orig. Price: $30
Market Value: $30

89

Just Married (set/2)
Issued: 1995 • Current
#54879 • Orig. Price: $25
Market Value: $25

90

Version 1   Version 2

Kids Around The Tree
Issued: 1986 • Retired: 1990
#5094-6 • Orig. Price: $15
Market Value: 1 – $65 (large) 2 – $48 (small)

Snow Village Accessories

	Date Purchased	Price Paid	Value
82.			
83.			
84.			
85.			
86.			
87.			
88.			
89.			
90.			

Totals

91

Kids, Candy Canes . . . And Ronald McDonald® (set/3)
Issued: 1997 • Retired: 1999
#54926 • Orig. Price: $30
Market Value: $32

92

Kids Decorating The Village Sign
Issued: 1990 • Retired: 1993
#5134-9 • Orig. Price: $12.50
Market Value: $32

93

Kids Love Hershey's™! (set/2)
Issued: 1997 • Current
#54924 • Orig. Price: $30
Market Value: $30

94

Kids Tree House
Issued: 1989 • Retired: 1991
#5168-3 • Orig. Price: $25
Market Value: $58

95

New!

Laundry Day
Issued: 1999 • Current
#55017 • Orig. Price: $13
Market Value: $13

96

Let It Snow, Let It Snow (track compatible)
Issued: 1997 • Current
#54923 • Orig. Price: $20
Market Value: $20

97

The Looney Tunes® Animated Film Festival (set/4)
Issued: 1999 • Current
#54983 • Orig. Price: $40
Market Value: $40

98

Mailbox
Issued: 1989 • Retired: 1990
#5179-9 • Orig. Price: $3.50
Market Value: $24

99

Mailbox
Issued: 1990 • Retired: 1998
#5198-5 • Orig. Price: $3.50
Market Value: $6

100

Man On Ladder Hanging Garland
Issued: 1988 • Retired: 1992
#5116-0 • Orig. Price: $7.50
Market Value: $21

Snow Village Accessories

	Date Purchased	Price Paid	Value
91.			
92.			
93.			
94.			
95.			
96.			
97.			
98.			
99.			
100.			

Totals

185

Snow Village – Accessories

101

Marshmallow Roast (set/3)
Issued: 1994 • Current
#5478-0 • Orig. Price: $32.50
Market Value: $32.50

102

McDonald's® . . . Lights Up The Night
Issued: 1997 • Retired: 1999
#54925 • Orig. Price: $30
Market Value: $32

103

Men At Work (set/5)
Issued: 1996 • Retired: 1998
#54894 • Orig. Price: $27.50
Market Value: $34

104

Monks-A-Caroling
Issued: 1983 • Retired: 1984
#6459-9 • Orig. Price: $6
Market Value: $70

105

Monks-A-Caroling
Issued: 1984 • Retired: 1988
#5040-7 • Orig. Price: $6
Market Value: $54

106

Moving Day (set/3)
Issued: 1996 • Retired: 1998
#54892 • Orig. Price: $32.50
Market Value: $42

Snow Village Accessories

	Date Purchased	Price Paid	Value
101.			
102.			
103.			
104.			
105.			
106.			
107.			
108.			
109.			
110.			
Totals			

107

Mush! (set/2)
Issued: 1994 • Retired: 1997
#5474-7 • Orig. Price: $20
Market Value: $27

108

Nanny And The Preschoolers (set/2)
Issued: 1992 • Retired: 1994
#5430-5 • Orig. Price: $27.50
Market Value: $38

109

Nativity
Issued: 1988 • Current
#5135-7 • Orig. Price: $7.50
Market Value: $7.50

110

On The Road Again (set/2)
Issued: 1996 • Current
#54891 • Orig. Price: $20
Market Value: $20

111

New!

On The Way To Ballet Class (set/3)
Issued: 1999 • Current
#55031 • Orig. Price: $27.50
Market Value: $27.50

112

Parking Meter (set/4)
Issued: 1989 • Retired: 1998
#5178-0 • Orig. Price: $6
Market Value: $8

113

Patrolling The Road
Issued: 1998 • Current
#54971 • Orig. Price: $20
Market Value: $20

114

Pets On Parade (set/2)
Issued: 1994 • Retired: 1998
#5472-0 • Orig. Price: $16.50
Market Value: $23

115

Version 1   *Version 2*

Pick-Up And Delivery
Issued: 1993 • Current
#5454-2 • Orig. Price: $10
Market Value:
1 – $10 (general release) 2 – $30 (St. Nick's)

116

Pint-Size Pony Rides (set/3)
Issued: 1993 • Retired: 1996
#5453-4 • Orig. Price: $37.50
Market Value: $45

117

Pizza Delivery (set/2)
Issued: 1995 • Retired: 1998
#54866 • Orig. Price: $20
Market Value: $30

118

Poinsettias For Sale (set/3)
Issued: 1995 • Retired: 1998
#54861 • Orig. Price: $30
Market Value: $39

119

Praying Monks
Issued: 1987 • Retired: 1988
#5103-9 • Orig. Price: $6
Market Value: $52

Snow Village Accessories

	Date Purchased	Price Paid	Value
111.			
112.			
113.			
114.			
115.			
116.			
117.			
118.			
119.			

Totals

120

Preparing For Halloween (set/2)
Issued: 1999 • Current
#54982 • Orig. Price: $40
Market Value: $40

121

Quality Service At Ford® (set/2)
Issued: 1998 • Current
#54970 • Orig. Price: $27.50
Market Value: $27.50

122

A Ride On The Reindeer Lines (set/3)
Issued: 1996 • Retired: 1997
#54875 • Orig. Price: $35
Market Value: $43

123

Round And Round We Go! (set/2)
Issued: 1992 • Retired: 1995
#5433-0 • Orig. Price: $18
Market Value: $31

124

Safety Patrol (set/4)
Issued: 1993 • Retired: 1997
#5449-6 • Orig. Price: $27.50
Market Value: $33

125

Santa Comes To Town, 1995 (LE-1995)
Issued: 1994 • Retired: 1995
#5477-1 • Orig. Price: $30
Market Value: $43

126

Santa Comes To Town, 1996 (LE-1996)
Issued: 1995 • Retired: 1996
#54862 • Orig. Price: $32.50
Market Value: $43

127

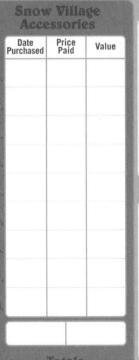

Santa Comes To Town, 1997 (LE-1997)
Issued: 1996 • Retired: 1997
#54899 • Orig. Price: $35
Market Value: $37

128

Santa Comes To Town, 1998 (LE-1998)
Issued: 1997 • Retired: 1998
#54920 • Orig. Price: $30
Market Value: $32

Snow Village Accessories

	Date Purchased	Price Paid	Value
120.			
121.			
122.			
123.			
124.			
125.			
126.			
127.			
128.			

Totals

Value Guide — Department 56® Villages

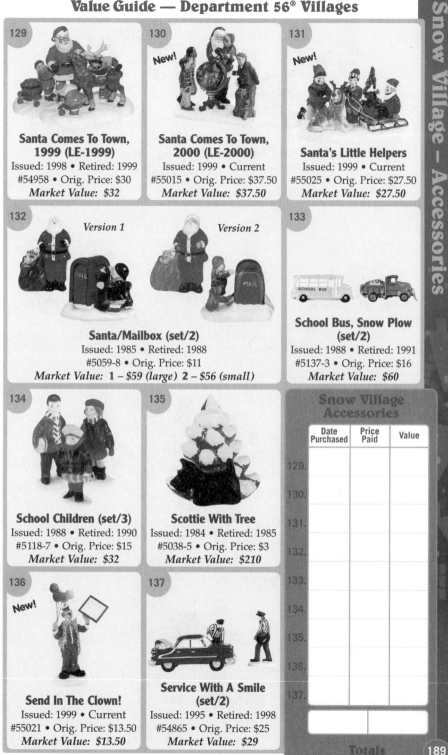

129

Santa Comes To Town, 1999 (LE-1999)
Issued: 1998 • Retired: 1999
#54958 • Orig. Price: $30
Market Value: $32

130

New!

Santa Comes To Town, 2000 (LE-2000)
Issued: 1999 • Current
#55015 • Orig. Price: $37.50
Market Value: $37.50

131

New!

Santa's Little Helpers
Issued: 1999 • Current
#55025 • Orig. Price: $27.50
Market Value: $27.50

132

Version 1   *Version 2*

Santa/Mailbox (set/2)
Issued: 1985 • Retired: 1988
#5059-8 • Orig. Price: $11
Market Value: 1 – $59 (large) 2 – $56 (small)

133

School Bus, Snow Plow (set/2)
Issued: 1988 • Retired: 1991
#5137-3 • Orig. Price: $16
Market Value: $60

134

School Children (set/3)
Issued: 1988 • Retired: 1990
#5118-7 • Orig. Price: $15
Market Value: $32

135

Scottie With Tree
Issued: 1984 • Retired: 1985
#5038-5 • Orig. Price: $3
Market Value: $210

136

New!

Send In The Clown!
Issued: 1999 • Current
#55021 • Orig. Price: $13.50
Market Value: $13.50

137

Service With A Smile (set/2)
Issued: 1995 • Retired: 1998
#54865 • Orig. Price: $25
Market Value: $29

Snow Village Accessories

	Date Purchased	Price Paid	Value
129.			
130.			
131.			
132.			
133.			
134.			
135.			
136.			
137.			
Totals			

189

138

Version 1

Version 2

Shopping Girls With Packages (set/2)
Issued: 1986 • Retired: 1988
#5096-2 • Orig. Price: $11
Market Value: 1 – $50 (large) 2 – $47 (small)

139

Singing Nuns
Issued: 1985 • Retired: 1987
#5053-9 • Orig. Price: $6
Market Value: $135

140

Sisal Tree Lot
Issued: 1988 • Retired: 1991
#8183-3 • Orig. Price: $45
Market Value: $92

141

Skate Faster Mom
Issued: 1989 • Retired: 1991
#5170-5 • Orig. Price: $13
Market Value: $30

142

Skaters & Skiers (set/3)
Issued: 1994 • Current
#5475-5 • Orig. Price: $27.50
Market Value: $27.50

143

Ski Slope
Issued: 1998 • Current
#52733 • Orig. Price: $75
Market Value: $75

144

Sleighride
Issued: 1990 • Retired: 1992
#5160-8 • Orig. Price: $30
Market Value: $57

145

Sno-Jet Snowmobile
Issued: 1990 • Retired: 1993
#5159-4 • Orig. Price: $15
Market Value: $30

Snow Village Accessories

	Date Purchased	Price Paid	Value
138.			
139.			
140.			
141.			
142.			
143.			
144.			
145.			
Totals			

Value Guide — Department 56® Villages

146

Snow Carnival Ice Sculptures (set/2)
Issued: 1995 • Retired: 1998
#54868 • Orig. Price: $27.50
Market Value: $36

147

Snow Carnival King & Queen
Issued: 1995 • Retired: 1998
#54869 • Orig. Price: $35
Market Value: $45

148

Snow Kids (set/4)
Issued: 1987 • Retired: 1990
#5113-6 • Orig. Price: $20
Market Value: $57

149

Snow Kids Sled, Skis (set/2)
Issued: 1985 • Retired: 1987
#5056-3 • Orig. Price: $11
Market Value: $50

150

Snow Village Promotional Sign
Issued: 1989 • Retired: 1990
#9948-1 • Orig. Price: N/A
Market Value: $25

151

Snowball Fort (set/3)
Issued: 1991 • Retired: 1993
#5414-3 • Orig. Price: $27.50
Market Value: $42

152

Snowman With Broom
Issued: 1982 • Retired: 1990
#5018-0 • Orig. Price: $3
Market Value: $15

153

Special Delivery (set/2)
Issued: 1989 • Retired: 1990
#5148-9 • Orig. Price: $16
Market Value: $54

154

Special Delivery (set/2)
Issued: 1990 • Retired: 1992
#5197-7 • Orig. Price: $16
Market Value: $35

155

Spirit Of Snow Village Airplane
Issued: 1992 • Retired: 1996
#5440-2 • Orig. Price: $32.50
Market Value: $44

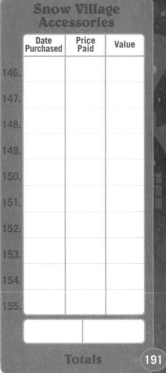

Snow Village Accessories

	Date Purchased	Price Paid	Value
146.			
147.			
148.			
149.			
150.			
151.			
152.			
153.			
154.			
155.			
Totals			

Snow Village – Accessories

156

Spirit Of Snow Village Airplane (2 assorted)
Issued: 1993 • Retired: 1996
#5458-5 • Orig. Price: $12.50 (ea.)
Market Value: $39 (ea.)

157

Starbucks® Coffee Cart (set/2)
Issued: 1995 • Current
#54870 • Orig. Price: $27.50
Market Value: $27.50

158

Statue Of Mark Twain
Issued: 1989 • Retired: 1991
#5173-0 • Orig. Price: $15
Market Value: $35

159

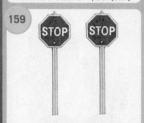

Stop Sign (set/2)
Issued: 1989 • Retired: 1998
#5176-4 • Orig. Price: $5
Market Value: $8

160

Street Sign (set/6)
Issued: 1989 • Retired: 1992
#5167-5 • Orig. Price: $7.50
Market Value: $15

161

Stuck In The Snow (set/3)
Issued: 1994 • Retired: 1998
#5471-2 • Orig. Price: $30
Market Value: $38

162

Taxi Cab
Issued: 1987 • Current
#5106-3 • Orig. Price: $6
Market Value: $6.50

163

Terry's Towing (set/2)
Issued: 1996 • Retired: 1999
#54895 • Orig. Price: $20
Market Value: $24

164

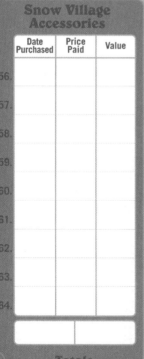

Through The Woods (set/2)
Issued: 1989 • Retired: 1991
#5172-1 • Orig. Price: $18
Market Value: $22

Snow Village Accessories

	Date Purchased	Price Paid	Value
156.			
157.			
158.			
159.			
160.			
161.			
162.			
163.			
164.			

Totals

165

New!

Through The Woods (set/4)
Issued: 1999 • Current
#52791 • Orig. Price: $75
Market Value: $75

166

Tour The Village
Issued: 1993 • Retired: 1997
#5452-6 • Orig. Price: $12.50
Market Value: $21

167

New!

Treats For The Kids (set/3)
Issued: 1999 • Current
#55016 • Orig. Price: $33
Market Value: $33

168

A Tree For Me (set/2)
Issued: 1990 • Retired: 1995
#5164-0 • Orig. Price: $7.50
Market Value: $15

169

Tree Lot
Issued: 1988 • Retired: 1999
#5138-1 • Orig. Price: $33.50
Market Value: $42

170

Treetop Tree House
Issued: 1996 • Current
#54890 • Orig. Price: $35
Market Value: $36.50

171

Trick-Or-Treat Kids (set/3)
Issued: 1998 • Current
#54937 • Orig. Price: $33
Market Value: $33

172

Two For The Road (track compatible)
Issued: 1998 • Current
#54939 • Orig. Price: $20
Market Value: $20

173

Uncle Sam's Fireworks Stand (set/2)
Issued: 1998 • Current
#54974 • Orig. Price: $45
Market Value: $45

174

Up On A Roof Top
Issued: 1988 • Current
#5139-0 • Orig. Price: $6.50
Market Value: $6.50

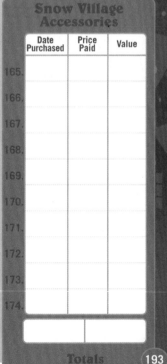

Snow Village Accessories

	Date Purchased	Price Paid	Value
165.			
166.			
167.			
168.			
169.			
170.			
171.			
172.			
173.			
174.			
Totals			

Snow Village – Accessories

175

Up, Up & Away Witch
Issued: 1998 • Current
#52711 • Orig. Price: $50
Market Value: $50

176

**Uptown Motors Ford®
Billboard**
Issued: 1998 • Current
#52780 • Orig. Price: $20
Market Value: $20

177

**Village Animated
Accessory Track**
Issued: 1996 • Current
#52642 • Orig. Price: $65
Market Value: $40

178

**Village Animated All
Around The Park (set/18)**
Issued: 1994 • Retired: 1996
#5247-7 • Orig. Price: $95
Market Value: $110

179

**Village Animated
Skating Pond (set/15)**
Issued: 1993 • Current
#5229-9 • Orig. Price: $60
Market Value: $60

180
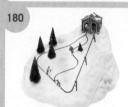

**Village Animated
Ski Mountain**
Issued: 1996 • Retired: 1998
#52641 • Orig. Price: $75
Market Value: N/E

181

**Village Animated
Sledding Hill**
Issued: 1997 • Current
#52645 • Orig. Price: $65
Market Value: $65

182

Village Birds (set/6)
Issued: 1989 • Retired: 1994
#5180-2 • Orig. Price: $3.50
Market Value: $16

Snow Village Accessories

	Date Purchased	Price Paid	Value
175.			
176.			
177.			
178.			
179.			
180.			
181.			
182.			
Totals			

Value Guide — Department 56® Villages

183

Village Express Electric Train Set (set/24)
Issued: 1998 • Current
#52710 • Orig. Price: $270
Market Value: $270

184

Village Fire Truck
Issued: 1998 • Current
#54952 • Orig. Price: $22.50
Market Value: $22.50

185

Village Gazebo
Issued: 1989 • Retired: 1995
#5146-2 • Orig. Price: $27
Market Value: $45

186

Village Greetings (set/3)
Issued: 1991 • Retired: 1994
#5418-6 • Orig. Price: $5
Market Value: $10

187

Village Marching Band (set/3)
Issued: 1991 • Retired: 1992
#5412-7 • Orig. Price: $30
Market Value: $64

188

Village News Delivery (set/2)
Issued: 1993 • Retired: 1996
#5459-3 • Orig. Price: $15
Market Value: $24

189

Village Phone Booth
Issued: 1992 • Current
#5429-1 • Orig. Price: $7.50
Market Value: $7.50

190

Village Potted Topiary Pair
Issued: 1989 • Retired: 1994
#5192-6 • Orig. Price: $5
Market Value: $15

191

Village Service Vehicles (set/3, track compatible)
Issued: 1998 • Current
#54959 • Orig. Price: $45
Market Value: $45

192

Village Streetcar (set/10)
Issued: 1994 • Retired: 1998
#5240-0 • Orig. Price: $65
Market Value: $67

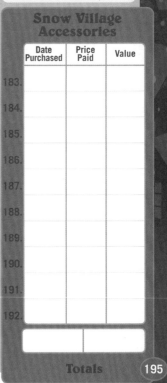

Snow Village Accessories

	Date Purchased	Price Paid	Value
183.			
184.			
185.			
186.			
187.			
188.			
189.			
190.			
191.			
192.			
Totals			

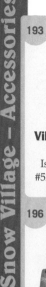

Snow Village – Accessories

193

Village Up, Up & Away, Animated Sleigh
Issued: 1995 • Current
#52593 • Orig. Price: $40
Market Value: $40

194

Village Used Car Lot (set/5)
Issued: 1992 • Retired: 1997
#5428-3 • Orig. Price: $45
Market Value: $55

195

Village Waterfall
Issued: 1996 • Current
#52644 • Orig. Price: $65
Market Value: $40

196

"A Visit With Santa"Versions
Bachman's (#07544) – $56
Fortunoff (#07676) – $57
Lemon Tree (#07684) – $52
Limited Edition (#07641) – $63
Pine Cone (#07730) – $50
Stats (#07650) – $50
William Glen (#07668) – $47
Young's Ltd. (#07692) – $45

A Visit With Santa (LE-1995)
Issued: 1995 • Retired: 1995
Various • Orig. Price: $25
Market Value: listed above

197
Version 1   Version 2

Water Tower
Issued: 1988 • Retired: 1991
#5133-0 • Orig. Price: $20
Market Value:
1 – $95 (general release)
2 – $680 (John Deere)

Snow Village Accessories

	Date Purchased	Price Paid	Value
193.			
194.			
195.			
196.			
197.			
198.			
199.			
200.			
201.			

198
New!

Welcome To The Congregation
Issued: 1999 • Current
#55014 • Orig. Price: $15
Market Value: $15

199

We're Going To A Christmas Pageant
Issued: 1992 • Retired: 1994
#5435-6 • Orig. Price: $15
Market Value: $30

200

The Whole Family Goes Shopping (set/3)
Issued: 1997 • Retired: 1999
#54905 • Orig. Price: $25
Market Value: $27

201

Winter Fountain
Issued: 1991 • Retired: 1993
#5409-7 • Orig. Price: $25
Market Value: $60

202

Winter Playground
Issued: 1992 • Retired: 1995
#5436-4 • Orig. Price: $20
Market Value: $40

203

Woodsman And Boy (set/2)
Issued: 1988 • Retired: 1991
#5130-6 • Orig. Price: $13
Market Value: $35

204

Woody Station Wagon
Issued: 1988 • Retired: 1990
#5136-5 • Orig. Price: $6.50
Market Value: $35

205

Wreaths For Sale (set/4)
Issued: 1991 • Retired: 1994
#5408-9 • Orig. Price: $27.50
Market Value: $47

SNOW VILLAGE – ORNAMENTS

Three ornaments have joined the *Classic Ornament Series* for the new year. The 11 ornaments, some lighted and battery operated, are replicas of existing Snow Village buildings. To date, only three have been retired.

1

J. Young's Granary
Classic Ornament Series
Issued: 1997 • Retired: 1998
#98632 • Orig. Price: $15
Market Value: $19

2

J. Young's Granary
Classic Ornament Series
Issued: 1998 • Current
#98644 • Orig. Price: $20
Market Value: $20

3

New!

Jingle Belle Houseboat
Classic Ornament Series
Issued: 1999 • Current
#98648 • Orig. Price: $20
Market Value: $20

4

Lighthouse
Classic Ornament Series
Issued: 1998 • Current
#98635 • Orig. Price: $20
Market Value: $20

Snow Village Accessories

	Date Purchased	Price Paid	Value
202.			
203.			
204.			
205.			

Snow Village Ornaments

1.			
2.			
3.			
4.			

Totals

197

Snow Village – Ornaments

5

Nantucket
Classic Ornament Series
Issued: 1997 • Retired: 1998
#98630 • Orig. Price: $15
Market Value: $20

6

Nantucket
Classic Ornament Series
Issued: 1998 • Current
#98642 • Orig. Price: $20
Market Value: $20

7

Pinewood Log Cabin
Classic Ornament Series
Issued: 1998 • Current
#98637 • Orig. Price: $20
Market Value: $20

8

New!

Queen Anne Victorian
Classic Ornament Series
Issued: 1999 • Current
#98646 • Orig. Price: $20
Market Value: $20

9

Steepled Church
Classic Ornament Series
Issued: 1997 • Retired: 1998
#98631 • Orig. Price: $15
Market Value: $17

10

Steepled Church
Classic Ornament Series
Issued: 1998 • Current
#98643 • Orig. Price: $20
Market Value: $20

11

New!

Street Car
Classic Ornament Series
Issued: 1999 • Current
#98645 • Orig. Price: $20
Market Value: $20

Snow Village Ornaments

	Date Purchased	Price Paid	Value
5.			
6.			
7.			
8.			
9.			
10.			
11.			
Totals			

Future Releases

Use this page to record future Snow Village releases.

Snow Village	Original Price	Status	Market Value	Date Purch.	Price Paid	Value

Page Total:	Price Paid	Value

Total Value Of My Collection

Add the "Page Totals" together to find the "Grand Total."

Snow Village – Buildings

Page Number	Price Paid	Value
Page 139		
Page 140		
Page 141		
Page 142		
Page 143		
Page 144		
Page 145		
Page 146		
Page 147		
Page 148		
Page 149		
Page 150		
Page 151		
Page 152		
Page 153		
Page 154		
Page 155		
Page 156		
Page 157		
Page 158		
Page 159		
Page 160		
Page 161		
Page 162		
Page 163		
Page 164		
Page 165		
Page 166		
Page 167		
Page 168		
Page 169		
Page 170		
Page 171		
Page 172		
Page 173		
Page 174		
Subtotal:		

Snow Village – Accessories

Page Number	Price Paid	Value
Page 175		
Page 176		
Page 177		
Page 178		
Page 179		
Page 180		
Page 181		
Page 182		
Page 183		
Page 184		
Page 185		
Page 186		
Page 187		
Page 188		
Page 189		
Page 190		
Page 191		
Page 192		
Page 193		
Page 194		
Page 195		
Page 196		
Page 197		
Subtotal:		

Snow Village – Ornaments

Page Number	Price Paid	Value
Page 197		
Page 198		
Subtotal:		

GRAND TOTAL:	Price Paid	Value

Other Department 56® Collectibles Overview

*T*hrough the years, Department 56 has expanded its community beyond the Heritage Village and Snow Village collections. Here's a look at some of the other Department 56 village collectibles:

Seasons Bay™

Introduced in 1998 and the first of its kind with its seasonal accessories, Seasons Bay offers charming buildings depicting life in a small 19th-century resort town. The village consists of lightly colored, porcelain buildings reminiscent of the American Shingle Style of architecture when roofs were gabled and porches were a must. Seasons Bay is a place where vacationers go to settle in and unwind, and go home with fond memories of a summer well spent.

The accessories are made of pewter, another first from Department 56 and offer many options when creating the perfect vacation setting; whether it's a snow-filled winter holiday or the annual flowers festival in the spring.

Perhaps the most popular Seasons Bay pieces are those which were released as "first editions" when the line debuted. The six buildings were "Bay Street Shops," "Chapel On The Hill," "The Grand Creamery," "Grandview Shores Hotel," "Inglenook Cottage," and "Side Porch Cafe." Each was available for just one year and had slight design and color differences from their general release counterparts.

Storybook Village®

The unique and intricately detailed pieces of Storybook Village, introduced in 1996, are based on the nursery rhymes we all know and love. The lighted, resin pieces come with their own accessories to help tell the story of childhood classics. There is also a collection of *Storybook Teapots*, with more famous titles that are sure to delight both young and old.

Other Collectibles

In recognition of their connection to the Bachman family, Department 56 has created several special pieces for the still-existing store, which is based in Minneapolis. The pieces, which are exclusive to the retail outlet, debut to collectors who attend the annual Bachman's Village Gathering. For 1999, the honor was bestowed upon "The Original Bachman Homestead."

Department 56 has also released a licensed series designed for specific companies. *The Profile Series* contains three buildings and one accessory so far, three pieces for the H.J. Heinz Co. and one for State Farm Insurance. Each piece was initially available to employees of the company and later was available in limited quantities to collectors.

In 1979, *Meadowland* was introduced, and although it was released along with several Snow Village buildings, it was never officially part of the village series. All of the pieces in the collection were retired just one year later. *Bachman's Hometown Series* was introduced several years later, in 1987 and was also available for only one year.

The Monopoly® Brand Citylights™ Collection, introduced in 1999, is made up of eight resin buildings painted in official Monopoly colors. Each building represents a plot of real estate on the game board and comes with a pewter accessory. Collectors who complete the entire set can send away to receive a complimentary "Monopoly® Bank & Trust" (set/2) building. In addition to these smaller series, several individual, stand-alone buildings have been released through the years, including Canadian exclusives, a piece from the *Literary Classics* series and several event pieces.

What's New For Other Department 56® Collectibles

*T*his section highlights the new releases for Seasons Bay and Storybook Village. One additional piece, "The Great Gatsby West Egg Mansion" (set/4) was also released.

Literary Classics™ Buildings

THE GREAT GATSBY WEST EGG MANSION (set/4, with book) . . . F. Scott Fitzgerald's literary classic is included with the purchase of this elaborate representation of Mr. Gatsby's mansion in West Egg Village. Characters from the novel, along with a yellow convertible complete the set.

Seasons Bay™ Buildings

PARKSIDE PAVILION . . . While taking a stroll in the park, be sure to ascend the magnificent stone staircase of the "Parkside Pavilion." This piece will debut as a general release (set/2, #53411), but will also be available during Department 56's Spring Promotion event (set/9, #53412), where it will be showcased with design and color changes and will be packaged in an exclusive gift set with the multiple-piece accessory set titled "Art Classes At Morning's Light."

SPRINGLAKE STATION . . . Families sit on charming white benches as they wait for their friends and relatives to arrive at "Springlake Station," one of the busiest spots in Seasons Bay.

STILLWATERS BOATHOUSE . . . Crew members looking for a rest from the water can be found at the "Stillwaters Boathouse." The regal green and brown building blends well into its beautiful setting, while the tall red ship weathervane can be seen from just about anywhere on the bay.

Seasons Bay™ Accessories

 SPRING ... It's springtime in Seasons Bay, and the perfect day to relax in "The Garden Swing." But for the many people who spent their day on the train, and are now "Arriving At The Station" (set/5), its time to move about and get ready for vacation.

 SUMMER ... "The Perfect Wedding" (set/7, with book) in Seasons Bay is one held in the summer. The day after the ceremony, guests enjoy "A Grand Day Of Fishing," or simply spend the day rowing "Gently Down The Stream." But do not row out to far because the "Lifeguard On Duty" keeps careful watch!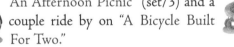

 FALL ... During the fall in Seasons Bay, villagers spend time enjoying the great outdoors. "Rocking Chair Readers" (set/2) indulge in their favorite literature, while at the park, three friends share "An Afternoon Picnic" (set/3) and a couple ride by on "A Bicycle Built For Two."

WINTER ... "The First Snow" of the winter has made it to Seasons Bay, giving children the day off to build snowmen. Other families spend "A Day Of Holiday Shopping" (set/3), while the evening, of course, is set aside for the "Singing Carols In Town."

GENERAL . . . One additional Seasons Bay accessory was released this year. "Seasons Bay Amusement Park Carousel" (animated) is a general village accessory that will fit into your collection no matter what the weather.

Storybook Village®

MOTHER GOOSE BOOK CELLAR (set/5) . . . Inspired by the classic nursery rhyme, the "Mother Goose Book Cellar" (set/5) is built in the shape of the famous goose. Alongside the unique structure, there is a bustle of activity with many villagers leafing through books outside the store.

LIL' BOY BLUE PETTING FARM (set/3) . . . The "Lil' Boy Blue Petting Farm" (set/3) captures the excitement of being a child with its pastel pink and blue colors and large, golden horn atop the roof. Visitors of all ages are welcome to buy their ticket and come inside to meet the animals!

QUEEN'S HOUSE OF CARDS (set/8) . . . All decked out in every suit, the "Queen's House Of Cards" (set/8) is a humorous reminder of Alice's journey through Wonderland. Even the Cheshire cat and his famous grin can be found in his favorite spot – the tree!

STORYBOOK VILLAGE COLLECTION SIGN . . . The collection would not be complete without the "Storybook Village Collection Sign." Flowers lace the bottom of this bright yellow sign supported by two brick pillars. A purple flag flies high above.

How To Use Your Collector's Value Guide™

1. Locate your piece in the Value Guide. The "Other Department 56 Collectibles" buildings are listed first, followed by their accessories, if applicable. Pieces are listed alphabetically within each section. To help locate your pieces, easy-to-use numerical and alphabetical indexes are provided in the back of the book.

Hometown Boarding House
Issued: 1987 • Retired: 1988
#670-0 • Original Price: $34
Market Value: $325

2. Find the market value of your piece. If no market value has been established, it is listed as "N/E" (not established). Pieces currently available at stores reflect the current retail price.

3. Record the year your piece was purchased, the retail price paid, and the secondary market value in the corresponding boxes at the bottom of the page.

4. Calculate the value for the page by adding all of the boxes in each column. Be sure to use a pencil so you can change the totals as your collection grows.

Bachman's Hometown Series Buildings		
Date Purchased	**Price Paid**	**Value**
1. *9/8/88*	*34.00*	*325.00*
2.		
3.		
Meadowland Buildings		
4.		
5.		
Miscellaneous Buildings		
6.		
Totals	*34.00*	*325.00*

5. Transfer the totals from each page to the "Total Value of My Collection" worksheets for Other Department 56 Collectibles on page 223.

6. Add the totals together to determine the overall value of your collection.

OTHER DEPARTMENT 56® COLLECTIBLES – BUILDINGS

In this section you will find Seasons Bay and Storybook Village, as well as several special collections and pieces released through the years.

Hometown Boarding House
Issued: 1987 • Retired: 1988
#670-0 • Original Price: $34
Market Value: $325

Hometown Church
Issued: 1987 • Retired: 1988
#671-8 • Original Price: $40
Market Value: $340

Hometown Drugstore
Issued: 1988 • Retired: 1989
#672-6 • Original Price: $40
Market Value: $585

Countryside Church
Issued: 1979 • Retired: 1980
#5051-8 • Original Price: $25
Market Value: $600

Thatched Cottage
Issued: 1979 • Retired: 1980
#5050-0 • Original Price: $30
Market Value: $660

**Bachman Greenhouse
(Bachman's Exclusive)**
Issued: 1998 • Retired: 1998
#2203 • Original Price: $60
Market Value: $80

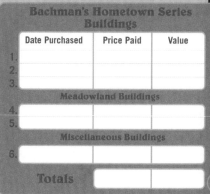

Bachman's Hometown Series Buildings

	Date Purchased	Price Paid	Value
1.			
2.			
3.			

Meadowland Buildings

4.			
5.			

Miscellaneous Buildings

6.			

Totals

Miscellaneous – Buildings

7

Bachman's Flower Shop (Bachman's Exclusive)
Issued: 1997 • Retired: 1997
#8802 • Original Price: $50
Market Value: $105

8

Canadian Trading Co. (Canadian Exclusive For *Dickens' Village*)
Issued: 1997 • Retired: 1998
#58306 • Original Price: $65 *(U.S.)*
Market Value: $140

9

Collectors' Club House (set/2)
Issued: 1998 • Retired: 1998
#54800 • Original Price: $56
Market Value: N/E

10

The First House That ❤ Built (Event Piece)
Issued: 1999 • Retired: 1999
#98774 • Original Price: $16.50
Market Value: N/E

11

New!

The Great Gatsby West Egg Mansion (set/4, with book)
Literary Classics
Issued: 1999 • Current
#58939 • Original Price: $135
Market Value: $135

12

Heinz Grocery Store (H.J. Heinz Co. Piece)
The Profile Series
Issued: 1998 • Retired: 1999
#05600 • Original Price: $34
Market Value: N/E

Miscellaneous Buildings

	Date Purchased	Price Paid	Value
7.			
8.			
9.			
10.			
11.			
12.			
13.			
Totals			

13

Heinz House (H.J. Heinz Co. Piece)
The Profile Series
Issued: 1996 • Retired: 1997
#7826 • Original Price: $27
Market Value: $95

14

The House That ♥ Built™ 1998 (Event Piece)
Issued: 1998 • Retired: 1998
#2210 • Original Price: N/A
Market Value: $390

15

Independence Hall (set/2)
Historical Landmark Series
Issued: 1998 • Current
#55500 • Original Price: $110
Market Value: $110

16

Main Street Memories (State Farm Piece)
The Profile Series
Issued: 1997 • Retired: 1997
#56000 • Original Price: $35.50
Market Value: $120

17

The Original Bachman Homestead (LE-7,500)
Issued: 1999 • Retired: 1999
#02255 • Original Price: $75
Market Value: N/E

18

Ronald McDonald House® "The House That ♥ Built" (Event Piece)
Issued: 1997 • Retired: 1997
#8960 • Original Price: N/A
Market Value: $320

19

The Times Tower (set/3)
Issued: 1999 • Current
#55510 • Original Price: $185
Market Value: $185

20

City Lights (set/12)
Issued: 1999 • Current
#13612 • Original Price: $335
Market Value: $335

Miscellaneous Buildings

	Date Purchased	Price Paid	Value
14.			
15.			
16.			
17.			
18.			
19.			
Monopoly Buildings			
20.			
Totals			

Monopoly – Buildings

21

Law Office, Inc.
Issued: 1999 • Current
#13606• Original Price: $50
Market Value: $50

22

Mediterranean Mortgage Co.
Issued: 1999 • Current
#13600 • Original Price: $30
Market Value: $30

23

Monopoly® Bank & Trust
Issued: 1999 • Current
N/A • Original Price: N/A
Market Value: N/E

24

Newsstand Daily
Issued: 1999 • Current
#13602 • Original Price: $37.50
Market Value: $37.50

25

Old St. James Hospital
Issued: 1999 • Current
#13603 • Original Price: $37.50
Market Value: $37.50

26

Opera Du Jardin
Issued: 1999 • Current
#13605 • Original Price: $45
Market Value: $45

27

Oriental Express
Issued: 1999 • Current
#13601 • Original Price: $37.50
Market Value: $37.50

Monopoly Buildings

	Date Purchased	Price Paid	Value
21.			
22.			
23.			
24.			
25.			
26.			
27.			
Totals			

28

Police Department
Issued: 1999 • Current
#13604 • Original Price: $37.50
Market Value: $37.50

29

Yorkshire Grand Hotel
Issued: 1999 • Current
#13607 • Original Price: $60
Market Value: $60

30

Bay Street Shops
(set/2, First Edition)
Issued: 1998 • Retired: 1999
#53301 • Original Price: $135
Market Value: N/E

31

Bay Street Shops (set/2)
Issued: 1998 • Current
#53401 • Original Price: $135
Market Value: $135

32

Chapel On The Hill
(First Edition)
Issued: 1998 • Retired: 1999
#53302 • Original Price: $72
Market Value: N/E

33

Chapel On The Hill
Issued: 1998 • Current
#53402 • Original Price: $72
Market Value: $72

34

The Grand Creamery
(First Edition)
Issued: 1998 • Retired: 1999
#53305 • Original Price: $60
Market Value: N/E

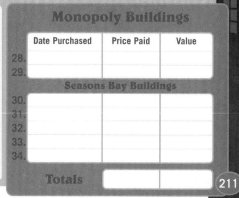

Monopoly Buildings

	Date Purchased	Price Paid	Value
28.			
29.			

Seasons Bay Buildings

30.			
31.			
32.			
33.			
34.			

Totals

Seasons Bay – Buildings

35

The Grand Creamery
Issued: 1998 • Current
#53405 • Original Price: $60
Market Value: $60

36

**Grandview Shores Hotel
(First Edition)**
Issued: 1998 • Retired: 1999
#53300 • Original Price: $150
Market Value: N/E

37

Grandview Shores Hotel
Issued: 1998 • Current
#53400 • Original Price: $150
Market Value: $150

38

**Inglenook Cottage #5
(First Edition)**
Issued: 1998 • Retired: 1999
#53304 • Original Price: $60
Market Value: N/E

39

Inglenook Cottage #5
Issued: 1998 • Current
#53404 • Original Price: $60
Market Value: $60

40

New!

Parkside Pavilion (set/2)
Issued: 1999 • Current
#53411 • Original Price: $65
Market Value: $65

41

New!

Parkside Pavilion (set/9, Event Piece)
Issued: 1999 • Current
#53412 • Original Price: $75
Market Value: $75

Seasons Bay Buildings

	Date Purchased	Price Paid	Value
35.			
36.			
37.			
38.			
39.			
40.			
41.			
Totals			

42

Side Porch Café
(First Edition)
Issued: 1998 • Retired: 1999
#53303 • Original Price: $50
Market Value: N/E

43

Side Porch Café
Issued: 1998 • Current
#53403 • Original Price: $50
Market Value: $50

44

New!

Springlake Station
Issued: 1999 • Current
#53413 • Original Price: $90
Market Value: $90

45

New!

Stillwaters Boathouse
Issued: 1999 • Current
#53414 • Original Price: $70
Market Value: $70

46

The Butcher, Baker And
Candlestick Maker
Issued: 1999 • Current
#13186 • Original Price: $75
Market Value: $75

47

Goldilocks Bed And Breakfast (set/4)
Issued: 1996 • Retired: 1999
#13193 • Original Price: $95
Market Value: N/E

48

H.D. Diddle Fiddles (set/4)
Issued: 1998 • Current
#13183 • Original Price: $75
Market Value: $75

Seasons Bay Buildings

	Date Purchased	Price Paid	Value
42.			
43.			
44.			
45.			

Storybook Village Buildings

46.			
47.			
48.			
Totals			

Storybook Village – Buildings

49

Hickory Dickory Dock (set/3)
Issued: 1996 • Retired: 1998
#13195 • Original Price: $95
Market Value: N/E

50

Humpty Dumpty Café (set/4)
Issued: 1997 • Current
#13181 • Original Price: $95
Market Value: $75

51

Lambsville School (set/5)
Issued: 1996 • Retired: 1999
#13194 • Original Price: $95
Market Value: N/E

52

New!

Lil' Boy Blue Petting Farm (set/3)
Issued: 1999 • Current
#13172 • Original Price: $75
Market Value: $75

53

Mary Quite Contrary Flower Shop (set/5)
Issued: 1997 • Current
#13180 • Original Price: $95
Market Value: $75

54

New!

Mother Goose Book Cellar (set/5)
Issued: 1999 • Current
#13171 • Original Price: $75
Market Value: $75

Storybook Village Buildings

	Date Purchased	Price Paid	Value
49.			
50.			
51.			
52.			
53.			
54.			
55.			
Totals			

55

An Old House In Paris That Was Covered With Vines (set/9)
Issued: 1998 • Current
#13185 • Original Price: $75
Market Value: $75

56

Old Woman Cobbler (set/5)
Issued: 1996 • Retired: 1999
#13191 • Original Price: $95
Market Value: N/E

57

P. Peter's (set/3)
Issued: 1998 • Current
#13184 • Original Price: $75
Market Value: $75

58

Peter Piper Pickle And Peppers (set/4)
Issued: 1996 • Retired: 1998
#13192 • Original Price: $95
Market Value: N/E

59

New!

Queen's House Of Cards (set/8)
Issued: 1999 • Current
#13173 • Original Price: $85
Market Value: $85

60

T.L. Pigs Brick Factory (set/6)
Issued: 1998 • Current
#13182 • Original Price: $95
Market Value: $75

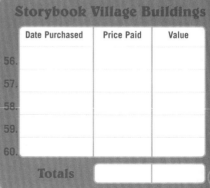

Storybook Village Buildings

	Date Purchased	Price Paid	Value
56.			
57.			
58.			
59.			
60.			
Totals			

OTHER DEPARTMENT 56® COLLECTIBLES – ACCESSORIES

Accessory pieces such as these can add that final, perfect touch to your display.

1

Aspen Trees
Issued: 1979 • Retired: 1980
#5052-6 • Orig. Price: $16
Market Value: $365

2

Sheep (set/12)
Issued: 1979 • Retired: 1980
#5053-4 • Orig. Price: $12
Market Value: $295

3

**Bachman's Wilcox Truck
(Bachman's Exclusive)**
Issued: 1997 • Retired: 1997
#8803 • Orig. Price: $29.95
Market Value: $55

4

**Heinz Hitch
(H.J. Heinz Co. Piece)**
The Profile Series
Issued: 1999 • Current
N/A • Orig. Price: $39
Market Value: $39

5

**Horse Drawn Squash Cart
(Bachman's Exclusive)**
Issued: 1995 • Retired: 1995
#0753-6 • Orig. Price: $50
Market Value: $90

Meadowland Accessories

	Date Purchased	Price Paid	Value
1.			
2.			

Miscellaneous Accessories

3.			
4.			
5.			
6.			
7.			
8.			
9.			

Totals

6

**New Year's Millennium
Waterglobe**
Issued: 1999 • Current
#20008 • Orig. Price: $32.50
Market Value: $32.50

7

**Ronald McDonald House®
Ornament (Event Piece)**
Issued: 1997 • Retired: 1997
#8961 • Orig. Price: $7.50
Market Value: N/E

8

**Say It With Flowers
(Bachman's Exclusive)**
Issued: 1998 • Retired: 1998
#2204 • Orig. Price: $30
Market Value: N/E

9

**Tending The Cold Frame
(Bachman's Exclusive)**
Issued: 1998 • Retired: 1998
#2208 • Orig. Price: $35
Market Value: $60

Value Guide — Department 56® Villages

10

Times Tower
Classic Ornament Series
Issued: 1999 • Current
#98775 • Orig. Price: $25
Market Value: $25

11

**Village Express Van
(Canadian Exclusive For
Heritage Village)**
Issued: 1992 • Retired: 1996
#5865-3 • Orig. Price: $25 *(U.S.)*
Market Value: N/E

12

New!

**Seasons Bay Amusement
Park Carousel
(animated, musical)**
Issued: 1999 • Current
#53410 • Orig. Price: $75
Market Value: $75

13

New!

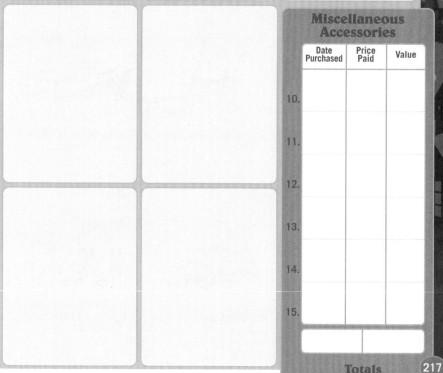

**Arriving At The Station
(set/5)**
Issued: 1999 • Current
#53416 • Orig. Price: $32.50
Market Value: $32.50

14

The Garden Cart
Issued: 1998 • Current
#53327 • Orig. Price: $27.50
Market Value: $27.50

15

New!

The Garden Swing
Issued: 1999 • Current
#53415 • Orig. Price: $13
Market Value: $13

Miscellaneous Accessories

	Date Purchased	Price Paid	Value
10.			
11.			
12.			
13.			
14.			
15.			
Totals			

20

I'm Wishing
Issued: 1998 • Current
#53309 • Orig. Price: $13
Market Value: $13

21

Relaxing In A Garden (set/3)
Issued: 1998 • Current
#53307 • Orig. Price: $25
Market Value: $25

22

A Stroll In The Park (set/5)
Issued: 1998 • Current
#53308 • Orig. Price: $25
Market Value: $25

23

Sunday Morning At The Chapel (set/2)
Issued: 1998 • Current
#53311 • Orig. Price: $17
Market Value: $17

24

4th Of July Parade (set/5)
Issued: 1998 • Current
#53317 • Orig. Price: $32.50
Market Value: $32.50

25

A Day At The Waterfront (set/2)
Issued: 1998 • Current
#53326 • Orig. Price: $20
Market Value: $20

26

Fishing In The Bay
Issued: 1998 • Current
#53313 • Orig. Price: $13
Market Value: $13

27

New!

Gently Down The Stream
Issued: 1999 • Current
#53418 • Orig. Price: $25
Market Value: $25

28

New!

A Grand Day Of Fishing
Issued: 1998 • Current
#53419 • Orig. Price: $25
Market Value: $25

29

Here Comes The Ice Cream Man (set/4)
Issued: 1998 • Current
#53314 • Orig. Price: $35
Market Value: $35

Seasons Bay Spring Accessories

	Date Purchased	Price Paid	Value
20.			
21.			
22.			
23.			

Seasons Bay Summer Accessories

24.			
25.			
26.			
27.			
28.			
29.			

Totals

30

New!

Lifeguard On Duty
Issued: 1999 • Current
#53423 • Orig. Price: $20
Market Value: $20

31

New!

The Perfect Wedding (set/7, with book)
Issued: 1999 • Current
#53417 • Orig. Price: $25
Market Value: $25

32

New!

An Afternoon Picnic (set/3)
Issued: 1999 • Current
#53420 • Orig. Price: $18
Market Value: $18

33

Back From The Orchard
Issued: 1998 • Current
#53320 • Orig. Price: $27.50
Market Value: $27.50

34

New!

A Bicycle Built For Two
Issued: 1999 • Current
#53421 • Orig. Price: $17.50
Market Value: $17.50

35

New!

Rocking Chair Readers (set/2)
Issued: 1999 • Current
#53422 • Orig. Price: $15
Market Value: $15

36

Trick Or Treat (set/4)
Issued: 1998 • Current
#53319 • Orig. Price: $25
Market Value: $25

37

Afternoon Sleigh Ride
Issued: 1998 • Current
#53322 • Orig. Price: $27.50
Market Value: $27.50

38

New!

A Day Of Holiday Shopping (set/3)
Issued: 1999 • Current
#53425 • Orig. Price: $25
Market Value: $25

39

New!

The First Snow
Issued: 1999 • Current
#53426 • Orig. Price: $15
Market Value: $15

Seasons Bay Summer Accessories		
Date Purchased	Price Paid	Value
30.		
31.		
Seasons Bay Fall Accessories		
32.		
33.		
34.		
35.		
36.		
Seasons Bay Winter Accessories		
37.		
38.		
39.		
Totals		

Seasons Bay – Accessories

40

Fun In The Snow (set/2)
Issued: 1998 • Current
#53323 • Orig. Price: $15
Market Value: $15

41
New!

Singing Carols In Town
Issued: 1999 • Current
#53427 • Orig. Price: $22.50
Market Value: $22.50

42

Skating On The Pond (set/2)
Issued: 1998 • Current
#53324 • Orig. Price: $20
Market Value: $20

43
New!

Storybook Village Collection Sign
Issued: 1999 • Current
#13169 • Orig. Price: $10
Market Value: $10

44

3 Men In A Tub Stackable Teapot And Cup (set/3)
Issued: 1997 • Current
#13329 • Orig. Price: $15
Market Value: $15

45

Cinderella (set/5)
Issued: 1997 • Current
#13326 • Orig. Price: $32.50
Market Value: $32.50

46

Cinderella Stackable Teapot And Cup (set/3)
Issued: 1997 • Current
#13327 • Orig. Price: $15
Market Value: $15

47

Hey Diddle Diddle (set/5)
Issued: 1996 • Current
#13303 • Orig. Price: $32.50
Market Value: $32.50

48

Hickory Dickory Dock (set/5)
Issued: 1996 • Current
#13302 • Orig. Price: $32.50
Market Value: $32.50

Seasons Bay Winter Accessories

	Date Purchased	Price Paid	Value
40.			
41.			
42.			

Storybook Village Accessories

43.			

Storybook Teapots

44.			
45.			
46.			
47.			
48.			

Totals

Value Guide — Department 56® Villages

49

Humpty Dumpty (set/5)
Issued: 1997 • Current
#13324 • Orig. Price: $32.50
Market Value: $32.50

50

Humpty Dumpty Stackable Teapot And Cup (set/3)
Issued: 1997 • Current
#13328 • Orig. Price: $15
Market Value: $15

51

Little Boy Blue (set/5)
Issued: 1996 • Current
#13316 • Orig. Price: $32.50
Market Value: $32.50

52

Little Miss Muffet (set/5)
Issued: 1996 • Current
#13318 • Orig. Price: $32.50
Market Value: $32.50

53

Little Red Riding Hood (set/5)
Issued: 1996 • Current
#13317 • Orig. Price: $32.50
Market Value: $32.50

54

Mother Goose (set/5)
Issued: 1996 • Current
#13300 • Orig. Price: $32.50
Market Value: $32.50

55

Mother Goose Stackable Teapot And Cup (set/3)
Issued: 1997 • Current
#13330 • Orig. Price: $15
Market Value: $15

56

Peter Pumpkin (set/5)
Issued: 1996 • Current
#13314 • Orig. Price: $32.50
Market Value: $32.50

57

Tea And Coffee (set/5)
Issued: 1997 • Current
#13325 • Orig. Price: $32.50
Market Value: $32.50

58

Three Bears (set/5)
Issued: 1996 • Current
#13301 • Orig. Price: $32.50
Market Value: $32.50

Storybook Teapots

	Date Purchased	Price Paid	Value
49.			
50.			
51.			
52.			
53.			
54.			
55.			
56.			
57.			
58.			
Totals			

Future Releases

Use this page to record future Department 56 releases.

Other Department 56 Collectibles	Original Price	Status	Market Value	Date Purch.	Price Paid	Value

Page Total:	Price Paid	Value

Total Value Of My Collection

Add the "Page Totals" together to find the "Grand Total."

Other Department 56 Collectibles

Page Number	Price Paid	Value
Page 207		
Page 208		
Page 209		
Page 210		
Page 211		
Page 212		
Page 213		
Page 214		
Page 215		
Page 216		
Page 217		
Page 218		
Page 219		
Page 220		
Page 221		
Subtotal:		

	Price Paid	Value
GRAND TOTAL:		

Secondary Market Overview

*W*hen looking for Department 56 pieces that are no longer in production, the collector should turn to the secondary market. While these pieces may be found through a local retailer or even at a garage sale, the secondary market is the most efficient way to locate hard-to-find collectibles.

The Mold Has Been Broken . . .

The secondary market is a place where collectors can buy, sell and trade items. For most collectible lines, a secondary market is born after pieces are retired – that is, removed from production and, therefore, is no longer available through retail stores. When a Department 56 piece is retired, the mold is destroyed which prevents the design from being introduced into the line again. As stores run low on stock for each retired piece, the demand for it grows, increasing its value and causing the piece to retain what is known as "secondary market value."

The secondary market for Department 56 began when the company announced the first Snow Village retirements in 1979. Since then, retired pieces have been announced annually through a large advertisement in *USA Today*. The retirement list can also be found on the Department 56 web site, *www.department56.com*.

Buy Them When You See Them!

Limited editions and exclusive pieces typically draw the highest prices on the secondary market, since they were available for the shortest amount of time and to the fewest number of collectors. The limited editions are pieces restricted either by production time ("LE-1999") or by the number of pieces produced ("LE-10,000").

Exclusive pieces include special event pieces available solely to collectors who attend a specific event and pieces made especially for select retailers, such as Lord & Taylor, William Glen and Fortunoff. Such collectibles sell out quickly, forcing the buyer to look to the secondary market for the desired piece.

Inspection For Perfection

Secondary market pricing is based on three criteria: availability, condition and packaging. The value of a piece depends on its condition. Stray wisps of paint, chips, cracks and water damage can each reduce the value of a piece on the secondary market. A piece that has been repaired or restored should be carefully inspected with the buyer keeping in mind that the resale price will decrease.

Pieces that are in perfect condition are often those that have never been removed from their original boxes and will, therefore, receive the highest value on the secondary market. They will be marked in listings as "mint in box" or "MIB." Pieces sold without their original boxes are often considered "incomplete" and are not worth as much on the secondary market.

Desperately Seeking . . . Snow Village

1. The search for a piece on the secondary market should begin with your *local retailer*. Most retailers are not active on the secondary market but can often direct you to other collectors in your area, give you information on where to find your piece or may be aware of secondary market shows.

2. *Exchange services* are another great place to help locate hard-to-find collectibles. These resources provide a listing of items that collectors are selling, along with the price they are asking. Exchanges usually issue a monthly or bi-weekly newsletter and charge a subscription or membership fee. The exchange acts as a broker and often expects a 10% to 20% service fee in order to complete a sale (a helpful list of exchanges, dealers and newsletters is provided for you on page 227).

3. The *Internet* is another method for accessing the secondary market. Searching through your computer can be very resourceful, giving you the freedom to obtain prices throughout the country – and perhaps the world – without ever leaving their homes. Bulletin boards welcome posts from collectors who are looking to buy, sell or trade pieces and auction sites allow for listing and bidding on items. There are also chat rooms in which the buyer can share information with other Department 56 collectors. Further more, several secondary market exchanges now have web sites were you can buy, sell and trade, as well as catch up on the latest news in the world of Department 56 collectibles.

4. Another place to look for secondary market pieces is through "Antiques & Collectibles" *classified advertisements* in your local newspaper or in various collectible magazines. Always keep in mind, however that newspapers target a general audience and this source may not be as effective as the other methods listed above.

Keep The Lights Burning . . .

The secondary market is a great way to build your Department 56 collection. But it is important to remember that the market can be unstable and there is no guarantee that values will continue to increase. If your sole reason for collecting is the investment, you may be disappointed. It would be wiser to relax and enjoy the view of your Department 56 villages.

EXCHANGES, DEALERS & NEWSLETTERS

Fifty-Six™ (formerly Quarterly)
(general information – *a must!*)
Department 56, Inc.
P.O. Box 44056
One Village Place
Eden Prairie, MN 55344-1056
(800) 548-8696
www.department56.com

56 Directions
Jeff & Susan McDermott
364 Spring Street Ext.
Glastonbury, CT 06033
(860) 633-8192
www.56directions.com

Collectible Exchange, Inc.
6621 Columbiana Road
New Middletown, OH 44442
(800) 752-3208
www.colexch.com

The Cottage Locator
Frank & Florence Wilson
211 No. Bridebrook Rd.
East Lyme, CT 06333
(860) 739-0705

Dickens' Exchange
Lynda W. Blankenship
5150 Highway 22, Suite C-16
Mandeville, LA 70471-2515
(504) 845-1954
www.dickensexchange.com

Donna's Collectible Exchange
703 Endeavor Drive South
Winter Springs, FL 32708
(800) 480-5105
www.donnascollexch.com

New England Collectibles Exchange
Bob Dorman
201 Pine Avenue
Clarksburg, MA 01247
(413) 663-3643
www.collectiblesbroker.com

The Village Chronicle
Peter & Jeanne George
757 Park Ave.
Cranston, RI 02910
(401) 467-9343

The Village Press
Roger Bain
P.O. Box 556
Rockford, IL 61105-0556
(815) 965-0901
http://elbourne.simplenet.com/village/vp.htm

Villages Classified
Paul & Mirta Burns
P.O. Box 34166
Granada Hills, CA 91394-9166
(818) 368-6765

What The Dickens
Judith Isaacson
2885 West Ribera Place
Tucson, AZ 85742
(520) 297-7019

Insuring Your Collection

*N*ow that you've devoted a lot of time, effort and money to build up your Department 56 collection, make sure that your collection is covered in the event of theft, flood, fire or other unforeseen circumstances. Insuring your collection is a wise move and it doesn't have to be costly or difficult.

1. Assess the value of your Department 56 collection. If it is quite extensive, you might want to have it professionally appraised. However, you can determine the current value of your collection yourself by consulting a reputable price guide such as the Collector's Value Guide™.

2. Determine the amount of coverage you need. Collectibles are often covered under a basic homeowner's or renter's policy, but ask your agent if your policy covers fire, theft, flood, hurricanes, earthquakes and damage or breakage from routine handling. Also, find out if your policy covers claims at "current replacement value" – the amount it would cost to replace items if they were damaged, lost or stolen. If the amount of insurance does not cover your collection, you may want to consider adding a Personal Articles Floater or a Fine Arts Floater ("rider") to your policy. Many insurance companies specialize in collectibles insurance and can help you ensure that your collection is adequately covered.

3. Keep up-to-date documentation of your collectible pieces and their values. Save all your receipts and consider photographing each item, taking special care to show variations, artist signatures and other special features in the photograph. Keep all of your documentation in a safe place, such as a safe deposit box, or make two copies and give one to a friend or relative.

Caring For Your Collection

*J*ust as your house may require the occasional repair, so, too may your Department 56 buildings. Here are some routine maintenance tips that will ensure that your village pieces keep looking as new as the day you bought them.

A Sticky Solution

Department 56 villages are handcrafted and, as a result, can be quite fragile. If, over the course of handling them, part of your piece comes loose or breaks off, a strong glue is your best bet to reattach the piece.

Spring Cleaning

The most common problem facing your villages is that they might get a bit dusty from being displayed in an open area. Department 56 recommends brushing the pieces lightly with a feather duster or using canned air to gently remove any dust or dirt. For those tough to reach nooks and crannies, use a small, moist paintbrush. Cleaning solvents, soaps and water should be avoided, as they could destroy the finish of your villages.

A Bright Idea

Keeping your lighted villages glowing will require replacement bulbs, should one happen to burn out. These bulbs are available from the retailer where you purchased your village.

Where There's Smoke. . .

Replacement smoke is also available for all of the village pieces that use the pine-scented magic smoking element, such as "Steen's Maple House." Once again, your local retailer is the place to turn to keep the homefires burning throughout the winter.

Variations

*S*ometimes a collector will find a Department 56 piece with slightly different characteristics than others of the same name. The piece that differs from the standard is considered to be a variation. Although not all variations affect the price of the piece, some changes can cause a substantial rise in the secondary market value. While some of the changes are unintentional or the result of human error; at times Department 56 will change the piece in an attempt to improve it.

A Little Dab Will Do Yah!

A common variation is a change in color. For example, the "Dickens' Village Church," which was originally painted white, has appeared in five different colors through the years. Soon after its release, the church showed up in a cream color. Then it changed to green, tan and finally butterscotch. The white version has the highest secondary market value because of its limited availability.

"Peggotty's Seaside Cottage" has also appeared with a color variation. It was first introduced in 1989 as a gray home. The second version is green.

"Small Double Trees" from Snow Village were featured at times with blue birds on the branches and, at other, times shown with red.

The "Knob Hill" house first appeared as off-white with black trim. The house was later released painted a bright yellow hue and came with white trim.

The *Dickens' Village* "Ox Sled" has gone through color changes as well. First the driver wore tan pants and was sitting on a green seat, while another version shows him with blue pants on a black seat.

Departmental Design

Sometimes Department 56 has to correct a design, as when the *New England Village* "Amish Family" (set/3) was introduced. At first the man with the basket was featured with a mustache but, after learning that Amish custom prohibits wearing a mustache, the piece was altered to show the man with only a beard.

Many other pieces have endured design changes as well. "The Flat Of Ebenezer Scrooge" in *Dickens' Village* appears with gold-colored window panes in some instances and without window panes at all in others.

"Train Station With 3 Train Cars" (set/4) in Snow Village originally appeared with six window panes and a circular window on the front door. Later the design was changed to feature eight window panes and two square windows on the door.

An example of an accessory with a change is the Snow Village piece "Auto With Tree." In the first version, the top of the car has a flattened look to it. The next version produced had a more inflated, or round, appearance.

Not So Carbon Copy

Misspellings are another common variation. The "Nicholas Nickleby Cottage" has also been seen with a bottomstamp with "Nickolas Nickelby," using a "k" instead of a "h."

"Kensington Palace" (set/23) first appeared with a misspelled word on its box. The text originally said "Princess of Whales" instead of the correct "Princess of Wales."

The bottomstamp of "Blythe Pond Mill House" in *Dickens' Village* was incorrectly labeled "By The Pond" in many instances.

In "Crooked Fence Cottage" the bottomstamp reads "Seires" instead of the correct "Series" on some pieces and some "J. Lytes Coal Merchant" pieces have a bottomstamp with the word "Village" misspelled as "Vallage."

Strategic Downsizing

Through the years, some Department 56 pieces have changed to a smaller size after their introduction. In addition to the size changing, sometimes characteristics of the piece were also altered. At some point between the time of release and the time of retirement, "Family Mom/Kids, Goose Girl" (set/2) decreased in size and became more detailed.

Exclusively Yours

Department 56 often issues exclusive pieces, however, these are not considered to be true variations though they often are based on a pre-existing piece in the collection. These unique collectibles are usually available through a specific retailer or group.

For a complete listing of Department 56 buildings and accessories with variations, please consult the Value Guide section of this book.

SO WHAT'S AN ARTIST PROOF?

Prototypes produced in the studios of Department 56 prior to the release of a piece are often used to "test run" various colors, patterns and/or design elements and are called "artist proofs." Although very few are made, on certain occasions they manage to make their way into collectors' hands and become highly valuable on the secondary market.

Production, Packaging And Pricing

*E*ach and every Department 56 building and accessory portrays the company's high standards of quality. The production process takes countless hours with each step carefully monitored to ensure customer satisfaction.

A Blueprint For Building A Village

All village pieces begin as a drawing on paper, which is then used as a guide, or blueprint. From the drawing, a building is sculpted. A mold of the piece is made into which "slip," or liquid clay, is poured. When the clay hardens, it is removed from the mold and sanded. The building is then ready for cosmetic touches, such as cutting the windows and adding attachments.

It's A Hot Time In The Old Town Tonight!

The piece is then placed in a kiln, heated to at least 1,000 degrees Fahrenheit and baked for a minimum of eight hours. When the firing process is complete and the buildings have cooled, they are hand-painted. Heritage Village pieces have a matte finish and do not need a coat of glaze. They only need to be refired long enough to dry and set the new paint. Snow Village pieces need to be fired for a longer period of time, at a higher temperature. This will set the top coat of glaze, producing their famous glossy finish.

Picture Perfect Packaging

Department 56 villages come packaged in styrofoam in either a "sleeve" or box, both of which might have a line drawing or a color picture of the piece on the front. Information regarding the piece and village is available on the sleeve. Snow Village and Heritage Village buildings normally range in price from $50 to $100, while accessories are generally $15 to $40. Ornaments cost approximately $20, while hinged boxes run between $15 and $25.

Department 56® Product Spotlight

*T*here are a number of other collectible and gift lines available from Department 56 that offer the same high quality and variety found in the village collections. Looking for something different? Perhaps one of these collections is for you!

Silhouette Treasures™ Collection

A line of white porcelain pieces featuring a Victorian lamplighter and three carolers was introduced in 1987 and was known as *Lamplighter*. New figurines were added and the line was renamed *Winter Silhouette*™. As the collection has grown to include more designs, sub-categories of "Special Occasion," "Family And Friends" and "Christmas" have been added to the *Silhouette Treasures*™*Collection*, as it is now called. Currently, there are 48 pieces available, including 15 new releases for 2000.

Snowbabies™ Figurines

In 1986 five small figures known as *Snowbabies*™ *Figurines* were introduced to the world. These highly detailed figures featuring winged children dressed in frosty crystal-covered parkas are the design of artist Kristi Jensen Pierro. Since the initial introduction of these figurines, the collection has grown to include more than 150 pieces including figurines, waterglobes, "Bootiebaby" ornaments, pewter miniatures, hinged boxes and the newest introduction – *Snowbabies Starlight Games*™ pieces. Featuring highlights of the annual athletic event held in *Frosty Frolic Land*™, these first four releases depict Snowbabies participating in soccer, baseball, diving and vaulting competitions. Each is a winner who has received a porcelain bisque star on a satin ribbon that is worn around the neck.

In 1998, *The Guest Collection*™ introduced familiar characters in vibrant colors from *The Wizard of Oz*, *Madeline* and the "Looney Tunes" to the *Snowbabies* line.

Instead of frosty winter parkas, the children of the *Snowbunnies*® *Figurines*, which were introduced in 1994, are wearing bunny suits with a hint of pastel colors to give them a touch of Spring. Easter eggs and springtime activities replace the wintery themes of the *Snowbabies* line. In addition to *Snowbunnies*, introductions of Easter bisque animal figurines are annual traditions that are anticipated by collectors.

Candle Crown™ Collections

This year, Department 56 introduced a new line of candle extinguishers, the *Candle Crown*™ *Collections*. There are currently three sets from which to choose: "Alice In Wonderland," "The Nutcracker Suite" and "The Wizard of Oz." Collectors can choose from numbered, limited edition pieces made of fine bone china accented with 23-karat gold, or open edition porcelain pieces.

Tabletop And Giftware

A wide variety of home decor items, including those for the kitchen and bathroom, rounds out the product line offered by Department 56. The most recent additions are fun but functional items featuring bright yellow ducks in the *Just Ducky*™ collection with soap dispensers, towels racks, pitchers, ice buckets, glasses and, of course, a lounge chair. For a taste of winter, cookie jars and mugs from the *Santa Clothes* collection or the *Under The Mistletoe* line will bring a whimsical touch to your holiday table.

On The Road With Department 56®

*D*epartment 56 has taken to the highways and byways of America and is sure to be making stops at a convention hall near you!

Now Appearing . . .

Stop by and introduce yourself to your favorite Department 56 artists; including Heritage Village artist Barbara Lund and master architect Neilan Lund, Seasons Bay designer Dennis Brose, Snow Village artist Scott Enter and *Snowbabies* artist Kristi Jensen Pierro.

In 1999, these talented people, along with "Ms. Lit Town," Judith Price; Rhonda Ritchie, editor of *Fifty-Six* and several Consumer Services specialists, visited over 50 locations from Connecticut to Arizona where they met with collectors, talked about their work and presented new display ideas using easy-to-find materials.

Department 56 will continue its travels throughout 2000, stopping at collectors' conventions from California to New York, including a stop at the famous International Collectibles Exposition in Rosemont, Illinois in June.

Make It A Date!

To find out when and where Department 56 will be appearing next, check the *Fifty-Six* (formerly *Quarterly*) magazine from Department 56 for a complete listing of dates and times. For collectors who also have internet access, the Department 56 web site, *www.department56.com*, lists upcoming appearances under the "Meet Department 56 Calendar" in the "What's New" section of the home page. Come join the fun!

Department 56 ®

Department 56

FIFTY-SIX

On The Road With Department 56

Display Ideas

*A*s a Department 56 village enthusiast, you have the wonderful opportunity to start your collection with one special piece; then slowly (or quickly!) add more buildings and accessories until you achieve your optimal display.

Starting Small?

If you do start out with only an individual piece, it can be attractively displayed just as well as a collection of village pieces. With a single building, you can surprise and delight visitors by placing it in an unexpected spot! Imagine finding this favorite lighthouse design perched on the edge of the bathtub (be sure it's distant enough from the water, as it may damage the buildings finish) with a few smooth stones or seashells surround-

ing its base. A lighthouse is the perfect piece to accessorize a bathroom that has a seashell, fish or undersea motif. Similar small displays can be placed on a dining table, in a kitchen cabinet or shelved on a bookcase. Or perhaps a series of small scenes leading up a staircase accented with Christmas lights and garland would be the perfect display for the holiday season.

Moving On Up . . .

Now that you've mastered the art of the small display, perhaps you're ready to move on to a medium-sized village scene. One collector chose the "Steeple Church" because it reminded her of the church she attended as a child in rural New England.

She added several Department 56 accessories (even choosing to mix and match from several different villages). With a display of this size, feel free to add various display elements which can be purchased at your local craft or hobby store. Department 56 also makes a wide variety of general display pieces, including trees, fences and snow, which will accentuate your display no matter what village, or season, you choose. The result is an impressive display with minimal effort and expense. A display of this size would also work well on a dining room buffet, showcased in a curio cabinet or on top of a dresser or bureau.

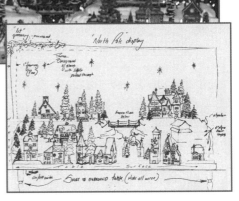

Think Big

Over a number of years, a collection can begin to take on a life of its own! New buildings and accessories are added and the question of where to display the growing village soon arises concerning. Many collectors decide to buy or make a large, table as a solution to their growing needs.

As you begin to accumulate numerous buildings and accessories you may, as opposed to breaking up pieces into smaller displays, chose to make a large, tabletop display of your village. If you are planning on a large display, the best way to start is to draw out a blueprint so that you can plan ahead in regards to the space and tools you will need.

Styrofoam is the perfect tool to provide you with a multi-level display, making realistic mountains and providing snowy ground cover. When managing a large display, take care to cover each of the electrical wires to give the display a realistic appearance. Large displays are fun as they provide you the opportunity to let your creative mind take over. It's easy to use your imagination and find new purposes for many, common household items. Try using cellophane to recreate a waterfall, a mirror for an icy lake and don't overlook the kitchen, as peppermints make the perfect sidewalk for busy *North Pole* elves. Aside from items in your house, there are several from outside the house you can use to create display magic (just be sure you thoroughly clean any items brought in from the great outdoors.) With a little bit of patience you can create your own accessories such as bales of hay, and rock walls. (By following the directions below and with a few sticks from your yard, this stick bridge can be yours!)

The Simple Stick Bridge

Begin bridge assembly by placing two long sticks parallel – about three inches apart. Apply hot glue to the ends of two small sticks and position them on each end of the parallel sticks. Continue gluing the remaining sticks on the base of the bridge, depending on the length.

Position and glue two, 2-inch sticks in an upright position (for handrails) at each end of the bridge. Add additional sticks in an upright position on each side, being sure to space them equally apart. Finally, attach string or yarn along the tops of the upright sticks to make a handrail. For a finishing touch, glue plastic icicles to the underside of the bridge and sprinkle the top with snow.

It's Not Just For Christmas Anymore

While many collectors prefer to keep their displaying specifically for the holidays, many are now choosing to display year-round. With the new Seasons Bay line, which features accessories for every season, creating spring, summer and fall scenes is just a shopping spree away. However, with the right accessories and a little creativity, you can also change any of the other Department 56 villages along with real-life seasonal splendor.

A display for the fall season can be achieved with a little planning and forethought. Luckily, snow may fall early in many parts of the country so the frosty covering on the roofs of the village buildings is appropriate for the season. (If you're working on a summer scenario, hide snow-capped roofs by the strategic placement of trees and the like.) Trees in autumnal splendor, "Farm Animals" (set/8) grazing, the "Harvest Pumpkin Wagon" and the "Sleepy Hollow Characters" (set/3) all can add a to the chill in the air making for the perfect Halloween display!

Display Success With "Dr. S"

isplay guru, "Dr. S" is back again, ready to help both beginners and experienced "displayers" enhance their growing village. This time, he's here to help with his easy-to-follow directions for sidewalks and walls, which are sure to add a special touch that will bring your village scene to life.

The third in our series of "always useful, never difficult" scenic articles leads us down the road to the issue of sidewalks, which are the perfect complement to those roads you built from the directions published in our 1998 edition of the *Collector's Value Guide to Department 56® Villages*.

The Quick Sidewalk

You will need:

- Newspaper

- 1/4" foam core board or similar material

- A black felt-tipped marker with a fine point

- Gray or tan latex paint in a spray can

- Stripwood or styrene

Step One: Arrange your Department 56 buildings, allowing room where you might want to have your streets, and prepare the surfaces of the street as described in our 1998 edition. Be certain to allow room for the sidewalks when you do your plan. And remember, cars have to drive past each other, not on top of each other as in police shows, so be sure to allow enough space so you can still have a two lane road.

Step Two: Cut your foam core board into 2" wide strips. Measure twice and cut once to avoid making large amounts of odd sidewalks (commonly called "scrap"). If you are planning a corner, cut a radius onto the corner of your sidewalk. The easiest way to do this is to place a dime at the corner and use the outside edge as a guide to the proper curve when you cut. Since your display does not have to comply with local zoning rules, we will not describe how to do curb cuts here. Feel free to experiment and report your results to us.

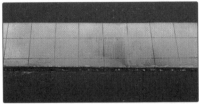

Step Three: Using a ruler and the black felt-tipped marker, draw a grid which looks like concrete sidewalk expansion joints (you know . . . the lines) on your pieces of foam core. The grid may be in 1/2" to 3/4" blocks. Try your design on a piece of scrap and see which one you like – remember, this is YOUR village and you are accountable to NO ONE.

Step Four: Take your pieces outside and carefully spray a fine mist of the gray or tan paint on them. Try to use one or two light coats rather than one heavy coat, as you do not want to hide the sidewalk lines. Your final coat should be uneven to represent the variations in color that are a part of every sidewalk. Make sure you spray your wood or styrene strips at this time. Let the paint dry 12 to 24 hours.

Step Five: Install your sidewalk pieces by coating the bottom (unpainted) side with white glue (or a thin coat of bubble gum if the flavor is gone) and carefully place the sidewalk onto your display. Weight the sidewalk with some light books and wait 24 hours – don't peek.

Step Six: Carefully bend your stripwood or styrene and glue them to the edges of your sidewalk. These pieces become your curbs. Use your favorite adhesive here, but apply sparingly. If you are really coordinated, you can apply the "curb" after Step Four then glue the entire piece in place, but I find it is easier to put the curbs in last, since this step offers another chance to carefully cover up any past errors.

Most of the material listed may be purchased in any office supply store, but you might want to visit your local hobby or model railroad shop for the stripwood and styrene. Remember, as always, this is another cheap project . . . if the result is not what you want, throw it away and try again. There is no failure – this is your world!

The Quick Concrete Retaining Wall

There are many ways to build a wall, either in a relationship or on a display, but neither requires a great deal of skill. As a follow-up to our "The Quick Wall" instructions in the 1999 edition, here's another quick and easy way to enhance your display.

You will need:

- Plywood cut to size

- A small can of artificial brick mortar like "Z Brick"

- Several paint mixing sticks (from your local paint or hardware store)

- Latex paint or craft paint to suit your color needs

- A putty knife or scraper with a 3" blade

Step One: Plan your display carefully. Decide where your wall needs to go and the effect you seek. The kind of wall which we describe here is used to separate levels of a city or railroad and highway interchanges. It is not used in water or wharf areas. Such walls are common all over the United States and many other countries.

Step Two: Cut your plywood to size. Often hardware and lumber stores will have scrap pieces they will sell (or even GIVE) to you so you do not have to rent a truck to build your display. Many stores will even cut

the pieces IF you are sure of your measurements. We recommend plywood for this type of wall over foam core board or any other material that might interact with the "concrete coating." The plywood will not warp, and can even be used to support levels of your display.

Step Three: Cut your paint mixing sticks to match the desired height of your wall and glue them to the plywood at approximately six to eight inch intervals. You are looking to simulate reinforcing buttresses often seen on higher walls. (Remember those Gothic cathedrals in Europe? Same idea, simpler design.) Set aside to dry.

Step Four: Open the can of "Z-Brick" or similar, and lightly coat the wall with a thin coat. The wall should be laid flat for this step. "Z-Brick" is a coarse, textured adhesive designed to simulate mortar for installation of faux stone (read "fake stone.") How logical for us to use the same stuff to simulate fake concrete! Remember, you can always add to low spots, but it is nearly impossible to remove this material when it dries. Err on the side of caution.

Step Five: After allowing the coating to dry, you are ready to paint! Dilute your paint with water and flow several light coats over the wall, allowing each coat to dry so you can examine the result. Brush quality is not an issue here, anything from a sponge to your cat's tail will do.

Step Six: Install your wall!

Current Display Pieces

*G*iving your village display that perfect and final "touch" is often accomplished by adding display accessories. Department 56 provides a wide variety from which to choose. In the following list, items that are designed for a specific village – Heritage Village, Snow Village, Seasons Bay or *Dickens' Village* – are labeled (HV), (SV), (SB) or (DV). New pieces for 2000 are marked with an asterisk (*).

Snow

- ❑ Blanket Of New
  Fallen Snow 49956
- ❑ Fresh Fallen Snow
  (7-oz. bag) 49979
- ❑ Fresh Fallen Snow
  (2-lb. box) 49980
- ❑ Ice Crystal Blanket
  Of Snow 52841*
- ❑ Real Plastic Snow
  (7-oz. bag) 49981
- ❑ Real Plastic Snow
  (2-lb. box) 49999

Fences

- ❑ Candy Cane Fence 52664
- ❑ Corral Fence 52746
- ❑ Halloween Fence
  (set/2) 52702
- ❑ Snow Fence, White (SV) . . 52657
- ❑ Twig Snow Fence 52598
- ❑ Victorian Wrought Iron
  Fence Extension (HV) 52531
- ❑ Victorian Wrought Iron
  Fence And Gate
  (set/5) (HV) 52523
- ❑ White Picket Fence (SV) . . 51004
- ❑ Wrought Iron Fence
  (set/4) (HV) 59994

Trees

- ❑ Autumn Birch/Maple
  Tree (set/4) 52655
- ❑ Bare Branch Trees
  (set/6) 52623

Trees, cont.

- ❑ Bare Branch Tree
  w/25 Lights 52434
- ❑ Birch Tree Cluster 52631
- ❑ Craggy Oak Tree 52748
- ❑ Decorated Sisal Trees
  (set/2, Asst.) 52714
- ❑ Flocked Pine Trees
  (set/3) 53367
- ❑ Frosted Spruce (set/2) 52637
- ❑ Frosted Topiary (set/2) 52000
- ❑ Frosted Topiary (set/4) 52019
- ❑ Frosted Topiary
  (set/8, Asst. Lg.) 52027
- ❑ Frosted Topiary
  (set/8, Asst. Sm.) 52035
- ❑ Halloween
  Spooky Tree 52770
- ❑ Holly Tree 52630
- ❑ Jack Pines (set/3) 52622
- ❑ Pine Trees With
  Pine Cones (set/3) 52771
- ❑ Porcelain Pine
  Trees (set/4) 59001
- ❑ Snowy Evergreen
  Trees, Lg. (set/5) 52614
- ❑ Snowy Evergreen
  Trees, Med. (set/6) 52613
- ❑ Snowy Evergreen
  Trees, Sm. (set/6) 52612
- ❑ Snowy Scotch Pines
  (set/3) 52615
- ❑ Storybook Village
  Collection Landcape
  Set (set/6) 13179*
- ❑ Towering Pines (set/2) 52632
- ❑ Twinkling Tip Tree 52781
- ❑ Village Flocked Pine
  Trees (set/2) 56715*
- ❑ Village Frosted
  Shrubbery (set/24) 52843*
- ❑ Village Frosted
  Topiaries (set/16) 52842*
- ❑ Village Frosty Light
  Trees (set/2) 52844*

Trees, cont.

- ❏ Village Icicle Trees
  (set/3) 56722*
- ❏ Village Palm Trees
  (set/2) 52820*
- ❏ Village Peppermint
  Trees (set/3) 56721*
- ❏ Village Pequot Pine,
  X-Lg. 52819*
- ❏ Village Pequot Pines
  (set/3) 52818*
- ❏ Village Twinkling Lit
  Shrubs, Green (set/4) 52824*
- ❏ Village Twinkling Lit
  Shrubs, White (set/4) 56724*
- ❏ Village Twinkling Lit
  Town Tree 52837*
- ❏ Village Twinkling Lit
  Trees, Green (set/3) 52823*
- ❏ Village Twinkling Lit
  Trees, White (set/3) 56723*
- ❏ Winter Birch (set/6) 52636
- ❏ Winter Pine Trees With
  Pine Cones (set/3) 52772
- ❏ Wintergreen Pines
  (set/3) 52660
- ❏ Wintergreen Pines
  (set/2) 52661

Miscellaneous Accent Pieces

- ❏ Acrylic Icicles (set/4) 52116
- ❏ Adirondack Chairs
  (set/4) (SB) 53436*
- ❏ Bears In The Birch 52743
- ❏ Blue Skies Backdrop 52685
- ❏ Brick Road (set/2) 52108
- ❏ Brick Town Square 52601
- ❏ Camden Park
  Cobblestone Road (set/2) . . 52691
- ❏ Camden Park Fountain 52705
- ❏ Camden Park Square
  (set/21) (DV) 52687
- ❏ Camden Park Square
  Stone Wall (DV) 52689
- ❏ Candy Cane Bench 52669
- ❏ Christmas Eave Trim 55115
- ❏ Clear Ice 52729
- ❏ Cobblestone Road (set/2) . . 59846
- ❏ Cobblestone Town
  Square 52602
- ❏ Country Road Lamp
  Posts (set/4) 52663
- ❏ Elf Tree House 56446*

Miscellaneous Accent Pieces, cont.

- ❏ Fallen Leaves
  (3-oz. bag) 52610
- ❏ Fieldstone Entry Gate 52718
- ❏ Fieldstone Stairway 52826
- ❏ Fieldstone Wall
  (3 Asst.) 52717
- ❏ Fieldstone Wall
  With Apple Tree 52768
- ❏ Flexible Autumn
  Hedges (set/2) 52703
- ❏ Flexible Sisal
  Hedge (set/3) 52596
- ❏ Flexible Sisal Hedge,
  Lg. (set/3) 52662
- ❏ Foxes In The Forest 52744
- ❏ Frosty Light Sprays
  (set/2) 52682
- ❏ Gazebo 52652
- ❏ Glistening Snow 53362
- ❏ Grassy Ground Cover
  (3.5-oz. bag) 53347
- ❏ Gravel Road 52756
- ❏ Gray Cobblestone
  Archway 52752
- ❏ Gray Cobblestone
  Capstones (set/2) 52755
- ❏ Gray Cobblestone
  Section (set/2) 52751
- ❏ Gray Cobblestone
  Tunnel 52753
- ❏ Green 52739
- ❏ Halloween Set (set/22) 52704
- ❏ Holiday Tinsel Trims
  (set/11) 52712
- ❏ Holly Split Rail Fence
  (set/4) 52722
- ❏ Holly Split Rail Fence
  With Seated Children 52723
- ❏ Hybrid Landscape
  (set/22) 52600
- ❏ Landscape (set/14) 52590
- ❏ Log Pile 52665
- ❏ Majestic Woodland
  Birds (set/2) 52814*
- ❏ Magic Smoke
  (6-oz. bottle) 52620
- ❏ Mill Creek Bridge 52635
- ❏ Mill Creek, Curved
  Section 52634
- ❏ Mill Creek Park Bench 52654
- ❏ Mill Creek Pond 52651
- ❏ Mill Creek, Straight
  Section 52633
- ❏. Mill Creek Wooden
  Bridge 52653
- ❏ Moose In The Marsh 52742
- ❏ Mountain Backdrop
  (set/2) 5257-4

Miscellaneous Accent Pieces, cont.

- ❑ Mountain Centerpiece..... 52643
- ❑ Mountain Tunnel 52582
- ❑ Mountain w/Frosted Sisal Trees, Lg. (set/14) ... 5228-0
- ❑ Mountain w/Frosted Sisal Trees, Med. (set/8) .. 5227-2
- ❑ Mountain w/Frosted Sisal Trees, Sm. (set/5) 5226-4
- ❑ Mylar Skating Pond (set/2) 5208-6
- ❑ Nativity Sand 41430*
- ❑ Peppermint Road, Curved Section......... 52667

- ❑ Peppermint Road, Straight Section 52666
- ❑ Personalize Your Village Accessories (set/5) 52811*
- ❑ Pine Point Pond 52618
- ❑ Pink Flamingos (set/4) 52595
- ❑ Putting Green 52740
- ❑ Radius Curved Track (set/4)................ 52809*
- ❑ Railroad Crossing Sign (set/2)......... 55018
- ❑ Remote Switches, Asst. Right & Left (set/2) 52807*
- ❑ Real Gray Gravel (12-oz. bag) 52754
- ❑ Revolving Display Stand 52640
- ❑ Road Construction Sign (set/2) (SV) 52680
- ❑ Sandy Beach (SB) 53433*
- ❑ Seasons Bay Christmas Garlands & Wreaths (set/14) (SB)............ 53429*
- ❑ Seasons Bay Park (set/8) (SB)............. 53428*
- ❑ Slate Stone Path 52719
- ❑ Slate Stone Path 52767
- ❑ Sled & Skis (set/2) 52337
- ❑ Starry Night Sky Backdrop.......... 52686
- ❑ Stone Curved Wall/Bench (set/4) 52650
- ❑ Stone Footbridge 52646
- ❑ Stone Holly Corner Posts & Archway (set/3) 52648
- ❑ Stone Holly Tree Corner Posts (set/2) 52649
- ❑ Stone Stairway 52725
- ❑ Stone Trestle Bridge...... 52647
- ❑ Stone Wall 52629

- ❑ Stone Wall With Sisal Hedge 52724
- ❑ Straight Track (set/4) 52809*
- ❑ Swinging Under The Old Oak Tree....... 52769
- ❑ Tacky Wax 52175
- ❑ Telephone Poles (set/6) (SV) 52656
- ❑ Television Antenna (set/4) (SV) 52658
- ❑ Thoroughbreds (set/5).... 52747
- ❑ Tinsel Trims (set/8) 52713
- ❑ Trout Stream, The........ 52834*
- ❑ Two Lane Paved Road (SV) 52668*
- ❑ Up In The Apple Tree..... 56640*
- ❑ Village Autumn Moss (4 Asst.) 52802*
- ❑ Village Cats & Dogs (set/6)................ 52828*
- ❑ Village Ground Cover (2 Asst.) 52840*

- ❑ Village Holiday Cobblestone Road 56447*
- ❑ Village Ice Crystal Gate & Walls (set/14)..... 56716*
- ❑ Village Ice Crystal Walls (set/6)........... 56717*
- ❑ Village Lookout Tower................. 52829*
- ❑ Village Real Gravel (3 Asst.) 52839*
- ❑ Village Red Wrought Iron Park Bench 56445*
- ❑ Village Spring/Summer Moss (4 Asst.) 52803*
- ❑ Village Square Clock Tower........... 52591
- ❑ Village Tall Stone Walls (set/4)............ 52825*
- ❑ Village Wooden Canoes (set/3).......... 52830*
- ❑ Walkway Lights (set/2) 52681
- ❑ Weather Vane (set/5) (SV) 52659
- ❑ Windmill (SV) 54569
- ❑ Wolves In The Woods..... 52765
- ❑ Wooden Pier (set/2) 52766
- ❑ Wooden Rowboats (set/3)................ 52797
- ❑ Woodland Animals At Cliff's Edge (set/3)....... 52816*

Miscellaneous Accent Pieces, cont.

- ❑ Woodland Animals At
  Mill Creek 52720
- ❑ Woodland Wildlife
  Animals, Lg. (set/6) 52813*
- ❑ Woodland Wildlife
  Animals, Sm. (set/5). 55525*
- ❑ Wrought Iron
  Park Bench. 52302

Lighted Accent Pieces

- ❑ 6-Socket Light Set 99279
- ❑ 20-Socket Light Set 99278
- ❑ 45 LED Light Strand 52678
- ❑ AC/DC Adapter 55026
- ❑ Boulevard Lampposts
  (set/4). 52627
- ❑ Bridge Over The
  Icy Pond. 56720*
- ❑ Carnival Carousel
  LED Light Set 52706
- ❑ Christmas
  LED Luminaries. 52715
- ❑ Double Light Socket
  Adapter 99280

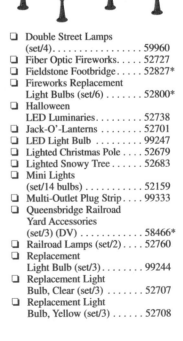

- ❑ Double Street Lamps
  (set/4). 59960
- ❑ Fiber Optic Fireworks. 52727
- ❑ Fieldstone Footbridge. 52827*
- ❑ Fireworks Replacement
  Light Bulbs (set/6) 52800*
- ❑ Halloween
  LED Luminaries. 52738
- ❑ Jack-O'-Lanterns 52701
- ❑ LED Light Bulb 99247
- ❑ Lighted Christmas Pole 52679
- ❑ Lighted Snowy Tree 52683
- ❑ Mini Lights
  (set/14 bulbs) 52159
- ❑ Multi-Outlet Plug Strip. . . . 99333
- ❑ Queensbridge Railroad
  Yard Accessories
  (set/3) (DV) 58466*
- ❑ Railroad Lamps (set/2) 52760
- ❑ Replacement
  Light Bulb (set/3). 99244
- ❑ Replacement Light
  Bulb, Clear (set/3) 52707
- ❑ Replacement Light
  Bulb, Yellow (set/3) 52708

Lighted Accent Pieces, cont.

- ❑ Replacement Round
  Light Bulb (set/3). 99245
- ❑ Single Cord Set 99028
- ❑ Spotlight (set/2). 52611
- ❑ Spotlight Replacement
  Bulbs (set/6). 99246
- ❑ Street Lamps (set/6) 36366
- ❑ String Of 12
  Pumpkin Lights 52700
- ❑ String Of 25
  Mini LED Lights 52728
- ❑ String Of Spotlights 52779
- ❑ String Of Starry Lights. . . . 52684
- ❑ Town Tree
  w/50 LED Lights 52639
- ❑ Traffic Light (set/2) 55000
- ❑ Turn-Of-The-Century
  Lamppost (set/4) 55042
- ❑ Utility Accessories
  (set/9) (SV) 52775
- ❑ Utility Accessories
  (set/11) (HV) 52776
- ❑ Village 3 Socket
  Light Set 52835*
- ❑ Village Frosted
  Fountain. 52831*
- ❑ Village Nativity
  Crèche 52822*
- ❑ Village Replacement
  Incandescent Bulbs
  (set/12). 13638*
- ❑ Village Stadium
  Lights (set/2) 52845*

Village Brite Lites

- ❑ Adapter 52256
- ❑ Angel 52671
- ❑ Candles (set/4) 52674
- ❑ Candy Canes (set/2) 52670
- ❑ Fence (set/4). 52361
- ❑ Holly Archway 52675
- ❑ "Merry Christmas" 52230
- ❑ Reindeer. 52248
- ❑ Santa 52396
- ❑ Santa In Chimney. 52673
- ❑ Snow Dragon 52672
- ❑ Snowman 52370
- ❑ Tree 52388

Glossary

accessory — pieces designed to enhance village buildings. Accessories are typically non-lit miniature figurines.

animated — a piece with motion.

bottomstamp — also called an "understamp," these are identifying marks on the underside of a collectible. Buildings have a bottomstamp which includes the village name, the title of the piece, the copyright date and the Department 56 logo.

collectibles — anything and everything that is "able to be collected," whether it is figurines, dolls, or even *yo-yos* can be considered a "collectible," but it is generally recognized that a true collectible should be something that increases in value over a period of time.

current — a piece that is in production and is available in stores.

event piece — a piece specially made for sale only at Department 56 promotional events which are held at retail stores.

exchange — a secondary market service that lists pieces that collectors wish to buy or sell. The exchange works as a middleman and usually requires a commission.

exclusive — a piece made especially for, and only available through, a specific store, exposition or buying group.

first edition — pieces with limited production. In *Seasons Bay*, there were first edition pieces with a special decal, as well as different colors and attachments than the open edition piece.

Gold Key Dealers — Showcase retailers who are recognized for their outstanding commitment to Department 56.

History List — Department 56 promotional material which lists the item number, title, issue year, retail price and retirement year of pieces.

issue date — for Department 56, the year of production is considered the year of "issue," although the piece may not become available to collectors until the following year.

issue price — the retail price of an item when it is first introduced.

limited edition — a piece scheduled for a predetermined production quantity or time period.

mid-year introductions — additional Department 56 pieces announced in May. These pieces are usually available in smaller allocations than January introductions at first, but become readily available in subsequent years.

mint-in-box — a secondary market term used when a piece comes in its original box that is in "good as new" condition. This usually adds to the value of the item.

new introductions — new pieces that are announced in December for release to retail stores the following year.

open edition — a piece with no predetermined limitation on time or size of production run.

primary market — the conventional collectibles purchasing process in which collectors buy at issue price through various retail outlets.

release date — the year a piece becomes available to collectors. For most pieces, the release date is the year following the issue date.

retired — a piece which is taken out of production, never to be made again, usually followed by a scarcity of the piece and a rise in value on the secondary market.

secondary market — the source for buying and selling collectibles according to basic supply-and-demand principles ("pay what the market will bear"). Popular pieces, or those that are retired or had low production quantities can appreciate in value far above the original price.

series — a grouping within a collection that is based on a certain theme, such as the *American Architecture Series.*

Showcase Dealers — a select group of retailers who receive early shipments of new and limited edition pieces.

sleeve — thin cardboard cover that slips over a foam box, usually featuring information such as the name of the collection, name of the piece and a photograph or drawing of the piece.

track compatible — pieces that can stand alone, but are made to go with animated tracks.

variations — items that have color, design or printed text changes from the "original" piece, whether intentional or not. Some of these changes are minor, while some are important enough to affect the value of a piece on the secondary market.

Numerical Index

– Key –

All Heritage and Snow Village pieces are listed below in numerical order by stock number. The first number refers to the piece's location within the Value Guide section and the second to the box in which it is pictured on that page. Items that are not pictured are listed as "NP."

	Pg.	Pic.
2203	207	6
2204	216	8
2208	216	9
2210	209	14
2255	209	17
670-0	207	1
671-8	207	2
672-6	207	3
7826	208	12
8802	208	7
8803	216	3
8960	209	18
8961	216	7
05600	208	12
0753-6	216	5
07544	196	196
07641	196	196
07650	196	196
07668	196	196
07676	196	196
07684	196	196
07692	196	196
07730	196	196
07740	183	79
07741	183	79
07742	183	79
07743	183	79
07744	183	79
07745	183	79
07746	183	79
07747	183	79
07748	183	79
07749	183	79

	Pg.	Pic.
07750	183	79
07751	183	79
07752	183	79
07753	183	79
07754	183	79
07755	183	79
07756	183	79
07757	183	79
07758	183	79
07759	183	79
07760	183	79
07761	183	79
07762	183	79
07763	183	79
13169	220	43
13171	214	54
13172	214	52
13173	215	59
13179	220	42
13180	214	53
13181	214	50
13182	215	60
13183	213	48
13184	215	57
13185	214	55
13186	213	46
13191	215	56
13192	215	58
13193	213	47
13194	214	51
13195	214	49
13300	221	54
13301	221	58
13302	220	48
13303	220	47
13314	221	56
13316	221	51
13317	221	53
13318	221	52
13324	221	49
13325	221	57
13326	220	45
13327	220	46
13328	221	50
13329	220	44
13330	221	55
13600	210	22
13601	210	27
13602	210	24
13603	210	25
13604	210	28
13605	210	26

	Pg.	Pic.
13606	210	21
13607	211	29
13612	209	20
13638	248	NP
20008	216	6
36366	248	NP
41430	246	NP
49956	245	NP
49979	245	NP
49980	245	NP
49981	245	NP
49999	245	NP
5000-8	170	209
5001-3	159	133
5001-6	152	90
5002-1	150	76
5002-4	171	218
5003-2	151	86
5003-9	154	106
5004-0	171	214
5004-7	146	48
5005-4	168	196
5005-9	157	122
5006-2	166	181
5006-7	164	168
5007-0	171	219
5007-5	169	202
5008-3	153	95
5008-8	158	125
5009-1	150	78
5009-6	168	198
5010-5	163	162
5011-2	154	103
5012-0	150	79
5012-1	147	54
5013-0	166	185
5013-8	142	22
5014-6	159	134
5015-3	166	180
5015-6	141	14
5016-1	166	182
5017-2	165	179
5018-0	191	152
5019-9		
Car	169	203
Church	143	28
5020-2	143	30
5021-0	142	25
5022-9	161	151

	Pg.	Pic.
5023-7	170	207
5024-5		
Bank	140	12
House	146	52
5025-3	151	81
5026-1	172	221
5027-0	168	193
5028-8	151	84
5029-6	161	148
5030-0	156	116
5031-8	174	236
5032-6	149	70
5033-4	148	64
5034-2	145	45
5035-0	170	212
5036-9	169	205
5037-7	159	137
5038-5	189	135
5039-3	161	147
5040-7	186	105
5041-5	173	232
5042-3	171	215
5043-1	139	3
5044-0	172	223
5045-8	169	204
5046-6	174	238
5047-4	162	153
5048-2	144	38
5049-0	168	194
5050-0	207	5
5050-4	147	60
5051-2	147	55
5051-8	207	4
5052-0	163	161
5052-6	216	1
5053-4	216	2
5053-9	190	139
5054-2	171	217
5054-7	155	112
5055-5	176	8
5055-9	156	113
5056-3	191	149
5056-7	142	21
5057-1	180	49
5057-5	157	120
5058-3	146	49
5059-1	168	199
5059-8	189	132
5060-1	156	117
5060-9	164	171
5061-7	171	213
5062-5	158	129
5062-8	167	190

Item	Pg.	Pic.
5063-3	158	130
5063-6	153	98
5064-1	176	16
5065-2	141	15
5065-8	150	80
5066-0	160	144
5066-6	139	4
5067-4	143	27
5067-9	162	157
5068-2	169	200
5068-7	164	169
5069-0	177	21
5070-9		
Church	140	7
House	145	44
5071-7		
Church	170	208
House	142	26
5072-5	174	237
5073-3		
Cottage	148	63
Shop	170	210
5074-1	141	13
5076-8		
Apoth.	140	9
Store	145	47
5077-6		
1981	140	10
1986	140	11
5078-4		
Church	148	62
Diner	147	57
5079-2	177	22
5080-6	156	114
5081-4		
Barn	163	158
House	150	77
5082-2		
School	155	110
Shop	150	75
5083-0	160	138
5084-9	143	33
5085-6	170	211
5089-0	148	65
5091-1	149	71
5092-0	167	186
5094-6	184	90
5095-4	182	67
5096-2	190	138
5097-0	144	37
51004	245	NP
5102-0	175	1
5103-9	187	119
5104-7	177	24
5105-5	177	18
5106-3	192	162
5107-1	178	29
5108-0	181	61
5113-6	191	148
5114-4	155	111
5116-0	185	100
5117-9	183	74
5118-7	189	134
5119-5	145	43
5120-9	160	140
5121-7	158	126
5122-5	173	229
5123-3	144	40
5124-1	145	46
5125-0	165	177
5126-8	154	102
5127-6	163	159
5128-4	165	174
5129-2	175	6
5130-6	197	203
5131-4	179	44
5132-2	181	55
5133-0	196	197
5134-9	185	92
5135-7	186	109
5136-5	197	204
5137-3	189	133
5138-1	193	169
5139-0	193	174
5140-3	169	201
5141-1	161	145
5142-0	161	146
5143-8	147	58
5144-6	146	50
5145-4	173	231
5146-2	195	185
5147-0	177	25
5148-9	191	153
5149-7	155	108
5150-0	161	150
5151-9	139	1
5152-7	159	131
5153-5	158	124
5154-3	173	227
5155-1	167	192
5156-0	162	154
5157-8	162	156
5158-6	179	45
5159-4	190	145
5160-8	190	144
5161-6	183	80
5162-4	184	85
5163-2	182	63
5164-0	193	168
5165-9	184	86
5166-7	181	62
5167-5	192	160
5168-3	185	94
5169-1	176	13
5170-5	190	141
5171-3	179	43
5172-1	192	164
5173-0	192	158
5174-8	176	14
5176-4	192	159
5177-2	181	60
5178-0	187	112
5179-9	185	98
5180-2	194	182
5192-6	195	190
5197-7	191	154
5198-5	185	99
52000	245	NP
52019	245	NP
52027	245	NP
52035	245	NP
5208-6	246	NP
52108	246	NP
52116	246	NP
5214-0	112	36
52159	247	NP
52175	247	NP
5218-3	89	41
5219-1	89	42
52230	248	NP
52248	248	NP
52256	248	NP
5226-4	246	NP
5227-2	246	NP
5228-0	246	NP
52298	116	15
5229-9		
HV	88	33
SV	194	179
52302	247	NP
52337	247	NP
52361	248	NP
52370	248	NP
52388	248	NP
52396	248	NP
5240-0		
HV	89	45
SV	195	192
52434	245	NP
5247-7		
HV	88	32
SV	194	178
5251-5	89	43
52523	245	NP
52531	245	NP
5257-4	246	NP
52582	246	NP
52590	246	NP
52591	247	NP
52593		
HV	90	47
SV	196	193
52595	246	NP
52596	246	NP
52598	245	NP
52600	246	NP
52601	246	NP
52602	246	NP
52610	246	NP
52611	248	NP
52612	245	NP
52613	245	NP
52614	245	NP
52615	245	NP
52618	246	NP
52620	246	NP
52621	115	3
52622	245	NP
52623	245	NP
52627	247	NP
52629	247	NP
52630	245	NP
52631	245	NP
52632	245	NP
52633	246	NP
52634	246	NP
52635	246	NP
52636	245	NP
52637	245	NP
52639	248	NP
52640	247	NP
52641		
HV	88	34
SV	194	180
52642		
HV	88	31
SV	194	177
52643	246	NP
52644		
HV	90	48
SV	196	195
52645		
HV	88	35
SV	194	181

	Pg.	Pic.		Pg.	Pic.		Pg.	Pic.		Pg.	Pic.
52646	247	NP	52711			52800	247	NP	53367	245	NP
52647	247	NP	*HV*	87	30	52802	247	NP	53400	212	37
52648	247	NP	*SV*	194	175	52803	247	NP	53401	211	31
52649	247	NP	52712	246	NP	52811	246	NP	53402	211	33
52650	247	NP	52713	247	NP	52813	247	NP	53403	213	43
52651	246	NP	52714	245	NP	52814	246	NP	53404	212	39
52652	246	NP	52715	247	NP	52816	247	NP	53405	212	35
52653	246	NP	52717	246	NP	52818	245	NP	53410	217	16
52654	246	NP	52718	246	NP	52819	245	NP	53411	212	40
52655	245	NP	52719	247	NP	52820	245	NP	53412	212	41
52656	247	NP	52720	247	NP	52822	248	NP	53413	213	44
52657	245	NP	52722	246	NP	52823	245	NP	53414	213	45
52658	247	NP	52723	246	NP	52824	245	NP	53415	217	19
52659	247	NP	52724	247	NP	52825	247	NP	53416	217	17
52660	246	NP	52725	247	NP	52826	246	NP	53417	219	31
52661	246	NP	52727	247	NP	52827	247	NP	53418	218	27
52662	246	NP	52728	248	NP	52828	247	NP	53419	218	28
52663	246	NP	52729	246	NP	52829	247	NP	53420	219	32
52664	245	NP	52731			52830	247	NP	53421	219	34
52665	246	NP	*HV*	84	1	52831	248	NP	53422	219	35
52666	246	NP	*SV*	176	12	52834	247	NP	53423	219	30
52667	246	NP	52732	117	25	52835	248	NP	53425	219	38
52668	247	NP	52733			52836	176	10	53426	219	39
52669	246	NP	*HV*	86	22	52837	245	NP	53427	220	41
52670	248	NP	*SV*	190	143	52839	247	NP	53428	247	NP
52671	248	NP	52738	247	NP	52840	247	NP	53429	247	NP
52672	248	NP	52739	246	NP	52841	245	NP	53433	247	NP
52673	248	NP	52740	246	NP	52842	245	NP	53436	246	NP
52674	248	NP	52742	246	NP	52843	245	NP	5350-3	81	2
52675	248	NP	52743	246	NP	52844	245	NP	5351-1		
52678	247	NP	52744	246	NP	52845	248	NP	*Set/2*	81	3
52679	247	NP	52746	245	NP				*Antiques I*	81	3a
52680	247	NP	52747	247	NP	53300	212	36	*Antiques II*	81	3b
52681	247	NP	52748	245	NP	53301	211	30	5352-0	81	1
52682	246	NP	52751	246	NP	53302	211	32	53521	82	4
52683	247	NP	52752	246	NP	53303	212	42	53522	82	5
52684	248	NP	52753	246	NP	53304	212	38	5353-8	119	3
52685	246	NP	52754	246	NP	53305	211	34	53539	119	1
52686	247	NP	52755	246	NP	53307	218	21	5354-6	119	2
52687	246	NP	52756	246	NP	53308	218	22	5355-4	119	4
52689	246	NP	52760	247	NP	53309	218	20			
52691	246	NP	52765	247	NP	53311	218	23			
52700	248	NP	52766	247	NP	53313	218	26	5400-3	160	141
52701	247	NP	52767	247	NP	53314	218	29	5401-1	154	104
52702	245	NP	52768	246	NP	53317	218	24	5402-0	172	222
52703	246	NP	52769	247	NP	53319	219	36	5403-8	167	191
52704	246	NP	52770	245	NP	53320	219	33	5404-6	151	85
52705	246	NP	52771	245	NP	53322	219	37	5405-4	149	69
52706	247	NP	52772	246	NP	53323	220	40	5406-2	155	109
52707	248	NP	52775	250	NP	53324	220	42	5407-0	147	59
52708	248	NP	52776	248	NP	53326	218	25	5408-9	197	205
52710			52779	248	NP	53327	217	18	5409-7	196	201
HV	88	36	52780	194	176	53347	246	NP	5410-0	179	38
SV	195	183	52791	87	25	53362	246	NP	5411-9	179	39

Numerical Index

	Pg.	Pic.		Pg.	Pic.		Pg.	Pic.		Pg.	Pic.
5412-7	195	187	5469-0	145	41	54893	184	82	54952	195	184
5413-5	178	28	5470-4	158	127	54894	186	103	54953	181	56
5414-3	191	151	5471-2	192	161	54895	192	163	54954	182	65
5415-1	179	42	5472-0	187	114	54896	177	19	54955	180	52
5418-6	195	186	5473-9	180	53	54897	183	76	54956	177	20
5420-8	152	88	5474-7	186	107	54898	182	71	54957	178	33
5421-6	164	170	5475-5	190	142	54899	188	127	54958	189	129
5422-4	172	225	5476-3	182	68	54900	182	70	54959	195	191
5423-2	140	6	5477-1	188	125	54901	182	72	54970	188	121
5424-0	151	83	5478-0	186	101	54902	160	143	54971	187	113
5425-9	162	155	5479-8	179	37	54903	160	142	54972	179	41
5426-7	152	93	54800	208	9	54904	159	136	54973	179	40
5427-5	173	230	5480-1	179	36	54905	196	200	54974	193	173
5428-3	196	194	5481-0	178	35	54910	144	34	54975	183	73
5429-1	195	189	5483-6	144	35	54911	155	107	54976	175	5
5430-5	186	108	5484-4	145	42	54912	148	66	54977	139	2
5431-3	180	47	54850	166	184	54913	153	96	54978	144	39
5432-1	178	31	54851	162	152	54914	158	128	54979	154	101
5433-0	188	123	5485-2	161	149	54915	152	87	54982	188	120
5434-8	183	77	54853	172	224	54916	163	165	54983	185	97
5435-6	196	199	54854	153	99	54917	156	118			
5436-4	197	202	54855	164	167	54918	142	20	55000	248	NP
5437-2	146	51	54856	148	61	54920	188	128	55001	143	32
5438-0	173	228	54857	141	16	54921	184	83	55002	172	220
5439-9	139	5	54858	141	19	54922	178	30	55003	153	100
5440-2	191	155	54859	168	195	54923	185	96	55004	152	89
5441-0	159	135	54860	182	64	54924	185	93	55006	168	206
5442-9	159	132	54861	187	118	54925	186	102	55008	165	175
5443-7	172	226	54862	188	126	54926	185	91	55009	143	29
5444-5	174	235	54863	177	26	54927	183	75	55010	174	238
5445-3	154	105	54864	181	57	54928	180	48	55011	157	121
5446-1	146	53	54865	189	137	54929	175	7	55012	156	115
5447-0	147	56	54866	187	117	54930	183	81	55013	184	88
5448-8	167	188	54867	182	69	54931	180	51	55014	196	198
5449-6	188	124	54868	191	146	54932	163	163	55015	189	130
5450-0	178	27	54869	191	147	54933	142	24	55016	193	167
5451-8	177	23	54870	192	157	54934	167	189	55017	185	95
5452-6	193	166	54871	160	139	54935	153	94	55018	246	NP
5453-4	187	116	54872	166	183	54936	181	59	55019	176	11
5454-2	187	115	54873	141	18	54937	193	171	55020	180	54
5455-0	183	78	54874	163	160	54938	176	15	55021	189	136
54569	247	NP	54875	188	122	54939	193	172	55022	184	84
5457-7	178	34	54879	184	89	54940	143	31	55023	181	58
5458-5	192	156	54880	163	164	54941	171	216	55024	175	4
5459-3	195	188	54881	144	36	54942	149	72	55025	189	131
5460-7	149	74	54882	141	17	54943	168	197	55026	247	NP
5461-5	149	73	54883	164	166	54944	153	97	55030	184	87
5462-3	167	188	54884	165	176	54945	140	8	55031	187	111
5463-1	177	17	54885	164	172	54946	148	67	55032	180	46
5464-0	174	234	54886	152	92	54947	157	119	55033		
5465-8	149	68	54887	157	123	54948	152	91	*HV*	85	9
5466-6	142	23	54890	193	170	54949	165	173	*SV*	180	50
5467-4	165	178	54891	186	110	54950	175	2	55035	182	66
5468-2	151	82	54892	186	106	54951	175	3	55036	176	9

	Pg.	Pic.		Pg.	Pic.		Pg.	Pic.		Pg.	Pic.
55042	248	NP	5561-1	96	52	56173	62	7	5637-5	118	38
55115	246	NP	5562-0	41	77	56174	62	6	5638-3	80	43
5513-1	87	26	5563-8	84	5	56175	108	9	56384	74	8
5516-6	109	6	5564-6	114	47	56176	62	8	56385	80	44
5517-4	112	35	5565-4	87	27	56177	62	11	56386	79	36
5523-9	86	20	5566-2	87	28	56178	63	15	56387	74	11
5530-1	85	10	5567-0	26	8	56180	108	13	56388	77	28
5531-0	71	44	5568-9	37	56	56182	107	1	56389	78	33
55311	71	44b	55690	37	56b	56183	108	10	56390	79	40
55312	71	44c	55691	37	56a	5618-9	60	2	56391	78	32
55313	71	44a	5569-7	100	87	56190	60	2b	56392	75	14
5532-8	111	24	5570-0	91	12	56191	60	2a	56393	73	2
5533-6	114	51	5571-9	96	53	56192	63	17	56394	74	12
5534-4	68	22	5572-7	89	44	5619-7	107	5	56395	75	18
5535-2	110	9	5573-5	95	47	5620-0	75	19	56396	75	13
5536-0	70	38	5574-3	48	99	56201	107	7	56397	78	34
5537-9	72	50	5575-1	100	93	56202	108	17	56398	74	10
5538-7	69	32	5577-8	96	56	56203	108	12	56400	73	4
5539-5	114	48	5578-6	98	74	56210	62	9	56401	80	42
5540-9	113	42	5579-4	93	32	56211	63	16	56402	74	6
5542-5	64	4	5580-8	101	97	56212	108	15	56403	78	30
5543-3	64	5	5581-6	96	54	56213	108	14	56404	78	31
5544-1	67	19	5582-4	37	59	56214	107	8	5640-5	54	27
5545-0	109	2	5583-2	30	24	56215	107	4	56407	79	37
5546-8	111	27	5584-0	47	96	5621-9			56408	75	16
5547-6	110	18	5585-9	46	88	*Set/2*	77	24	5641-3	104	28
5548-4	110	10	5586-7	35	46	*Orly's*	77	24a	5642-1	51	7
5549-2	66	12	5587-5	34	40	*Rimpy's*	77	24b	5643-0	59	49
55500	209	15	5588-3	93	23	5622-7	79	41	56431	119	45
55501	85	16	5589-1	93	24	5623-5	78	29	56434	115	7
55502	87	24				5624-3	77	26	56435	115	9
5550-6			56000	209	16	5625-1	74	7	56436	117	32
Set/3	30	28	5600-6	79	39	5626-0	76	21	56437	116	20
Peggotty	31	28c	5601-4	76	20	5627-8	76	23	56438	115	8
Trotwood	30	28a	56015	76	20b	5628-6	79	38	56439	116	13
Wickfield	30	28b	56016	76	20a	5629-4	78	35	56442	118	40
55510	209	19	5602-2	118	42	5630-8	119	46	56443	116	19
5551-4	94	33	5603-0	114	1	5631-6	118	35	56444	117	31
55515	84	8	5604-9	117	24	5632-4	117	28	56445	247	NP
5552-2	34	39	5605-7	118	41	5633-2	74	9	56446	246	NP
55523	85	11	5607-3	108	11	5634-0	73	1	56447	247	NP
55524	89	40	5608-1	119	43	5635-9	76	22	5644-8	58	43
55525	247	NP	5609-0	118	33	56363	117	30	5645-6	103	19
5553-0			56100	85	13	56364	115	5	5646-4	106	42
Set/2	42	81	5610-3	118	34	56365	116	22	5647-2	50	6
Brownlow	42	81a	5611-1	118	37	56366	114	2	5648-0	49	1
Maylie	42	81b	5612-0	63	18	56368	117	27	56481	49	1b
5554-9	97	65	5613-8	107	6	56369	116	14	56482	49	1a
5555-7	25	3	5614-6	62	5	56370	116	17	5649-9	104	21
5556-5	86	17	5615-4	61	4	56371	116	21	5650-2	102	4
5557-3	40	70	5616-2	108	16	56372	115	11	5651-0	50	4
5558-1	91	7	5617-0	63	14	56373	115	10	5652-9	51	10
5559-0	98	71	56171	63	13	56374	119	44	5653-7	56	33
5560-3	93	31	56172	50	3				5654-5	105	34

Numerical Index

	Pg.	Pic.		Pg.	Pic.		Pg.	Pic.		Pg.	Pic.
5655-3	105	33	56640	247	NP	5815-7	92	17	58341	26	7
5656-1	87	29	56700	73	5	5816-5	92	14	58344	40	71
56568	51	9a	56701	77	27	5817-3	101	98	58345	40	69
56569	51	9b	56702	75	17	5818-1	91	10	58346	42	80
5657-0	51	9	56703	73	3	5819-0	91	6	58347	39	67
56571	52	13	56704	77	25	5820-3	84	7	58348	45	86
56572	59	48	56705	75	15	5821-1	48	100	5835-1	98	67
56573	56	32	56706	116	18	5822-0	34	42	58352	28	18
56574	53	22	56707	115	12	5823-8	35	47	58353	33	36
56575	54	29	56708	118	39	5824-6	44	84	5836-0	100	90
56576	51	8	56709	115	4	58247	45	84c	58378	99	86
56577	59	46	56710	118	36	58248	44	84b	58379	95	48
56578	53	16	56711	115	6	58249	44	84a	58381	95	46
56579	58	41	56712	117	26	5825-4	101	99	58382	99	79
56580	57	36	56713	117	29	5826-2	92	20	58383	98	75
56581	53	17	56714	116	16	5827-0	92	15	58384	94	37
56587	105	38	56715	245	NP	5828-9	98	69	58385	97	63
56588	103	14	56716	247	NP	5829-7	99	85	58386	99	82
56589	104	24	56717	247	NP	5830-0	98	68	58387	100	89
56590	104	25	56720	247	NP	58301	38	64	58390	91	8
56591	103	18	56721	245	NP	58302	34	38	58391	99	81
56592	103	17	56722	245	NP	58303	38	60	58392	92	19
56593	105	32	56723	245	NP	58304	30	26	58393	101	100
56594	102	6	56724	245	NP	58305	25	4	58394	93	30
56595	102	9				58306	208	8	58395	99	84
56596	102	5	57501	121	4	58307	47	97	58396	91	13
56597	102	8	57502	121	5	58308	46	89	58397	101	101
56598	102	7	57505	121	9	58309	36	55	58400	95	43
56599	106	41	57506	121	8	58310	35	45	58401	98	73
56601	53	18	5750-9	30	27	58311	47	94	58402	96	49
56602	54	28	5751-7	44	83	58313	35	48	58403	93	27
56604	52	15	5752-5	31	29	58314	47	95	58404	93	28
56605	53	20	5753-3	46	90	58315	38	62	58405	90	3
56606	54	26	57534	34	43	58316	41	74	58406	95	45
56610	53	19	57535	34	41	5831-9	93	26	58407	95	41
56611	59	45				58322	33	34	58408	93	29
56612	53	21	5800-9	35	49	58323	36	53	58410	96	51
56613	57	34	5801-7	37	57	58324	26	6	58411	99	78
56614	57	35	5802-5	97	64	58326	94	34	58413	94	38
56615	105	35	5803-3	90	4	5832-7	47	93	58414	100	92
56616	103	12	5804-1	100	94	58328	36	52	58415	92	21
56617	105	37	58050	94	39	58329	33	37	58416	99	83
56619	106	47	5806-8	84	6	58330	26	9	58417	90	2
56620	104	26	5807-6	84	4	58331	48	102	58420	96	50
56621	104	22	5808-4	45	85	58332	48	102c	58430	121	1
56622	103	11	58085	45	85a	58333	48	102a	58431	121	6
56623	104	29	58086	45	85b	58334	48	102b	58432	121	3
56630	104	23	58087	45	85c	5833-5	38	63	58433	121	7
56631	106	43	5809-2	27	11	58336	46	87	58434	121	2
56633	103	16	5810-6	27	12	58337	27	15	58440	38	65
56635	106	45	5811-4	37	58	58338	27	14	58441	25	1
56637	103	15	5812-2	35	44	58339	28	21	58442	25	2
56638	102	3	5813-0	92	18	5834-3	33	35	58443	42	78
56639	103	20	5814-9	92	16	58340	35	50	58444	39	66
									58445	46	92

	Pg.	Pic.		Pg.	Pic.		Pg.	Pic.		Pg.	Pic.
58446	38	61	58894	111	22	5926-9			5970-6	68	25
58447	28	20	58895	111	26	Set/5	39	68	5971-4	111	19
58448	46	91	58896	112	29	Bakery	40	68e	5972-2	71	46
58449	48	101	58897	112	32	Fish	39	68b	5973-0	70	40
58453	42	79	58898	113	45	Poulterer	39	68c	5974-9	67	20
58454	98	72	58899	112	34	Tailors	40	68d	5975-7	83	3
58455	97	61	58900	109	5	Watch	39	68a	59759	120	2
58456	96	55	58901	110	11	5927-7	36	51	5977-3	64	2
58457	97	60	58902	114	49	5928-5	95	42	5978-1	64	3
58458	97	59	58903	111	21	5929-3	97	62	5979-0	110	12
58460	100	91	58906	109	1	5930-7	52	14	59791	120	1
58461	100	88	58907	113	41	5931-5	59	47	59792	120	5
58462	95	44	58909	109	7	5932-3	56	31	59793	120	4
58464	91	9	58910	110	16	5934-0	91	5	59794	120	3
58465	97	58	58939	208	11	5938-2	86	23	59795	83	2
58466	249	NP	58940	69	34	5939-0			59796	83	4
58467	90	1	58941	70	37	Set/3	52	12	59797	83	1
58500	47	98	58943	72	47	Barber	52	12b	5980-3	88	37
58501	41	76	58945	71	43	Butcher	52	12c	5981-1	90	46
5864-5	96	57	58947	70	36	Toys	52	12a	5982-0	85	15
5865-3			58948	72	49	5940-4	50	2	5983-8	110	17
U.S.	89	39	58950	64	1	5941-2	106	44	59846	246	NP
Canadian	217	11	58951	67	18	5942-0	50	5	5985-4	113	44
5866-1	84	2	58952	69	34	5943-9	54	25	5986-2	106	46
5880-7	72	48	58953	69	33	5944-7	54	24	5987-0	105	36
58808	72	48a	58954	67	17	5945-5	103	13	59960	247	NP
58809	72	48b	58955	109	8	5946-3	57	37	5997-8	88	41
5881-5	65	7	58956	114	50	5947-1	51	11	59994	245	NP
5882-3	67	21	58957	111	28	5948-0	102	2			
5883-1	68	25	58958	111	25	5949-8	101	1	6459-9	186	104
5884-0	110	13	58959	113	39	5950-1	99	77	6500-5		
5885-8	112	30	58960	109	3	5951-0	97	66	Set/3	28	22
5886-6	112	31				5952-8	63	12	Cottage	29	22a
58870	68	23	59000	86	18	5953-6	62	10	Fezziwig's	29	22b
58871	70	41	59001	245	NP	5954-4			Scrooge	29	22c
5887-4	69	29	5900-5			Set/3	57	38	6501-3	93	25
58875	69	28	Set/2	25	5	Cottage	57	38a	6502-1	41	73
58876	65	6	Barn	26	5a	Manor	58	38c	6507-2		
58877	65	8	House	26	5b	School	57	38b	Set/3	32	31
58878	65	8a	5901-3	94	40	5955-2	58	39	Coffee	32	31b
58879	65	8b	5902-1	30	25	5956-0	105	39	Pub	32	31c
58880	72	46	5903-0	92	22	5957-9	113	38	Toy	32	31a
58881	68	22	5904-8	28	16	5958-7	113	40	6508-0	27	10
58882	65	9	5905-6	41	75	5959-5	113	43	6510-2	85	14
58883	67	15	5916-1	36	54	5960-9	110	15	6511-0	106	40
58884	68	26	5924-2			5961-7	71	42	6512-9		
58885	113	46	Set/3	29	23	5962-5	66	11	Set/3	66	14
58886	69	30	Booter	29	23a	5963-3	70	36	Bakery	66	14a
58887	65	10	T. Wells	29	23b	5964-1	109	4	Tower	66	14b
58888	70	40	Wool	29	23c	5965-0	111	20	Toy Shop	66	14c
58890	114	52	5925-0			5966-8	98	76			
58891	112	37	Set/2	40	72	5967-6	111	23			
58892	110	14	Cottage	40	72a	5968-4	66	13			
58893	112	33	School	41	72b	5969-2	67	16			

	Pg.	Pic.		Pg.	Pic.		Pg.	Pic.
6515-3			8183-3	190	140	99247	247	NP
Set/7	43	82				99278	247	NP
Baker	43	82e	98630	198	5	99279	247	NP
Butcher	43	82a	98631	198	9	99280	247	NP
Candle	43	82c	98632	197	1	99333	247	NP
Grocer	44	82f	98635	197	4	9948-1	191	150
Inn	43	82d	98637	198	7	9953-8	85	12
Jones	44	82g	98642	198	6			
Smithy	43	82b	98643	198	10			
6516-1	33	32	98644	197	2			
6518-8			98645	198	11			
Set/3	31	30	98646	198	8			
Stone	31	30a	98648	197	3			
Thatched	31	30b	9870-1	123	13			
Tudor	32	30c	9871-0	98	70			
6519-6	33	33	98711	84	3			
6526-9	91	11	9872-8	122	3			
6527-7	100	95	98729	122	9			
6528-5	28	17	98730	122	2			
6530-7			98731	123	12			
Set/7	55	30	98732	122	8			
Apothecary	55	30a	98733	122	6			
Church	56	30g	98734	124	27			
Fabrics	56	30e	98737	122	4			
School	56	30f	98738	123	10			
Stable	55	30d	98739	123	16			
Store	55	30c	98740	124	22			
Town Hall	55	30b	98741	124	20			
6531-5	102	10	98742	125	30			
6532-3	105	31	98745	122	1			
6537-4	86	19	98756	123	15			
6538-2	54	23	98757	123	18			
6539-0	58	42	98758	124	25			
6540-4	61	3	98759	123	19			
65405	61	3b	98762	124	29			
65406	61	3d	98763	124	26			
65407	61	3a	98766	122	7			
65408	61	3c	98767	122	5			
65409	61	3e	98768	123	11			
6541-2	60	1	98769	123	17			
6542-0	107	3	98770	124	23			
6543-9	58	40	98771	124	21			
6544-7	58	44	98772	125	32			
6545-5	86	21	98773	125	31			
6546-3	99	80	98774	208	10			
6547-1	101	96	98775	217	10			
6549-8	27	13	98780	123	14			
6568-4	28	19	98781	124	28			
6569-2	94	35	98782	124	24			
6570-6	105	30	99028	248	NP			
6571-4	107	2	99244	247	NP			
6589-7	104	27	99245	248	NP			
6590-0	94	36	99246	248	NP			

Alphabetical Index

– Key –

All village pieces are listed below in alphabetical order. The first number refers to the piece's location within the Value Guide section and the second to the box in which it is pictured. Items that are not pictured are listed as "NP."

	Pg.	Pic.
3 Men In A Tub Stackable Teapot And Cup	220	44
3 Nuns With Songbooks	175	1
4th Of July Parade	218	24
5¢ Pony Rides	70	41
5th Avenue Salon	64	1
6-Socket Light Set	247	NP
12 Days of Dickens' Village Sign, The	90	1
20-Socket Light Set	247	NP
45 LED Light Strand	247	NP
56 Flavors Ice Cream Parlor	139	1
1919 Ford® Model-T	109	1
1955 Ford® Automobiles	175	2
1964½ Ford® Mustang	175	3
2000 Holly Lane	139	2
2101 Maple	139	3
5607 Park Avenue Townhouse	64	2
5609 Park Avenue Townhouse	64	3
. . . Another Man's Treasure Accessories	175	5
. . . Another Man's Treasure Garage	140	8
A. Bieler Farm	49	1
Abbey (see Brick Abbey)		
Abel Beesley Butcher	43	82a
AC/DC Adapter	247	NP
Acrylic Icicles	246	NP
Ada's Bed And Boarding House	50	2
Adirondack Chairs	246	NP
Adobe House	139	4
Afternoon Picnic, An	219	32
Afternoon Sleigh Ride	219	37
Airport	140	6
Al's TV Shop	140	7
Aldeburgh Music Box Shop (#58441)	25	1
Aldeburgh Music Box Shop (#58442)	25	2
Ale Mates	90	2
All Around The Town	109	2
All In Together Girls	109	3
All Saints Church	140	7
All Saints Corner Church	64	4
"Alpen Horn Player" Alpine Village Sign	107	1
Alpine Church	60	1
Alpine Shops	60	2
Alpine Village	61	3
Alpine Village Sign	107	2
Alpine Villagers (#6542-0)	107	3
Alpine Villagers (#56215)	107	4
Amish Buggy	101	1
Amish Family	102	2

	Pg.	Pic.
Angels In The Snow	175	4
Anne Shaw Toys	52	12a
Antique Shop (see Cobblestone Antique Shop)		
Apothecary	140	9
Apothecary Shop	55	30a
Apotheke	61	3a
Apple Girl/Newspaper Boy	175	6
Apple Valley School	50	3
Arlington Falls Church	50	4
Arriving At The Station	217	17
Artist's Touch, An	102	3
Arts Academy	64	5
Ashbury Inn	25	3
Ashley Pond Skating Party	90	3
Ashwick Lane Hose & Ladder	25	4
Aspen Trees	216	1
At The Barn Dance, It's Allemande Left	175	7
Auto With Tree	176	8
Automobiles	109	4
Autumn Birch/Maple Tree	245	NP
Bachman Greenhouse	207	6
Bachman's Flower Shop	208	7
Bachman's Wilcox Truck	216	3
Back From The Orchard	219	33
Backwoods Outhouse	176	9
Backyard Patio, The	176	10
Bah Humbug	121	1
Bahnhof	61	4
Baker Elves	114	1
Bakery & Chocolate Shop	62	5
Bakery (#6512-9)	66	14a
Bakery (#5077-6, 1981)	140	10
Bakery (#5077-6, 1986)	140	11
Balloon Seller	119	1
Bank	140	12
Bare Branch Tree w/25 Lights	245	NP
Bare Branch Trees	245	NP
Barley Bree	25	5
Barmby Moor Cottage	26	6
Barn (#5074-1)	141	13
Barn (#5900-5)	26	5a
Bay Street Shops (#53301)	211	30
Bay Street Shops (#53401)	211	31
Bayport	141	14
Beacon Hill House	141	15
Beacon Hill Victorian	141	16
Bean And Son Smithy Shop	43	82b
Beard Barber Shop	73	1
Bears In The Birch	246	NP
Beekman House	65	8a
Before The Big Game	176	11
Ben's Barbershop	52	12b
Berkshire House	50	5
Bernhardiner Hundchen	62	6
Besson Bierkeller	61	3b
Betsy Trotwood's Cottage	30	28a
Bicycle Built For Two, A	219	34
Big Ben	26	7
Big Smile For The Camera	109	5
Bill's Service Station (see Service Station)		
Biplane Up In The Sky (HV)	84	1

	Pg.	Pic.
Biplane Up In The Sky (SV)	176	12
Birch Run Ski Chalet	141	17
Birch Tree Cluster	245	NP
Bird Seller, The	90	4
Bishops Oast House	26	8
Blacksmith	91	5
Blanket of New Fallen Snow	245	NP
Blenham Street Bank	26	9
Blue Skies Backdrop	246	NP
Blue Star Ice Co.	50	6
Blue Star Ice Harvesters	102	4
Bluebird Seed And Bulb	51	7
Blythe Pond Mill House	27	10
Boarding & Lodging School (#5809-2)	27	11
Boarding & Lodging School (#5810-6)	27	12
Bobwhite Cottage	51	8
Booter And Cobbler	29	23a
Boulder Springs House	141	18
Boulevard	109	6
Boulevard Lampposts	247	NP
Bowling Alley	141	19
Brandon Bungalow, The	142	20
Brewster Bay Cottages	51	9
Brick Abbey	27	13
Brick Road	246	NP
Brick Town Hall	55	30b
Brick Town Square	246	NP
Bridge Over The Icy Pond	247	NP
Brighton School	65	6
Brighton Train (see Village Train)		
Bringing Fleeces To The Mill	91	6
Bringing Home The Baby	109	7
Bringing Home The Tree	176	13
Bringing Home The Yule Log	91	7
Brixton Road Watchman	91	8
Brokerage House	65	7
Browning Cottage	44	84a
Brownlow House	42	81a
Brownstone	142	21
Brownstones On The Square	65	8
Bumpstead Nye Cloaks & Canes	45	85a
Busy City Sidewalks	109	8
"Busy Elf, A" North Pole Sign	114	2
Busy Railway Station	91	9
Busy Sidewalks	110	9
Butcher (see Abel Beesley Butcher)		
Butcher, Baker And Candlestick Maker, The	213	46
Butter Tub Barn	27	14
Butter Tub Farmhouse	27	15
Buying Bakers Bread	107	5
By The Pond (see Blythe Pond)		
C. Bradford, Wheelwright & Son	91	10
C. Fletcher Public House	28	16
C.H. Watt Physician	37	56a
Cafe Caprice French Restaurant	65	9
Calling All Cars	176	14
Camden Park Cobblestone Road	246	NP
Camden Park Fountain w/Pump	246	NP
Camden Park Square	246	NP
Camden Park Square Stone Wall	246	NP
Canadian Trading Co.	208	8
Candle Shop	43	82c
Candy Cane Bench	246	NP
Candy Cane Elves	79	40
Candy Cane Fence	245	NP
Candy Cane Lampposts	115	3
Candy Cane Lane	79	40
Candy Cane & Peppermint Shop	79	40
Canine Courier	115	4
Cape Cod	142	22
Cape Keag Fish Cannery	51	10
Capitol, The	65	10
Captain's Cottage (#5947-1)	51	11
Captain's Cottage (#98756)	123	15
Carmel Cottage	142	23
Carnival Carousel, The	142	24
Carnival Carousel LED Light Set w/Adapter	247	NP
Carnival Tickets & Cotton Candy	176	15
Carolers (#5064-1)	176	16
Carolers (#6526-9)	91	11
Carolers On The Doorstep	91	12
Caroling At The Farm	177	17
Caroling Elf	121	8
Caroling Family	177	18
Caroling Through The Snow	177	19
Caroling Thru The City	110	10
Caroling With The Cratchit Family	91	13
Carriage House (#5021-0)	142	25
Carriage House (#5071-7)	142	26
Carriage Ride For The Bride, A	110	11
Catch Of The Day, The	177	20
Cathedral, The	66	11
Cathedral Church (#5019-9)	143	28
Cathedral Church (#5067-4)	143	27
Cathedral Church Of St. Mark (#5549-2)	66	12
Cathedral Church Of St. Mark (#98759)	123	19
Cedar Point Cabin	143	29
Centennial House	143	30
Center For The Arts	143	31
Central Park Carriage	110	12
Ceramic Car	177	21
Ceramic Sleigh	177	22
Chadbury Station And Train	28	17
Chamber Orchestra	110	13
Champsfield Stadium®	143	32
Chancery Corner	28	18
Chapel On The Hill (#53302)	211	32
Chapel On The Hill (#53402)	211	33
Charting Santa's Course	115	5
Chateau	143	33
Check It Out Bookmobile	177	23
Check This Out	115	6
Chelsea Lane Shoppers	92	14
Chelsea Market Curiosities Monger & Cart	92	15
Chelsea Market Fish Monger & Cart	92	16
Chelsea Market Flower Monger & Cart	92	17
Chelsea Market Fruit Monger & Cart	92	18
Chelsea Market Hat Monger & Cart	92	19
Chelsea Market Mistletoe Monger & Cart	92	20
Cherry Lane Shops	52	12
Chesterton Manor House	28	19
Child's Play	92	21
Childe Pond & Skaters	92	22

	Pg.	Pic.
Children In Band	177	24
Chimney Sweep	121	2
China Trader, The	28	20
Chocolate Shoppe	66	13
Choir Kids	177	25
Choirboys All-In-A-Row	110	14
Chop Shop, The	48	102a
Chopping Firewood	177	26
Chowder House	52	13
Christmas Apples	46	89
Christmas At The Farm	178	27
Christmas At The Park	84	2
Christmas Barn Dance	144	34
Christmas Bazaar . . . Flapjacks & Hot Cider	102	5
Christmas Bazaar . . . Handmade Quilts	102	6
Christmas Bazaar . . . Sign	102	7
Christmas Bazaar . . . Toy Vendor & Cart	102	8
Christmas Bazaar . . . Woolens & Preserves	102	9
Christmas Bells	84	3
Christmas Bread Bakers	73	2
Christmas Cadillac	177	28
Christmas Carol Christmas Morning Figures	93	23
Christmas Carol Christmas Spirits Figures	93	24
Christmas Carol Cottage	28	21
Christmas Carol Cottages (#6500-5)	28	22
Christmas Carol Cottages (#98745)	122	1
Christmas Carol Figures	93	25
Christmas Carol Holiday Trimming Set	93	26
"Christmas Carol, A" Reading By Charles Dickens (#58403)	93	27
"Christmas Carol, A" Reading By Charles Dickens (#58404)	93	28
Christmas Children	178	29
Christmas Cove Lighthouse	144	35
Christmas Eave Trim	246	NP
Christmas Fun Run	115	7
Christmas In The City	66	14
Christmas In The City Sign	110	15
Christmas Kids	178	30
Christmas Lake High School	144	36
Christmas LED Luminaries	247	NP
Christmas Pudding Costermonger	93	29
Christmas Puppies	178	31
Christmas Shop, The	144	37
Christmas Trash Cans	178	32
Christmas Visit To The Florist	178	33
Church Of The Open Door	144	38
Churchyard Fence Extensions	84	4
Churchyard Fence Gate	84	5
Churchyard Gate And Fence	84	6
Cinderella	220	45
Cinderella Stackable Teapot And Cup	220	46
Cinema 56	144	39
City Ambulance, The	110	16
City Bus & Milk Truck	110	17
City Clockworks	71	44a
"City Fire Dept.," Fire Truck	110	18
City Globe, The	67	15
City Hall (#5969-2)	67	16
City Hall (#98741)	124	20
City Hall (#98771)	124	21
City Lights	209	20
City Newsstand	111	19
City People	111	20
City Police Car	111	21
City Taxi	111	22
City Workers	111	23
Clark Street Automat	67	17
Classic Cars	178	34
Clear Ice	246	NP
Climb Every Mountain	107	6
Cobb Cottage	44	84b
Cobbler & Clock Peddler	93	30
Cobblestone Antique Shop	144	40
Cobblestone Road	246	NP
Cobblestone Shops	29	23
Cobblestone Town Square	246	NP
Cobles Police Station	30	24
Coca Cola® Brand Bottling Plant	145	41
Coca-Cola® Brand Billboard	178	35
Coca-Cola® Brand Corner Drugstore	145	42
Coca-Cola® Brand Delivery Men	179	36
Coca-Cola® Brand Delivery Truck	179	37
Coffee House (see Thomas Kersey Coffee House)		
Cold Care Clinic	73	3
Cold Weather Sports	179	38
Collectors' Club House	208	9
Colonial Church	145	43
Colonial Farm House	145	44
Come Into The Inn	93	31
Come Join The Parade	179	39
Congregational Church	145	45
Constables	93	32
Consulate, The	67	18
Corner Cafe	145	46
Corner Store	145	47
Corner Wall Topiaries	46	87
Corral Fence	245	NP
Costumes For Sale	179	40
Cottage of Bob Cratchit & Tiny Tim, The (#6500-5)	29	22a
Cottage of Bob Cratchit & Tiny Tim, The (#98745)	122	1
Cottage Toy Shop	32	31a
Couldn't Wait Until Christmas	179	41
Counting House & Silas Thimbleton Barrister	30	25
Country Church	146	48
Country Harvest	179	42
Country Road Lamp Posts	246	NP
Countryside Church (#5051-8)	207	4
Countryside Church (#5058-3)	146	49
Courthouse	146	50
Covered Wooden Bridge	102	10
Crack The Whip	179	43
Craftsman Cottage	146	51
Craggy Cove Lighthouse (#5930-7)	52	14
Craggy Cove Lighthouse (#98739)	123	16
Craggy Cove Lighthouse (#98769)	123	17
Craggy Oak Tree	245	NP
Crooked Fence Cottage	30	26
Crown & Cricket Inn (#5750-9)	30	27
Crown & Cricket Inn (#98730)	122	2
Crowntree Inn	43	82d

	Pg.	Pic.
Cumberland House.	146	52
Custom House.	38	64
Custom Stitchers	73	4
Dairy Barn	146	53
Dairy Delivery Sleigh	103	11
Danube Music Publisher	62	7
Dash Away Delivery	115	8
Dashing Through The Snow	84	7
David Copperfield	30	28
David Copperfield Characters	94	33
Day At The Waterfront, A.	218	25
Day Of Holiday Shopping, A.	219	38
Deacon's Way Chapel.	52	15
Decorate The Tree	167	189
Decorated Sisal Trees	245	NP
Dedlock Arms (#5752-5).	31	29
Dedlock Arms (#9872-8).	122	3
Delivering Coal For The Hearth	94	34
Delivering Real Plastic Snow	115	9
Delivering The Christmas Greens	115	10
Delta House.	147	54
Depot & Train With Two Train Cars.	147	55
Dickens' Cottages	31	30
Dickens' Lane Shops.	32	31
Dickens' Sleighride (see Sleighride, #6511-0)		
Dickens' Village Church (#6516-1)	33	32
Dickens' Village Church (#98737)	122	4
Dickens' Village Church (#98767)	122	5
Dickens' Village Mill (#6519-6)	33	33
Dickens' Village Mill (#98733)	122	6
Dickens' Village Mill (#98766)	122	7
Dickens' Village Sign	94	35
Dickens' Village Start A Tradition Set.	33	34
Dinah's Drive-In	147	56
Diner	147	57
Disney Parks Family	119	2
Disneyland Fire Department #105.	81	1
Doctor's House	147	58
Doctor's House Call	103	12
Doctor's Office, The	67	19
Doghouse/Cat In Garbage Can.	179	44
Don't Break The Ornaments.	115	11
Don't Drop The Presents!	111	24
Dorothy's Dress Shop (#5974-9)	67	20
Dorothy's Dress Shop (#98740)	124	22
Dorothy's Dress Shop (#98770)	124	23
Dorothy's Skate Rental	84	8
Double Bungalow	147	59
Double Light Socket Adapter.	247	NP
Double Street Lamps.	247	NP
Dover Coach	94	36
Down The Chimney He Goes	179	45
Downhill Daredevils.	115	12
Downhill Elves	116	13
Dragon Parade, The	180	46
Dudden Cross Church	33	35
Dudley Docker	33	36
Duplex	147	60
Dursley Manor	33	37
Dutch Colonial	148	61
E. Staubr Backer	61	3c
Early Morning Delivery	180	47
Early Rising Elves	116	14
East Indies Trading Co.	34	38
East Willet Pottery.	53	16
Eight Maids-A-Milking.	94	37
Eleven Lords A-Leaping.	94	38
Elf Bunkhouse (#56016)	76	20a
Elf Bunkhouse (#98763)	124	26
Elf Mountain Ski Resort	73	5
Elf On A Sled	121	9
Elf Spa, The	74	6
Elf Tree House	246	NP
Elfie's Sleds & Skates	74	7
Elfin Forge & Assembly Shop	74	8
Elfin Snow Cone Works	74	9
Elsie's Gingerbread	74	10
Elves On Ice	116	15
Elves On Track	116	16
Elves' Trade School	74	11
Emily Louise, The	53	17
End Of The Line	116	17
English Church	148	62
English Cottage	148	63
English Post Box	94	39
English Tudor	148	64
Entrance	76	22
Everybody Goes Skating At Rollerama	180	48
Excellent Taste	111	25
Factory (see Snow Village Factory)		
Fagin's Hide-A-Way	34	39
Fallen Leaves	246	NP
Falstaff Inn (see Sir John Falstaff Inn)		
Family Mom/Kids, Goose/Girl.	180	49
Family Tree, The	111	26
Family Winter Outing (HV).	85	9
Family Winter Outing (SV).	180	50
Farm Accessory Set.	180	51
Farm Animals (#56588).	103	14
Farm Animals (#5945-5).	103	13
Farm House (#5089-0).	148	65
Farm House (#54912)	148	66
Farm People & Animals.	94	40
Farmer's Co-op Granary, The	148	67
Farmer's Flatbed	180	52
Farmer's Market	103	15
Farmhouse	26	5b
Father Christmas's Journey	95	41
Faversham Lamps & Oil.	47	93
Federal House	149	68
Federbetten Und Steppdecken.	62	8
Feeding The Birds	180	53
Fezziwig And Friends.	95	42
Fezziwig Delivery Wagon, The	95	43
Fezziwig's Warehouse (#6500-5)	29	22b
Fezziwig's Warehouse (#98745)	122	1
Fiber Optic Fireworks.	247	NP
Fieldstone Entry Gate.	246	NP
Fieldstone Footbridge.	247	NP
Fieldstone Stairway.	246	NP
Fieldstone Wall	246	NP
Fieldstone Wall With Apple Tree.	246	NP
Finding The Bird's Song.	180	54
Fine Asian Antiques.	95	44
Finklea's Finery: Costume Shop	149	69
Fire Brigade Of London Town, The	95	45
Fire Brigade, The	111	27
Fire Hydrant And Mailbox.	181	55
Fire Station.	149	70
Fire Station No. 2.	149	71

	Pg.	Pic.
Fire Station #3	149	72
Fireman To The Rescue	181	56
Firewood Delivery Truck	181	57
Fireworks Replacement Light Bulbs	247	NP
First Deposit	181	58
First House That ♥ Built, The	208	10
First Metropolitan Bank	67	21
First Round Of The Year	181	59
First Snow, The	219	39
Fisherman's Nook Bass Cabin	149	73
Fisherman's Nook Cabins	149	73
Fisherman's Nook Resort	149	74
Fisherman's Nook Trout Cabin	143	69
Fishing In The Bay	218	26
Five Golden Rings	95	46
Flag Pole	181	60
Flat Of Ebenezer Scrooge, The	34	40
Flexible Autumn Hedges	246	NP
Flexible Sisal Hedge	246	NP
Flexible Sisal Hedge, Lg.	246	NP
Flocked Pine Trees	245	NP
Flower Shop	150	75
Fly-casting In The Brook	103	16
Flying Scot Train, The	95	47
For Sale Sign (#5108-0)	181	61
For Sale Sign (#5166-7)	181	62
Four Calling Birds	95	48
Foxes In The Forest	246	NP
Franklin Hook & Ladder Co.	53	18
Fresh Fallen Snow (#49979)	245	NP
Fresh Fallen Snow (#49980)	245	NP
Fresh Flowers For Sale	111	28
Fresh Frozen Fish	182	63
"Fresh Paint" New England Village Sign	103	17
Frogmore Chemist	38	64
Frosted Spruce	245	NP
Frosted Topiary (#52000)	245	NP
Frosted Topiary (#52019)	245	NP
Frosted Topiary (#52027)	245	NP
Frosted Topiary (#52035)	245	NP
Frosty Light Sprays	246	NP
Frosty Playtime	182	64
Fruit & Spice (see T. Wells Fruit & Spice Shop)		
Fun At The Firehouse	182	65
Fun In The Snow	220	40
G. Choir's Weights & Scales	38	64
Gabled Cottage	150	76
Gabled House	150	77
Gad's Hill Place (#57535)	34	41
Gad's Hill Place (#98732)	122	8
Galena House	150	78
Garden Cart, The	217	18
Garden Swing, The	217	19
Gasthof Eisl	61	3d
Gate House	85	10
Gatekeeper's Dwelling	83	1
Gazebo	246	NP
General Store (#5012-0)	150	79
General Store (#6530-7)	55	30c
Gently Down The Stream	218	27
Geo. Weeton Watchmaker	39	68a
Giant Trees	150	80
Gift Wrap & Ribbons	79	40
Gifts On The Go	182	66
Giggelswick Mutton & Ham	34	42
Gingerbread House	151	81
Gingerbread Vendor	96	49
Girl/Snowman, Boy	182	67
Glacier Gazette, The	74	12
Glass Ornament Works	75	13
Glenhaven House	151	82
Glistening Snow	246	NP
Glockenspiel®	62	9
God Bless Us Every One	121	3
Going Home For The Holidays	112	29
Going To The Chapel	182	68
Golden Swan Baker	43	82e
Goldilocks Bed And Breakfast	213	47
Good Day's Catch, A	96	50
Good Shepherd & His Animals, The	120	1
Good Shepherd Chapel & Church School	151	83
Gothic Church	151	84
Gothic Farmhouse	151	85
Governor's Mansion	151	86
Gracie's Dry Goods & General Store	152	87
Grand Central Railway Station	68	22
Grand Creamery, The (#53305)	211	34
Grand Creamery, The (#53405)	212	35
Grand Day of Fishing, A	218	28
Grand Movie Theater, The	68	23
Grand Ole Opry Carolers	182	69
Grandma's Cottage	152	88
Grandview Shores Hotel (#53300)	212	36
Grandview Shores Hotel (#53400)	212	37
Grapes Inn, The (#57534)	34	43
Grapes Inn, The (#98729)	122	9
Grassy Ground Cover	246	NP
Gravel Road	246	NP
Gray Cobblestone Archway	246	NP
Gray Cobblestone Capstones	246	NP
Gray Cobblestone Section	246	NP
Gray Cobblestone Tunnel	245	NP
Great Denton Mill	35	44
Great Gatsby West Egg Mansion, The	208	11
Great Expectations Satis Manor	35	45
Green	246	NP
Green Gate Cottage	35	46
Green Grocer	44	82f
Grimsly Manor	152	89
Grist Mill	62	10
Grocery	152	90
H.D. Diddle Fiddles	213	48
Haberdashery	71	44b
Hale & Hardy House	53	19
Hall Of Records	75	14
Halloween Fence	245	NP
Halloween LED Luminaries	247	NP
Halloween Set	246	NP
Halloween Spooky Tree	245	NP
Hank's Market	68	24
Happy Harley® Day, A	116	18
Happy New Year!	116	19
Harley-Davidson® Fat Boy & Softail	182	70
Harley-Davidson® Holiday, A	182	71
Harley-Davidson® Manufacturing	152	91
Harley-Davidson® Motorcycle Shop	152	92
Harley-Davidson® Sign	182	72

	Pg.	Pic.
Harley-Davidson® Water Tower	183	73
Harper's Farm	53	20
Harper's Farmhouse	53	21
Hartford House	152	93
Harvest Pumpkin Wagon	103	18
Harvest Seed Cart	103	19
Hather Harness	35	47
Haunted Mansion	153	94
Have A Seat	116	20
Haversham House	153	95
Hayride	183	74
He Led Them Down The Streets Of Town	183	75
Heading For The Hills	183	76
Hear Ye, Hear Ye	85	11
Heathmoor Castle	35	48
Heavy Snowfall, A	183	77
Heidi & Her Goats	107	7
Heidi's Grandfather's House	62	11
Heinz Grocery Store	208	12
Heinz Hitch	216	4
Heinz House	208	13
Hembleton Pewterer	35	49
Heralding Angels	120	2
Herd Of Holiday Heifers, A	183	78
Here Comes Santa	183	79
Here Comes The Ice Cream Man	218	29
Here We Come A Caroling	183	80
Here We Come A-Wassailing	96	51
Heritage Museum Of Art	68	25
Heritage Village Promotional Sign	85	12
Hershey's™ Chocolate Shop	153	96
Hey Diddle Diddle	220	47
Hi-De-Ho Nightclub	68	26
Hickory Dickory Dock (#13195)	214	49
Hickory Dickory Dock (#13302)	220	48
Hidden Ponds House	153	97
Highland Park House	153	98
Hitch Up The Buckboard	183	81
Holiday Coach	96	52
Holiday Deliveries	116	21
Holiday Field Trip	112	30
Holiday Hoops	184	82
Holiday Sleigh Ride Together, A	184	83
Holiday Spirit Baptistery	184	84
Holiday Tinsel Trims	246	NP
Holiday Travelers	96	53
Holly Brothers Garage	153	99
Holly & The Ivy, The	85	13
Holly Split Rail Fence	246	NP
Holly Split Rail Fence With Seated Children	246	NP
Holly Tree	245	NP
Hollydale's Department Store (#5534-4)	68	27
Hollydale's Department Store (#98782)	124	24
Holy Name Church	69	28
Holy Spirit Baptistery	184	84
Holy Spirit Church	153	100
Home Delivery	184	85
Home For The Holidays, A	184	86
Home In The Making, A	154	101
Home Sweet Home/House & Windmill	154	102
Homestead	154	103
Hometown Boarding House	207	1
Hometown Church	207	2
Hometown Drugstore	207	3
Honeymooner Motel, The	154	104
Horse And Hounds Pub, The	35	50
Horse Drawn Squash Cart	216	5
Hot Dog Vendor	112	31
House That ❤ Built™ 1998, The	209	14
Humpty Dumpty	221	49
Humpty Dumpty Café	214	50
Humpty Dumpty Stackable Teapot And Cup	221	50
Hunting Lodge	154	105
Hybrid Landscape	246	NP
Ice Crystal Blanket Of Snow	245	NP
Ichabod Crane's Cottage	57	38a
I'll Need More Toys	116	22
I'm Wishing	218	20
Independence Hall	209	15
Inglenook Cottage #5 (#53303)	212	38
Inglenook Cottage #5 (#53404)	212	39
Inn, The	154	106
Innkeeper's Caravansary	83	2
Is That Frosty?	184	87
Italianate Villa	155	107
It's Almost Thanksgiving	103	20
It's Time For An Icy Treat	184	88
Ivy Glen Church	36	51
Ivy Terrace Apartments	69	29
J.D. Nichols Toy Shop	36	52
J. Hudson Stoveworks	53	22
J. Lytes Coal Merchant	36	53
J. Young's Granary (#5149-7)	155	108
J. Young's Granary (#98632)	197	1
J. Young's Granary (#98644)	197	2
Jack In The Box Plant No. 2	75	15
Jack-O'-Lanterns	247	NP
Jack Pines	245	NP
Jack's Corner Barber Shop	155	109
Jacob Adams Farmhouse And Barn	54	23
Jannes Mullet Amish Barn	54	24
Jannes Mullet Amish Farm House	54	25
Jefferson School	155	110
Jeremiah Brewster House	51	9a
Jingle Belle Houseboat (#5114-4)	155	111
Jingle Belle Houseboat (#98648)	197	3
Johnson's Grocery & Deli	69	30
Johnson's Grocery ... Holiday Deliveries	112	32
Jones & Co. Brush & Basket Shop	44	82g
Josef Engel Farmhouse	63	12
Just Married	184	89
Kamm Haus	63	13
Kenilworth Castle	36	54
Kensington Palace	36	55
Kenwood House	155	112
"Key To The City, A" Christmas In The City Sign	112	33
Kids Around The Tree	184	90
Kids, Candy Canes ... And Ronald McDonald®	185	91
Kids Decorating The Village Sign	185	92
Kids Love Hershey's™!	185	93
Kids Tree House	185	94
King's Road	37	56
King's Road Cab	96	54
King's Road Market Cross	96	55

	Pg.	Pic.
King's Road Post Office	37	57
Kingsford's Brew House	37	58
Knife Grinder	104	21
Knob Hill	156	113
Knottinghill Church	37	59
Konditorei Schokolade (see Bakery & Chocolate Shop)		
Kringle's Toy Shop	160	143
Kukuck Uhren	60	2a
Lafayette's Bakery	69	31
Lambsville School	214	51
Lamplighter w/Lamp	96	56
Landscape	246	NP
Large Single Tree	156	114
Last Minute Delivery	117	23
Last Stop Gas Station	156	115
Laundry Day	185	95
Law Office, Inc.	210	21
Leacock Poulterer	38	60
Leading The Bavarian Cow	107	8
LED Light Bulb	247	NP
Leed's Oyster House	38	61
Let It Snow, Let It Snow	185	96
Let's Go One More Time	104	22
Let's Go Shopping In The City	112	34
Letters For Santa	117	24
Lifeguard On Duty	219	30
Lighted Christmas Pole	249	NP
Lighted Snowy Tree	249	NP
Lighted Tree w/Children And Ladder	85	14
Lighthouse (#5030-0)	156	116
Lighthouse (#98635)	197	4
Lil' Boy Blue Petting Farm	214	52
Lincoln Park Duplex	156	117
Linden Hills Country Club	156	118
Lionel® Electric Train Shop	157	119
Lionhead Bridge	96	57
Little Boy Blue	221	51
"Little Italy" Ristorante	69	32
Little Miss Muffet	221	52
Little Red Riding Hood	221	53
Little Town Of Bethlehem	83	3
Little Women The March Residence	54	26
Livery Stable & Boot Shop	55	30d
Load Up The Wagon	104	23
Loading The Sleigh	117	25
Lobster Trappers	104	24
Locomotive Shed & Water Tower, The	97	58
Log Cabin	157	120
Log Pile	246	NP
Lomas Ltd. Molasses	45	85b
Looney Tunes® Animated Film Festival, The	185	97
Lucky Dragon Restaurant	157	121
Lumberjacks	104	25
Lydby Trunk & Satchel Shop	38	64
Lynton Point Tower	38	62
Magic Smoke	246	NP
Mailbox (#5179-9)	185	98
Mailbox (#5198-5)	185	99
Mailbox & Fire Hydrant (#5214-0)	112	36
Mailbox & Fire Hydrant (#5517-4)	112	35
Main Street House	157	122
Main Street Memories	209	16
Mainstreet Gift Shop	157	123
Mainstreet Hardware Store	158	124
Majestic Woodland Birds	246	NP
Making The Christmas Candles	104	26
Maltings, The	38	63
Man On Ladder Hanging Garland	185	100
Manchester Square	38	64
Manchester Square Accessory	38	64
Mansion	158	125
Maple Ridge Inn	158	126
Maple Sugaring Shed	104	27
Margrove Orangery	38	65
Marie's Doll Museum	75	17
Market Day	104	28
Marshmallow Roast	186	101
Marshmallows Around The Campfire	117	26
Marvel's Beauty Salon	158	127
Mary Quite Contrary Flower Shop	214	53
Master Gardeners	97	59
Maylie Cottage	42	81b
McDonald's®	158	128
McDonald's® . . . Lights Up The Night	186	102
McGrebe-Cutters & Sleighs	54	27
McShane Cottage	39	66
Mediterranean Mortgage Co.	210	22
Meeting Family At The Railroad Station	97	60
Melancholy Tavern, The	39	67
Members Of Parliament	97	61
Men At Work	186	103
Merchant Shops	39	68
Mermaid Fish Shoppe, The	39	68b
Metterniche Wurst	60	2b
Mickey & Minnie	119	3
Mickey's Christmas Carol	81	2
Mickey's Diner (see Diner)		
Milch-Kase	61	3e
Mill Creek Bridge	246	NP
Mill Creek Crossing	104	29
Mill Creek, Curved Section	246	NP
Mill Creek Park Bench	246	NP
Mill Creek Pond	246	NP
Mill Creek, Straight Section	246	NP
Mill Creek Wooden Bridge	246	NP
Mini-Donut Shop	75	16
Mini Lights	249	NP
Mission Church	158	129
Mobile Home	158	130
Moggin Falls General Store	54	28
Molly O'Brien's Irish Pub	69	33
Monks-A-Caroling (#5040-7)	186	105
Monks-A-Caroling (#6459-9)	186	104
Monopoly™ Bank & Trust	210	23
Moose In The Marsh	246	NP
Morningside House	159	131
Morston Steak & Kidney Pie	47	93
Mother Goose	221	54
Mother Goose Book Cellar	214	54
Mother Goose Stackable Teapot And Cup	221	55
Mount Olivet Church	159	132
Mountain Backdrop	246	NP
Mountain Centerpiece	246	NP
Mountain Lodge	159	133
Mountain Tunnel	246	NP

	Pg.	Pic.
Mountain w/Frosted Sisal Trees, Lg.	246	NP
Mountain w/Frosted Sisal Trees, Med.	246	NP
Mountain w/Frosted Sisal Trees, Sm.	246	NP
Moving Day	186	106
Mr. & Mrs. Pickle	45	84c
Mr. Wickfield Solicitor	30	28b
Mrs. Claus' Greenhouse	75	18
Mulberrie Court	40	69
Multi-Outlet Plug Strip	247	NP
Mush!	186	107
Music Emporium	71	44c
Mylar Skating Pond	246	NP
Nanny And The Preschoolers	186	108
Nantucket (#5014-6)	159	134
Nantucket (#98630)	198	5
Nantucket (#98642)	198	6
Nantucket Renovation	159	135
Nathaniel Bingham Fabrics	56	30e
Nativity (#5135-7)	186	109
Nativity (#59796)	83	4
Nativity Sand	246	NP
Navigational Charts & Maps	54	29
Neenee's Dolls & Toys	75	19
Nephew Fred's Flat	40	70
Nettie Quinn Puppets & Marionettes	40	71
New Batch Of Christmas Friends, A	108	9
New England Village	55	30
New England Village Sign	105	30
New England Winter Set	105	31
New Hope Church	159	136
New Potbellied Stove For Christmas, A	105	32
New School House	159	137
New Stone Church	160	138
New Year's Millennium Waterglobe	216	6
Newsstand Daily	210	24
Nicholas Nickleby	40	72
Nicholas Nickleby Characters	97	62
Nicholas Nickleby Cottage	40	72a
Nick The Tree Farmer	160	139
Nick's Tree Farm	160	139
Nikki's Cocoa Shop	160	143
Nine Ladies Dancing	97	63
Norman Church	41	73
North Creek Cottage	160	140
North Eastern Sea Fisheries Ltd.	41	74
North Pole	76	20
North Pole Chapel	76	21
North Pole Dolls	76	22
North Pole Dolls & Santa's Bear Works	76	22
North Pole Express	117	27
North Pole Express Depot	76	23
North Pole Gate	117	28
North Pole Santa's Workshop	124	28
North Pole Shops	77	24
Northern Lights Tinsel Mill	77	25
Nutcracker Vendor & Cart	108	10
Oak Grove Tudor	160	141
Obbie's Books & Letrinka's Candy	77	26
Old Chelsea Mansion	160	142
Old Curiosity Shop, The (#5905-6)	41	75
Old Curiosity Shop (#98738)	123	10
Old Curiosity Shop, The (#98768)	123	11
Old East Rectory	33	34
Old Globe Theatre, The	41	76
Old House In Paris That Was Covered In Vines, An	214	55
Old Man And The Sea, The	105	33
Old Michaelchurch	41	77
Old North Church	56	31
Old Puppeteer, The	97	64
Old Queensbridge Station	42	78
Old Royal Observatory, The	42	79
Old St. James Hospital	210	25
Old Trinity Church	69	34
Old Woman Cobbler	215	56
Olde Camden Town Church, The	42	80
Olde World Antiques I	81	3a
Olde World Antiques II	81	3b
Olde World Antiques Gate	119	4
Olde World Antiques Shops	81	3
Oliver Twist	42	81
Oliver Twist Characters	97	65
On The Road Again	186	110
On The Way To Ballet Class	187	111
One Horse Open Sleigh	85	15
One-Man Band And The Dancing Dog	112	37
Open Wide!	117	29
Opera Du Jardin	210	26
Organ Grinder	113	38
Oriental Express	210	27
Original Bachman Homestead, The	209	17
Original Shops Of Dickens' Village, The	43	82
Original Snow Village Start A Tradition Set, The	160	143
Orly's Bell & Harness Supply	77	24a
Otis Hayes Butcher Shop	52	12c
Over The River And Through The Woods	105	34
Ox Sled	97	66
P. L. Wheeler's Bicycle Shop	57	34
P. Peter's	215	57
Pacific Heights House	160	144
Painting Our Own Village Sign	85	16
Palace Fountain	46	87
Palace Gate	46	87
Palace Guards	46	87
Palace Theatre	70	39
Palos Verdes	161	145
Paramount Theater	161	146
Parish Church	161	147
Parking Meter	187	112
Parkside Pavilion (#53411)	212	40
Parkside Pavilion (#53412)	212	41
Parkview Hospital	70	36
Parsonage	161	148
Partridge In A Pear Tree, A	98	67
Patrolling The Road	187	113
Peaceful Glow On Christmas Eve, A	98	68
Peanut Brittle Factory, The	77	27
Peggotty's Seaside Cottage	31	28c
Pennsylvania Dutch Barn	49	1a
Pennsylvania Dutch Farmhouse	49	1b
Pennyfarthing Pedaling	105	35

	Pg.	Pic.
Peppermint Porch Day Care	161	149
Peppermint Road, Curved Section	246	NP
Peppermint Road, Straight Section	246	NP
Peppermint Skating Party	117	30
Perfect Wedding, The	219	31
Personalize Your Village Accessories	246	NP
Peter Piper Pickle And Peppers	215	58
Peter Pumpkin	221	56
Pets On Parade	187	114
Photo With Santa	117	31
Pick-Up And Delivery	187	115
Pickford Place	65	8b
Picking Out The Christmas Tree	113	39
Pied Bull Inn, The	44	83
Pied Bull Inn Ornament, The	123	12
Pierce Boat Works	56	32
Pigeonhead Lighthouse	56	33
Pine Point Pond	246	NP
Pine Trees With Pine Cones	245	NP
Pinewood Log Cabin (#5150-0)	161	150
Pinewood Log Cabin (#98637)	198	7
Pink Flamingos	246	NP
Pint-Size Pony Rides	187	116
Pioneer Church	161	151
Pisa Pizza	162	152
Pizza Delivery	187	117
Plantation House	162	153
Platt's Candles & Wax	57	35
Playing In The Snow	86	17
Poinsettia Delivery Truck	86	18
Poinsettias For Sale	187	118
Police Department	211	28
Polka Fest	108	11
Popcorn & Cranberry House	77	28
Popcorn Vendor	113	40
Porcelain Pine Trees	245	NP
Porcelain Trees	86	19
Portobello Road Peddlers	98	69
Portobello Road Thatched Cottages	44	84
Post Office	78	29
Postern	98	70
Potter's Tea Seller	72	48a
Poulterer	39	68c
Poultry Market	98	71
Prairie House	162	154
Praying Monks	187	119
Precinct 25 Police Station	70	37
Preparing For Halloween	188	120
Print Shop & Village News	162	155
Pump Lane Shoppes	45	85
Putting Green	246	NP
Quality Service At Ford®	188	121
Queen Anne Victorian (#5157-8)	162	156
Queen Anne Victorian (#98646)	198	8
Queen's House Of Cards	215	59
Queen's Parliamentary Coach, The	98	72
Queensbridge Railroad Yard Accessories	247	NP
Quilly's Antiques	45	86
Radius Curved Track	246	NP
Railroad Crossing Sign	246	NP
Railroad Lamps	247	NP
Ramsey Hill House	162	157
Ramsford Palace	46	87
Ready For The Road	113	41
Real Gray Gravel	247	NP
Real Plastic Snow (#49981)	245	NP
Real Plastic Snow (#49999)	245	NP
Real Plastic Snow Factory (#56403)	78	30
Real Plastic Snow Factory (#98781)	124	28
Red Barn	162	158
Red Brick Fire Station (#5536-0)	70	38
Red Brick Fire Station (#98758)	124	25
Red Christmas Sulky	98	73
Red Covered Bridge	105	36
Red Schoolhouse	56	30f
Redeemer Church	163	159
Reindeer Barn (#56015)	76	20b
Reindeer Barn (#98762)	124	29
Reindeer Bus Depot	163	160
Reindeer Flight School	78	31
Reindeer Training Camp	117	32
Relaxing In A Garden	218	21
Remote Switches, Asst. Right & Left	247	NP
Replacement Light Bulb	247	NP
Replacement Light Bulb, Clear	248	NP
Replacement Light Bulb, Yellow	248	NP
Replacement Round Light Bulb	248	NP
Resort Lodge (see Snow Village Resort Lodge)		
Rest Ye Merry Gentlemen	113	42
Revolving Display Stand	247	NP
Ride On The Reindeer Lines, A	188	122
Ridgewood	163	161
Rimpy's Bakery	77	24b
Ritz Hotel	70	39
River Road House	163	162
River Street Ice House Cart	113	43
Riverside Row Shops	70	40
Road Construction Sign	247	NP
Rock Creek Mill	163	163
Rockabilly Records	163	164
Rocking Chair Readers	219	35
Rollerama Roller Rink	163	165
Remote Switches, Assorted Right & Left	248	NP
Ronald McDonald House® Ornament	216	7
Ronald McDonald House® "The House That ♥ Built"	209	18
Rosita's Cantina	164	166
Round And Round We Go!	188	123
Route 1, North Pole, Home Of Mr. & Mrs. Claus	78	32
Royal Coach (#5578-6)	98	74
Royal Coach (#57501)	121	4
Ruth Marion Scotch Woolens	46	88
Ryman Auditorium®	164	167
Safety Patrol	188	124
Sailors' Knot, The	105	37
St. Anthony Hotel & Post Office	164	168
St. Bernard Puppies (see Bernhardiner Hundchen)		
Saint James Church	164	169
St. Luke's Church	164	170
St. Nicholas	108	12
St. Nikolaus Kirche	63	16
Salvation Army Band	113	44
Sandy Beach	247	NP
Santa & Mrs. Claus	118	33
Santa Comes To Town, 1995	188	125

	Pg.	Pic.
Santa Comes To Town, 1996	188	126
Santa Comes To Town, 1997	188	127
Santa Comes To Town, 1998	188	128
Santa Comes To Town, 1999	189	129
Santa Comes To Town, 2000	189	130
Santa's Bear Works	76	22
Santa's Bell Repair	78	33
Santa's Light Shop	78	34
Santa's Little Helpers (#5610-3)	118	34
Santa's Little Helpers (#55025)	189	131
Santa's Lookout Tower (#5629-4)	78	35
Santa's Lookout Tower (#98742)	125	30
Santa's Lookout Tower (#98773)	125	31
Santa's Rooming House	79	36
Santa's Visiting Center	79	37
Santa's Woodworks	79	38
Santa's Workshop (#5600-6)	79	39
Santa's Workshop (#98772)	125	32
Santa/Mailbox	189	132
Saturday Morning Downtown	160	143
Say It With Flowers	216	8
School Bus, Snow Plow	189	133
School Children	189	134
School House	164	171
Scottie With Tree	189	135
Scottie's Toy Shop	70	41
Scrooge & Marley Counting House (#6500-5)	29	22c
Scrooge & Marley Counting House (#98745)	122	1
Sea Captain & His Mates	105	38
Season's Bay Amusement Park Carousel	217	16
Season's Bay Christmas Garlands & Wreaths	247	NP
Season's Bay Park	247	NP
Secret Garden Florist, The	164	172
Secret Garden Greenhouse, The	165	173
Semple's Smokehouse	57	36
Send In The Clown!	189	136
Service Station	165	174
Service With A Smile	189	137
Seton Morris Spice Merchant	46	89
Seven Swans A-Swimming	98	75
Shady Oak Church	167	187
Sheep	216	2
Shelly's Diner	165	175
Shingle Creek House	57	37
Shingle Victorian	165	176
Shopkeepers	98	76
Shopping Girls With Packages	190	138
Side Porch Café (#53303)	213	42
Side Porch Café (#53403)	213	43
Silent Night	108	13
Silo & Hay Shed	99	77
Silversmith	82	4
Sing A Song For Santa	118	35
Singing Carols In Town	220	41
Singing Nuns	190	139
Single Car Garage	165	177
Single Cord Set	248	NP
Sir John Falstaff Inn (#5753-3)	46	90
Sir John Falstaff Inn (#9870-1)	123	13
Sisal Tree Lot	190	140
Sisters Of The Abbey	108	14
Sitting In Camden Park	99	78
Six Geese A-Laying	99	79
Skate Faster Mom	190	141
Skate & Ski Shop	165	178
Skaters & Skiers	190	142
Skating On The Pond	220	42
Skating Party	86	20
Skating Pond (#5017-2)	165	179
Skating Pond (#6545-5)	86	22
Skating Rink/Duck Pond Set	166	180
Ski Bums	118	36
Ski Slope (HV)	86	22
Ski Slope (SV)	190	143
Slate Stone Path (#52719)	247	NP
Slate Stone Path (#52767)	247	NP
Sled & Skis	247	NP
Sleepy Hollow	57	38
Sleepy Hollow Characters	105	39
Sleepy Hollow Church	58	39
Sleepy Hollow School	57	38b
Sleigh & Eight Tiny Reindeer	118	37
Sleighride (#5160-8)	190	144
Sleighride (#57502)	121	5
Sleighride (#6511-0)	106	40
Small Chalet	166	181
Small Double Trees	166	182
Smithy (see Bean And Son Smithy Shop)		
Smokey Mountain Retreat	166	183
Smythe Woolen Mill	58	40
Sno-Jet Snowmobile	190	145
Snow Carnival Ice Palace	166	184
Snow Carnival Ice Sculptures	191	146
Snow Carnival King & Queen	191	147
Snow Children	86	23
Snow Cone Elves	118	38
Snow Fence, White	245	NP
Snow Kids	191	148
Snow Kids Sled, Skis	191	149
Snow Village Factory	166	185
Snow Village Promotional Sign	191	150
Snow Village Resort Lodge	167	186
Snow Village Starter Set	167	187
Snowball Fort	191	151
Snowman With Broom	191	152
Snowy Evergreen Trees, Lg.	245	NP
Snowy Evergreen Trees, Med.	245	NP
Snowy Evergreen Trees, Sm.	245	NP
Snowy Hills Hospital	167	188
Snowy Pines Inn	167	189
Snowy Scotch Pines	247	NP
Sonoma House	167	190
Sound of Music® Gazebo, The	108	15
Sound of Music® von Trapp Villa, The	63	15
Sound Of Music® Wedding Church, The	63	16
Southern Colonial	167	191
Spanish Mission Church	167	192
Special Delivery (#5148-9)	191	153
Special Delivery (#5197-7)	191	154
Spielzeug Laden	63	17
Spider Box Locks, The	46	91
Spirit Of Christmas, The	121	6
Spirit Of Giving, The	33	34
Spirit Of Snow Village Airplane (#5440-2)	191	155
Spirit Of Snow Village Airplane (#5458-5)	192	156
Spirit Of The Season	113	45
Sport Laden	63	18

	Pg.	Pic.
Spotlight	248	NP
Spotlight Replacement Bulbs	248	NP
Spring St. Coffee House	72	48b
Springfield House	168	193
Springlake Station	213	44
Spruce Place	168	194
Staghorn Lodge	46	92
Starbucks® Coffee	168	195
Starbucks® Coffee Cart	192	157
Starry Night Sky Backdrop	247	NP
Stars And Stripes Forever	87	24
Start A Tradition Set (#56390)	79	40
Start A Tradition Set (#5832-7)	47	93
Statue Of Mark Twain	192	158
Steen's Maple House	58	41
Steeple Church (#6530-7)	56	30g
Steeple Church (#6539-0)	58	42
Steeple Church (#98757)	123	18
Steepled Church (#5005-4)	168	196
Steepled Church (#98631)	198	9
Steepled Church (#98643)	198	10
Steppin' Out On The Town	113	46
Stick Style House	168	197
Stillwaters Boathouse	213	43
Stone Bridge	99	80
Stone Church (#5009-6)	168	198
Stone Church (#5059-1)	168	199
Stone Cottage	31	30a
Stone Curved Wall/Bench	247	NP
Stone Footbridge	247	NP
Stone Holly Corner Posts & Archway	247	NP
Stone Holly Tree Corner Posts	247	NP
Stone Mill House	169	200
Stone Stairway	247	NP
Stone Trestle Bridge	247	NP
Stone Wall	247	NP
Stone Wall With Sisal Hedge	247	NP
Stonehurst House	169	201
Stoney Brook Town Hall	58	43
Stop Sign	192	159
Storybook Village Collection Landscape Set	245	NP
Storybook Village Collection Sign	220	43
Straight Track	247	NP
Stratford House	169	202
Street Car (#5019-9)	169	203
Street Car (#98645)	198	11
Street Lamps	248	NP
Street Musicians	114	47
Street Sign	192	160
String Of 12 Pumpkin Lights	248	NP
String Of 25 Mini LED Lights	248	NP
String Of Spotlights	248	NP
String Of Starry Lights	248	NP
Stroll In The Park, A	218	22
Stucco Bungalow	169	204
Stuck In The Snow	192	161
Sudbury Church	33	34
Summit House	169	205
Sunday Morning At The Chapel	218	23
Sunday School Serenade	167	187
Super Suds Laundromat	169	206
Sutton Place Brownstones	71	42
Swinging Under The Old Oak Tree	247	NP
Swiss Chalet	170	207
T.L. Pigs Brick Factory	215	60
T. Puddlewick Spectacle Shop	48	102b
T. Wells Fruit & Spice Shop	29	23b
Tacky Wax	247	NP
"Tallyho!"	99	81
Tangled In Tinsel	118	39
Tapping The Maples	106	41
Tassy's Mittens & Hassel's Woolies	79	41
Tattyeave Knoll	47	94
Taxi Cab	192	162
Tea And Coffee	221	57
Teaman & Crupp China Shop	47	95
Tee Time Elves	118	40
Telephone Poles	247	NP
Television Antenna	247	NP
Ten Pipers Piping	99	82
Tending The Cold Frame (#2208)	216	9
Tending The Cold Frame (#58416)	99	83
Tending The New Calves	99	84
Terry's Towing	192	163
Testing The Toys	118	41
Thatched Cottage (#5050-0)	207	5
Thatched Cottage (#6518-8)	31	30b
Thatchers	99	85
Theatre Royal	47	96
Thomas Kersey Coffee House	32	31b
Thomas Mudge Timepieces	47	97
Thomas T. Julian House	51	9b
Thoroughbreds	247	NP
Three Bears	221	58
Three French Hens	99	86
Through The Woods (#5172-1)	192	164
Through The Woods (#52791)	87	25
Tillie's Tiny Cup Café	80	42
Timber Knoll Log Cabin	58	44
Times Tower, The (#55510)	209	19
Times Tower, The (#98775)	217	10
Tin Soldier Shop	80	43
Tinker Bell's Treasures	82	5
Tinsel Trims	247	NP
'Tis The Season	114	48
To Protect And To Serve	114	49
Tour The Village	193	166
Tower Of London	47	98
Tower Restaurant	66	14b
Towering Pines	245	NP
Town Church	170	208
Town Crier	121	7
Town Crier & Chimney Sweep	100	87
Town Gate	120	3
Town Hall	170	209
Town Square Carolers	47	93
Town Square Gazebo	87	25
Town Square Shops	47	93
Town Tinker	106	42
Town Tree	87	27
Town Tree Trimmers	87	28
Town Tree w/50 LED Lights	248	NP
Town Well & Palm Trees	120	4
Toy Peddler, The	108	16
Toy Shop	170	210
Toy Shop And Pet Store	66	14c
Toymaker Elves	118	42
Traffic Light	248	NP
Train Station With 3 Train Cars	170	211
Transport (see City Bus & Milk Truck)		
Treasure From The Sea, A	100	88
Treats For The Kids	193	167

	Pg.	Pic.
Tree For Me, A	193	168
Tree Lot	193	169
Treetop Tree House	193	170
Trekking In The Snow	108	17
Trick Or Treat	219	36
Trick-Or-Treat Kids	193	171
Trimming The North Pole	119	43
Trinity Church	170	212
Trinity Ledge	59	45
Trout Stream, The	247	NP
Tudor Cottage	32	30c
Tudor House	171	213
Turn Of The Century	171	214
Turn-Of-The-Century Lamppost	248	NP
Tutbury Printer	37	56b
Tuttle's Pub	32	31c
Twelve Drummers Drumming	100	89
Twin Peaks	171	215
Twinkling Tip Tree	245	NP
Twig Snow Fence	245	NP
Two For The Road	193	172
Two Lane Paved Road	247	NP
Two Rivers Bridge	87	29
Two Turtle Doves	100	90
Uncle Sam's Fireworks Stand	193	173
Under The Bumbershoot	100	91
Under The Mistletoe	106	43
University Club, The	71	43
Untangle The Christmas Lights	119	44
Until We Meet Again	100	92
Up In The Apple Tree	247	NP
Up On A Roof Top	193	174
Up, Up & Away Witch (HV)	87	30
Up, Up & Away Witch (SV)	194	175
Uptown Motors Ford®	171	216
Uptown Motors Ford® Billboard	194	176
Uptown Shoppes	71	44
Utility Accessories (#52775)	248	NP
Utility Accessories (#52776)	248	NP
Van Guilder's Ornamental Ironworks	59	46
Van Tassel Manor	58	38c
Variety Store	71	45
Victoria Station (#5574-3)	48	99
Victoria Station (#98780)	123	14
Victoria Station Train Platform	100	93
Victorian	171	217
Victorian Cottage	171	218
Victorian House	171	219
Victorian Wrought Iron Fence Extension	245	NP
Victorian Wrought Iron Fence And Gate	245	NP
Village 3 Socket Light Set	248	NP
Village Animated Accessory Track (HV)	88	31
Village Animated Accessory Track (SV)	194	177
Village Animated All Around The Park (HV)	88	32
Village Animated All Around The Park (SV)	194	178
Village Animated Skating Pond (HV)	88	33
Village Animated Skating Pond (SV)	194	179
Village Animated Ski Mountain (HV)	88	34
Village Animated Ski Mountain (SV)	194	180
Village Animated Sledding Hill (HV)	88	35
Village Animated Sledding Hill (SV)	194	181
Village Autumn Moss	247	NP
Village Bank & Trust	172	220
Village Birds	194	182
Village Brite Lites	248	NP
Adapter	248	NP
Angel	248	NP
Candles	248	NP
Candy Canes	248	NP
Fence	248	NP
Holly Archway	248	NP
"Merry Christmas"	248	NP
Reindeer	248	NP
Santa	248	NP
Santa In Chimney	248	NP
Snow Dragon	248	NP
Snowman	248	NP
Tree	248	NP
Village Cats & Dogs	247	NP
Village Church	172	221
Village Express Electric Train Set (HV)	88	36
Village Express Electric Train Set (SV)	195	183
Village Express Train (#5980-3)	88	37
Village Express Train (#5997-8)	88	38
Village Express Van (HV)	89	39
Village Express Van (Canadian)	217	11
Village Fire Truck	195	184
Village Flocked Pine Trees	245	NP
Village Frosted Fountain	248	NP
Village Frosted Shrubbery	245	NP
Village Frosted Topiaries	245	NP
Village Frosty Light Trees	245	NP
Village Gazebo	195	185
Village Greenhouse	172	222
Village Greetings	195	186
Village Ground Cover	247	NP
Village Harvest People	106	44
Village Holiday Cobblestone Road	249	NP
Village Ice Crystal Gate & Walls	247	NP
Village Ice Crystal Walls	247	NP
Village Icicle Trees	245	NP
Village Lookout Tower	247	NP
Village Marching Band	195	187
Village Market	172	223
Village Monuments	89	40
Village Nativity Crèche	248	NP
Village News Delivery	195	188
Village Palm Trees	245	NP
Village Peppermint Trees	245	NP
Village Pequot Pine	245	NP
Village Pequot Pines	245	NP
Village Phone Booth	195	189
Village Police Station	172	224
Village Porcelain Pine, Large	89	41
Village Porcelain Pine, Small	89	42
Village Porcelain Pine Trees	89	43
Village Post Office	172	225
Village Potted Topiary Pair	195	190
Village Public Library	172	226
Village Real Gravel	247	NP
Village Realty	173	227

	Pg.	Pic.
Village Red Wrought Iron Park Bench	247	NP
Village Replacement Incandescent Bulbs	248	NP
Village Service Vehicles	195	191
Village Sign With Snowman	89	44
Village Spring/Summer Moss	247	NP
Village Square Clock Tower	247	NP
Village Stadium Lights	248	NP
Village Station	173	228
Village Station And Train	173	229
Village Street Peddlers	100	94
Village Streetcar (HV, #5240-0)	89	45
Village Streetcar (SV, #5240-0)	195	192
Village Tall Stone Walls	247	NP
Village Train	100	95
Village Train Trestle	90	46
Village Twinkling Lit Shrubs (#52824)	245	NP
Village Twinkling Lit Shrubs (#56724)	245	NP
Village Twinkling Lit Town Tree	245	NP
Village Twinkling Lit Trees (#52823)	245	NP
Village Twinkling Lit Trees (#56723)	245	NP
Village Up, Up & Away (HV)	90	47
Village Up, Up & Away (SV)	196	193
Village Used Car Lot	196	194
Village Vet And Pet Shop	173	230
Village Warming House	173	231
Village Waterfall (HV)	90	48
Village Waterfall (SV)	196	195
Village Well & Holy Cross	101	96
Village Wooden Canoes	247	NP
Violet Vendor/Carolers/ Chestnut Vendor	101	97
Vision Of A Christmas Past	101	98
Visit With Santa, A	196	196
Visiting The Nativity	114	50
Volunteer Firefighters	106	45
W.M. Wheat Cakes & Puddings	45	85c
Wackford Squeers Boarding School	41	72b
Walkway Lights	247	NP
Wall Hedge	46	87
Walpole Tailors	40	68d
Washington Street Post Office	72	46
Water Tower	196	197
Waverly Place	173	232
Wayside Chapel (see Country Church)		
We're Going To A Christmas Pageant	196	199
Weather & Time Observatory	80	44
Weather Vane	249	NP
Wedding Chapel	174	234
Wedding Gallery, The	72	48
Welcome Home	114	51
Welcome To Elf Land	119	45
Welcome To The Congregation	196	198
West Village Shops	72	49
Weston Train Station	59	47
White Horse Bakery	40	68e
White Picket Fence	245	NP
Whittlesbourne Church	48	100
Whole Family Goes Shopping, The	196	200
Wickfield Solicitor (see Mr. Wickfield Solicitor)		
William Glen Johnson's Grocery Holiday Deliveries	112	32
Williamsburg House	174	234
Windmill	247	NP
Wingham Lane Parrot Seller	48	101
Winter Birch	246	NP
Winter Fountain	196	201
Winter Pine Trees With Pine Cones (#52772)	246	NP
Winter Playground	197	202
Winter Sleighride	101	99
Wintergarten Cafe	72	49
Wintergreen Pines (#52660)	246	NP
Wintergreen Pines (#52661)	246	NP
Wise Men From The East	120	5
Wolves In The Woods	247	NP
Wong's In Chinatown	72	51
Woodbridge Post Office	59	48
Woodbury House	174	235
Woodcutter And Son	106	46
Wooden Church	174	236
Wooden Clapboard	174	237
Wooden Pier	247	NP
Wooden Rowboats	247	NP
Woodland Animals At Cliff's Edge	247	NP
Woodland Animals At Mill Creek	247	NP
Woodland Wildlife Animals (#52813)	247	NP
Woodland Wildlife Animals (#55525)	247	NP
Woodsman And Boy	197	203
Woodsmen Elves	119	46
Woodworker, The	106	47
Woody Station Wagon	197	204
Wool Shop, The	29	23c
Wreaths For Sale	197	205
Wrenbury Baker	48	102c
Wrenbury Shops	48	102
Wrought Iron Fence	245	NP
Wrought Iron Park Bench	247	NP
WSNO Radio	174	238
Yankee Jud Bell Casting	59	49
"Ye Olde Lamplighter" Dickens' Village Sign	101	100
Yeomen Of The Guard	101	101
"Yes, Virginia . . ."	114	52
Yorkshire Grand Hotel	211	29

Acknowledgements

CheckerBee Publishing would like to thank Frank & Florence Wilson, Jeff & Susan McDermott, Mr. Sierakowski, Stan & Linda Jones, Enet Y. Silvestri and all the Department 56 retailers and collectors who contributed their valuable time to assist us with this book.

Alphabetical Index